ROGUE CLERICS

ROGUE CLERICS

THE SOCIAL PROBLEM OF CLERGY DEVIANCE

ANSON SHUPE

Transaction Publishers

New Brunswick (U.S.A.) and London (U.K.)

Library of Congress Catalog Number: 2007035196
ISBN: 978-1-4128-0704-3
Printed in the United States of America

Library of Congress Cataloging-in-Publication Data

Shupe, Anson D.
    Rogue clerics : the social problem of clergy deviance / Anson Shupe.
        p. cm.
    Includes bibliographical references and index.
    ISBN 978-1-4128-0704-3
    1. Clergy—Professional ethics. 2. Clergy—Conduct of life. I. Title..

BV4011.5.S56 2007
262'.14—dc22   2007035196

To two pioneers in different ways . . .
Jeanne M. Miller and A.W. Richard Sipe, my esteem.

A.S.

Contents

Preface

This is a book that I have felt for some time was missing in sociology and particularly in the sub-discipline of deviance. I have researched religious elite deviance for two decades. During that time I have been mystified that criminologists and sociologists of deviance as well as sociologists of religion have generally ignored the problem of clergy deviance. For any literature to speak of on this subject we owe our thanks to therapists, counselors, religionists, journalists, and not a few victims. Certainly, a perusal of current leading texts and readers on general deviance, elite deviance, and corporate criminality (randomly picking titles by, say, Simon [2006], McGaghy *et al.* [2006], or Thio and Calhoun [2006]) reveals *absolutely nothing* on a topic with such a venerable history and high current visibility in the mass media and on the internet.

I believe this situation exists because of a fundamental discomfort within both sub-disciplines: criminology-deviance colleagues, by training and/or personal inclination, are ill equipped to study religious institutions, and alternately, this dark side of religion is treated by many sociologists of religion in an embarrassed *sotto voce* only. There are exceptions, but they are rare. My own past works on the subject, which I have had to cite liberally through this volume by default, have been relatively lonely in sociology except for individual articles which I obtained by culling conference programs or querying graduate advisors for inclusion in edited volumes.

I have retained some "classic" examples and cases of clergy malfeasance (or misconduct) in this volume, but so much has occurred since 1995 when I published *In the Name of All That's Holy: A Theory of Clergy Malfeasance* that the pages to follow also monitor important developments of the early years of the twenty-first century. The cases change, but the phenomenon remains the same. Readers will recognize many familiar concepts taken from theorists as diverse as Robert Michels and Gaetano Mosca to Amitai Etzioni. Sociology (particularly political sociology) already possesses adequate conceptual tools for understanding what is occurring as revelations of clergy malfeasance continue to unfold. Thus, I have been eclectic in applying them.

Acknowledgments

Several colleagues assisted in reading earlier drafts of the *Rogue Clerics* manuscript when it was a project thought out much differently. I am indebted to Professors Diane Taub and Christopher Bradley for their questions, suggestions, and criticisms. Even if I did not always agree with them, they helped me later address issues in the text. One of my original inspirations, A. W. Richard Sipe, was a true long distance supporter. And, as always, thanks go to Roberta (Bobbi) Shadle of Indiana University Purdue University Fort Wayne's Learning Resource Center for her artistry and patience.

1

Introduction

The president of the religiously conservative Baptist-based Hillsdale College in Michigan eventually resigned after it was learned that he had conducted an affair with his daughter-in-law (mother of his grandson) for fifteen years even after he divorced a wife and remarried.

When the families of forty-three children molested by Roman Catholic priests as far back as the 1960s first tried to bring the problem to their archbishop in 1983, they were threatened with legal action if they said anything more. They eventually sued the Church and in 2005 won a punitive settlement for $22 million.

A Philadelphia rabbi was convicted in 2002 for hiring two men to beat his wife to death during the time he was having an affair with a woman he met while ministering to her dying husband.

The Director of Development for (televangelist) Jimmy Swaggart Ministries in Baton Rouge, Louisiana was arrested in 1999 on charges of pilfering more than $750,000 from the organization through leases and trust documents. He spent the money, state and federal prosecutors learned, on girlfriends, flowers, World Series tickets, rented limousines, a sport utility vehicle, and a furnished apartment.

The Boston Roman Catholic Archdiocese, after 2002's ongoing revelations of many dozens of lawsuits resulting from child sexual abuse committed by pedophile priests over the years, sold the Cardinal's residence and other Church property for a total of $189 million to pay off the lawsuit settlements.

Between 1950 and 1971 in a West African boarding school for the school-aged children of Presbyterian missionaries working in that country, the young wards were routinely subjected to cruelties ranging from belt whippings to rape. ,

In late 2005, it was learned that over five years the business manager of a Roman Catholic parish in Buffalo Grove, Illinois stole more than $600,000 from collections and donations to Church charities to support a gambling habit that cost at least $1.8 million.

Clergy malfeasance, or deviant behavior, is not merely a current or recent problem; it is old and will invariably recur due to the nature of religious groups themselves. That is, such antisocial behavior is not new, and it is inevitable for explainable reasons. This is a sociological axiom (a self-evident beginning principle) which this book will establish by argument and plentiful detailed examples similar to ones sampled at the beginning of this introduction.

Clergy malfeasance is old. How old is "old?" It reaches back into antiquity. In fact, noted historian Ernest Gellner, in *Plough, Sword and Book: The Structure of Human History* (1988), writes that despite the familiar cliché that prostitution is the world's oldest profession, that distinction actually belongs to two early occupations: the warrior and priestly castes. The latter's rise as specialists paralleled the transition from hunting/gathering (nomadic) to agrarian (settled) modes of production; the holy men and women went from being shamanistic spiritual experts of small bands and tribes to the ritual/sacrament dispensers of organized religions. As anthropologists have richly demonstrated in their studies of non-Western societies (see, as only one example, Dow, 1986), the clergy have always relied for their authority and ability to awe the crowd on a certain amount of ritualistic manipulation which can sometimes turn into sleight-of-hand or be misused. It is doubtful that human nature has changed much in thousands of years, therefore the temptation and opportunities to exploit believers' vulnerabilities, as we are now seeing, is likely as venerable as civilization itself.

For example, Ladurie (1978), a historian of medieval Europe, recounts how widespread were the potential situations for sexual exploitation within the inequitable status relationships between Roman Catholic priests and other cleric grades. Homosexual relations in ecclesiastical medieval Christendom among priests and monks, brothers, and novitiates (trainees) were so rampant, according to another historian (Boswell, 1981: 182) that:

Saint Peter Damian . . . complained bitterly about the widespread practice of gay priests confessing to each other in order to avoid detection and obtained milder penance, and he alleged that spiritual advisors commonly had sexual relations with those entrusted to their care, a circumstance which would presumably render confessions from the advisee considerably less awkward.

Historian Graciela S. Daichman (1990: 106) also testifies to parallel instances of heterosexual exploitation of nuns and sisters by priests who could conveniently switch from their roles as tempters to absolvers of sins. Doyle, Sipe, and Wall (2006: 29), in an extensive review of literature on the medieval Catholic Church's repeated attempts to outlaw clerical sexual immorality and activities, concluded that:

> It is clear that the bishops were not as preoccupied with secrecy as they are today. Clergy sexual abuse of all kinds was apparently well-known by the public, the clergy, and secular law enforcement authorities. There was a constant stream of disciplinary legislation from the church but none of it was successful in changing clergy behavior.

Half a millennium later on this continent there was a steady parade during the eighteenth and nineteenth centuries of religious hustlers, charlatans, and lecherous clergy persons (Jenkins, 2000). There seems to be something about sex and spirituality that can bring out both the noblest, sacrificial and basest, avaricious behaviors in human beings, and this culture's legacy of continuous renewal of religious pluralism has virtually ensured a rich subculture of deviant behavior.

One audaciously classic case was Robert Matthews, a mid-nineteenth-century modestly educated man (a carpenter by trade) who proclaimed himself the Prophet of the God of the Jews. His charismatic personality attracted followers, particularly women whom he seduced (claiming privileged right of access to all the wives of men in his movement). He collected all his followers' financial assets, meanwhile keeping them in a state of communal poverty as he lived extravagantly. Matthews renamed himself in Hebrew Mattias and actually served jail time for assault during the 1830s (Johnson and Wilentz, 1994). A precursor to the 1990s' David Koresh, the self-appointed Waco, Texas messiah-prophet who also claimed he had a sacred mandate to make adultery a perverse sort of sacrament and sign of group loyalty, Mattias was one of a gallery of sexually voracious religious leaders during the prudish Victorian Era.

The twentieth and twenty-first centuries have supplied a similar trove of accused and actual deviant clergy who made special claims that enriched themselves sexually and/or financially. Sinclair Lewis' *Elmer Gantry (1927)* was a fictitious sawdust-trail tent evangelist, a womanizing, hard-drinking, Bible-quoting hypocrite who actually represented a thinly disguised caricature of a generation of real-life pastors abroad in the United States between the two world wars, such as the charismatic Pentecostal Aimee Semple McPhearson (Blumhoffer, 1993). As we move now into the twenty-first century, or what I term "modern times," the Protestant/Roman Catholic/Jewish/non-Christian examples become legion and these are what this book is about.

What is Clergy Malfeasance?

Clergy malfeasance is a special type of elite deviance, from the Latin meaning bad or evil actions, committed by religious leaders. It signifies the exploitation and abuse of a religious group's rank-and-file believers by the elites of that religion whom those members trust.

There are four important elements in this short definition to consider.

First, the term *malfeasance* in this book is used synonymously with deviance, misconduct, misdeeds, misbehavior, exploitation, and abuse. This malfeasance can be psychological as well as physical. There is no implication that is necessarily illegal, only that it is harmful. It injures those who trust in religious leaders and as an activity is, *by the standards of the particular organization where it occurs*, immoral. The difference between legal and immoral in a given situation can be illustrated, say, by a minister who every Sunday skims charitable contributions from the collection plate given by unknowing persons sitting in the pews in order to secretly buy himself a yacht, as opposed to a pastor who counsels any emotionally vulnerable married woman contemplating a divorce and ends up sleeping with her in the name of therapy. Clergy malfeasance can also be likened to malpractice (though this term is usually reserved for norm-violating or incompetent physicians, therapists, accountants, and lawyers).

Second, in this definition *clergy* broadly refers to religious functionaries with formal or delegated or self-delegated authority. Such clerics include bishops and cardinals, superintendents, pastors, deacons and elders, church youth leaders, educational or choral directors, treasurers, and fund raisers. (A dictionary definition of "a minister" suggests not just an ordained congregational leader but also a diplomat or any agent acting on a higher authority's orders or—again in the religious sense—simply one who applies spiritual principles in order to help all-around growth and well-being in others.)

Religious leaders are therefore *fiduciaries*. This is a critical concept. In legal terms, a fiduciary is one who has special expert knowledge to help or minister to another person; is responsible for looking out for that other's best interests; and, because of that special expert knowledge, holds a unique confidence by the other. Fiduciaries are found in a broad range of occupations: clergy, doctors and nurses, professors and teachers, elected politicians, accountants and lawyers, and counselors. The important common denominator for all fiduciaries is that they ought to be looking out for what is best for their clients, patients, students, citizens, and parishioners—not for themselves. They should not be exploiting these vulnerable persons in order to enrich themselves. If they choose the latter course, it means the betrayal of their special responsibilities and the trust placed in them.

Third, this key fiduciary relationship in religion is one of *social exchange*, often of financial support, reverence, and obedience by laypersons. In return, clergy offer benefits of well-being, spiritual solace and assurance, and perhaps even membership into an elect group of eternally "saved" believers. The relationship of exchange is not so legalistic as a contract with specified limits, warranties, and enforceable obligations. It is more a *covenant* within primary group relations, with no more limits or boundaries than found among family members or that marriage ever puts on partners. And covenants are found in an emotional context while contracts rarely are.

Who decides if elites' actions are abusive? The terms of the religious covenantal social exchange come into play here. Otherwise, couldn't such a decision always be subjective? For example, if what "they" in that group are expected to do by their leaders far exceeds what I think is normal or appropriate, I may conclude that the group's leaders are abusive. This subjectivity can be a knotty problem for outside observers, particularly if they disapprove of the group in question from the start. The key, however, is using the group's own standards as part of gauging malfeasance (remember the first element in the definition above). Most important is the issue of *voluntariness* in the covenantal social exchange. For example, submitting oneself to a rigid lifestyle of discipline (which could include strict, permanent celibacy, unswerving obedience to a superior on every matter, fasting, or periodic ceremonies of humiliation) does not necessarily render those behaviors "abusive" if they are understood as part of a voluntarily embraced lifestyle.

As illustrations, consider two real potentially abusive cases and evaluate them by the voluntariness dimension.

1. Jesus People USA is a Chicago based urban fundamentalist Christian communal group started in the 1970s and still thriving into the twenty-first century. This group has continuously reinvented itself by experimenting with the demands of literal communal service and sacrificial poverty for entire families, based on how members interpret the New Testament's Book of Acts. Among other things, the group is

internally organized into "clans," or biblically named "tribes," each with its own leader.

Jesus People USA developed a practice by internal consent that infractions of the sort that could occur in any group of persons living in tight quarters were to be punished, after due process hearings, by leaders literally spanking other adults with light wooden switches. However, after a year and a half the general conclusion was reached that the practice of humiliations, intended to foster spiritual growth, had been a bust for what it was supposed to accomplish, and the adult membership unanimously voted to abandon the practice. By 1994, the group members themselves looked back and regarded the failed experiment as embarrassingly bizarre.

This is the important point: submission to spanking for an infraction was purely voluntary (and only done to adults) and more symbolic than painful. In terms of the voluntariness criterion, this curious practice of corporal punishment was no more abusive, or malfeasant, to the persons who democratically accepted it than periodic fasting in Roman Catholic or Zen Buddhist monasteries (see Trott, 2000).

A second alternative case, also from the Midwestern United States:

2. The late Hobart Freeman, an independent fundamentalist Protestant preacher in Indiana during the 1980s, vehemently railed in his Faith Assembly movement against the use of medicine of any kind. He preached that biomedical care was grounded in paganism, Satanism, and sin, claiming that prayer alone was sufficient for true Christians' health. By 1983, a total of twenty-eight babies and seven other children had died mostly from lack of any prenatal medical care or treatment, or from preventable childhood diseases such as chicken pox. Some adults as well died from preventable/treatable ailments ranging from kidney disease to bronchitis. By 1988, altogether over one hundred adults and children died of illnesses when the state of Indiana intervened.

According to Indiana law, it is a felony to withhold medical treatment from a minor. Not long after juries began handing down convictions of Faith Assembly parents and Freeman himself for child neglect and manslaughter to Hoosier prosecutors, Freeman (an elderly man) eventually passed away. His followers held a three-day vigil by his corpse expecting him to arise at the end of that time (violating another Indiana public hygiene law). But Freeman never arose (Barron, 1987: 26ff; *Journal Gazette*, 1991; *News-Sentinel*, 1983).

The first amendment to the U.S. Constitution permits complete freedom of belief and conscience but not freedom of *any* actions based on those beliefs without *any* consequences whatsoever. Hobart Freeman's adult followers willingly obeyed his prohibitions on modern medicine. But there are limits for those rendered vulnerable by age and their involuntary presence in any extremist group. For the children and babies there was no covenant with Faith Assembly freely entered into any more than they chose to be the children of their parents in the first place. A religious belief adopted in order to promote spiritual growth, even purity and salvation, but which ends up endangering the very lives of persons—especially minors the civil state has a duty to protect—crosses a line into abuse. Again, voluntariness in accepting the norms and terms of the social exchange with a religious fiduciary becomes a criterion here for defining abuse.

Thus, triangulating or combining information based on outside and inside observers' accounts, knowing the level of voluntariness for all participants in what appears to be a covenantal social exchange, civil laws, and most importantly having clear statements of a religious group's norms, goals, and expectations for a member are not always perfect guides. But the multi-method approach offers a practical, reasonably objective way of recognizing misconduct from the pulpit, rectory, youth outing, collection tallies, or wherever clergy members are found.

Fourth and finally, it is important to emphasize what clergy deviance, or malfeasance, is *not*. The term certainly does not refer to religious groups (or their leaders) as deviant merely because in a particular society they are considered culturally "odd," unpopular, or non-mainstream, such as cults and sects. (One religious scholar critiquing unconventional religious groups did incorporate the word "deviations" into his book's title, but the author clearly admitted his own bias that his own beliefs were the absolute standards by which to judge other groups—see Davies, 1972. Sociologists of religion strive for cultural relativism in analyzing various religious groups and try to avoid prejudging or assigning derogatory labels to groups whenever possible—see Bromley and Shupe, 1981.) To judge some group's beliefs as "deviant" or "false" (departing presumably from a known "truth") would create for sociologists a quagmire of age-old disagreements and jealousies among varieties of Roman Catholics, Protestants, Jews, Muslims, Buddhists, and other non-Christians, some of which in the past involved violence and repression. To evaluate a clergy person as deviant or malfeasant in no way passes a judgment on the validity of the group itself, though sometimes it is difficult to separate the image of an outspoken, even unusual pastor from the group he or she heads. But social science does not deal with absolutes of religious "truth"; these are matters of faith.

With such dry, formal definitional matters completed, we can now turn to the heart of this introduction: laying out the possible types of clergy elite deviance and illustrating them with sometimes shocking but real examples.

Clergy Misconduct and Levels of Crime and Deviance

Sociologists of crime and deviance usually sort regular offenses into one of three categories:

Street crimes produce the most visible, dramatic reactions and often involve violence against persons or their property, or at least the threat of such violence. Harm from street crimes, therefore, is usually easy for victims to recognize. Such crime is also the most likely to receive media attention because it so clearly violates laws and fears about security, it is sensational, and with it most of the public can identify.

White-collar crime, if committed on a large enough scale, may occasionally receive media attention but generally much more limited public awareness. Here the perpetrators steal from their employers. It is much less sensational than street crime because it typically entails guile and cleverness, not physical violence. Its perpetrators are more likely to be found in banks, financial offices, and corporate boardrooms. Examples would be embezzlement, fraud, and phony accounting ("cooking the books"). If street crime is stereotyped as being committed by persons of lower socio-economic status, then white-collar crime (so first named in 1939 by that famous researcher of professional thieves, Edwin H. Sutherland) is more upper class. That is, perpetrators with access to other peoples' resources are more likely to wear suits and white shirts than factory clothes and to be otherwise "respectable" citizens. And both detection and awareness of being a victim is subtle and less dramatic (see, for example, Coleman, 2002; Shower and Wright, 2001).

Corporate crime is the most invisible and least dramatic compared to the previous two levels, therefore it receives the least overall public concern and media coverage. Its perpetrators are often "pillars" of their respective communities: solid family members, wealthy but known for extensive charitable donations, and success stories of American enterprise. The latter criterion is important *because corporate leaders who commit or approve this type of offence must have organizational power close to the top.* Yet corporate offenses are often the most incredibly expensive and damaging to society of all levels. In fact, in terms of a "body count," this level often produces more victims than the first two types combined (see, for examples overall, Simon, 2006; and for detailed analyses of the enormous Enron and Archer-Daniels-Midland scandals that bilked billions of dollars from American consumers and investors, Eichenwald, 2005, 2000). This is because *both the perpetration and the later cover-up of deviance are part of organizational, or corporate, policy.* Not merely individuals but whole networks of policymakers and functionaries are involved and often, when caught by law enforcement, they are not nearly as stigmatized as street criminals are.

Usually these three levels are treated by sociologists and criminologists as *discrete*, i.e., non-overlapping categories of bad actions. This is not the case, however, with many instances of clergy malfeasance. These can have elements of all three levels running simultaneous through them.

One illustration (by no means unique) is Father James Porter, a Roman Catholic priest who was a bisexual pedophile active in his vocation during the 1960s and 1970s. Porter, and others like him, caused a wave of Church sex scandals a decade before the infamous Boston Archdiocese pedophile priest revelations of 2002 so often cited (see later in this chapter).

Porter was relentlessly tracked down and exposed years after his abuses by a private investigator who had been one of Porter's adolescent victims. As it came to light, Porter was one of the premier sex offenders in U.S. history. His sins included engaging children in oral sex (sometimes with more than one child at the same time), mutual masturbation, erotic wrestling and "rough-house" grabbing and groping, and forced anal intercourse with boys and vaginal digital penetration of girls. He had adolescent girls in the confessional booth demonstrate *on him* what they told him their boyfriends and dates had done with them (Berry, 1992: 360; Woodward *et al.*, 1992). Porter in particular had a predilection for altar boys, a readily available victim pool for a priest regularly serving mass. He often had different forms of sex with boys at parochial schools (such as in locker-room showers and wrestling rooms or in church rectories and sacristies) as well as in their home bedrooms when their well-meaning parents invited the friendly (presumably "safe") young priest to meals.

Porter admitted on a television program to having sex with at least 125 male and female youths (with many repeatedly) during the 1960s, though a close reading of one detailed journalistic account (Burkett and Bruni, 1993: 22-24) suggests that a more realistic victim estimate surpasses 200. At one time Porter was sent by church officials to the Villa

Louis Martin, a rehabilitation retreat center for alcoholic and sexually disturbed priests in Jemez Spring, New Mexico. While there, however, he was repeatedly released to do part-time sacramental work (due to a priest shortage) in nearby parishes and while on release molested four youth. After discharge from the villa he later perpetrated abuse again in Houston and *again* at a small-town church in Minnesota (sixteen youths this last time). His most outrageous case after "rehabilitation" undoubtedly occurred when he was a chaplain and sexually abused a young patient confined in a full-body cast at a children's hospital (Burkett and Bruni, 1993: 20; Cafardi, 1993: 148-49).

Later, in their adult lives, Porter's victims pursued him by legal channels. Porter was eventually tried for crimes in more than one locale because his diocesan officials had apparently moved him repeatedly from parish to parish within New England hoping to bury or conceal the trail of his malfeasance. One Massachusetts grand jury, for example, indicted him (thanks to victims' dogged complaints) on forty-six counts of assault, battery, sodomy, and unnatural acts. And they sued. On December 3, 1993 sixty-eight persons in the Fall River, Massachusetts diocese settled claims against the church over his misconduct for over $5 million. But Porter did not stop his perpetration even after he had successfully petitioned the pope in 1974 to dismiss him from the priesthood. He returned to criminal court in the fall of 1992 on charges of fourth-degree felony sexual molestation against a fifteen year-old female baby sitter. (Ex-priest Porter by this time had married and had several children of his own whom he claimed he had never sexually abused.) Ultimately, he was sentenced to up to eighteen years in prison on child endangerment and molestation and scheduled to serve a minimum of six years.

The Father James Porter case clearly demonstrates overlapping levels of street crime (rapes: oral, vaginal, anal; intimidation; various and numerous forms of illegal sexual conduct between an adult and minors), white-collar crime (no pun intended, Porter's deeds were performed to satisfy personal needs and desires during moments "stolen" from his official duties and employer which hurt, and in no way helped, the latter), and corporate crime (Porter's superiors knew of his illegal/immoral actions, choosing at one time to have him seek counseling for his problems. This proved not only ineffective but actually opened up new victim pools in other states, but mostly it covered up his deviance and quietly moved him from parish to parish, hoping his deviant urges would subside *but as a policy the new parish was never warned about his sordid actions in the previous one!*).

Clergy malfeasance, thus, covers the gamut of deviance-crime levels, in large part because (as we will see further) the religious institution inherently provides a wide array of opportunities for deviance, and no other hierarchical institution is so trusted by average members thus rendering them emotionally and spiritually vulnerable in *criminogenic* fashion.

Three Types of Clergy Misconduct

Throughout this volume, we will be focused on three general types of clergy deviance for our examples: sexual violation, economic exploitation, and excessive authoritarian control of congregants and parishioners. Moreover, virtually every case considered here deals with what is criminologically called *recidivism*, or repeated offenses by the same person. Sociologist Edwin M. Lemert (1958, 1951) referred to this pattern as *secondary deviance* as opposed to *primary deviance*. Primary deviance by an actor occurs a few times for whatever reason, perhaps even by accident, but its commission is not part of that actor's self-identity. It is basically situational deviance minimally explainable in a sociological sense. But, according to Lemert, secondary deviance—like recidivism—involves a sequence of actions that go beyond just any number of repetitions. These also influence and alter the actor's role network of interaction with others as well as his or her lifestyle and fundamental self-concept.

Revelations of secondary deviance require some public audience(s). Whether these actions entail child molestation, a homosexual ring of novitiates in a celibate or married seminary, or a corrupt televangelist with a small inner circle of associates who are aware of the former's cynical, fraudulent appeals for charitable donations, the three most important audiences recurring through the following chapters are the perpetrators themselves, their fellow elites who either witness or learn of the deviance before others, and the victims (and their advocates). (Other possible audiences are considered in Chapter 6.) Without audiences to react, there is for all practical purposes no meaningful secondary deviance.

Primary deviance, while intrinsically interesting because it takes up the "Why do they do it?" question, deals more with the social psychology of motives. As I earlier have (1995: 47) observed,

Most patterns of secondary deviance, we can assume, began as acts of primary deviance. In the case of clergy persons, for primary deviance to evolve into secondary deviance the actions' rewards must outweigh any ethical or moral reservations. Moreover . . . it is likely that the particularly elevated moral status of religious elites not only enhances whatever "forbidden fruit" attractions exist in sexual affairs but aids in the rationalization of economic exploitation [and inflation of self-importance beyond mundane ethical restraints] as well. (Bracketed phrase addition mine.)

This issue is considered again in Chapter 3. Until then, below is an abbreviated sample representing merely the tip of a staggering malfeasance iceberg of the three types of clergy deviance.

Sexual Violations

It is safe to say that the most famous and best-publicized American clergy sex scandal was revealed in spring of 2002 in the nation's largest Christian denomination: the Roman Catholic Church, specifically the Archdiocese of Boston under Cardinal Bernard Law. The Boston Archdiocese is the fourth largest in the U.S. Indeed, Roman Catholics make up more than one-half of Boston's total population. During the numerous lawsuit proceedings, Cardinal Law was deposed for two days by attorneys representing dozens of clients alleging to have been victims of priestly sexual misconduct. It was embarrassing for a prelate so prominent (and proud) as His Eminence to have to testify. More than humiliating, however, was Law's often-foggy memory on questions of church disciplinary policy for wayward priests that seemed to imply attempts to evade answering questions directly. Later, it came out that Law had been warned by bishops and others that his Boston priesthood was a ticking time bomb as archdiocesan officials had secretly shuffled malfeasant priests from parish to parish, as in the Porter *et al.* case, without notifying the new parishes of incoming trouble. As writers for the *Boston Globe* (2002: 6) concluded, "Law, his bishops, and their predecessors had moved abusive priests around like pawns on a chessboard." When a judge later unsealed court records from previously settled lawsuits against the church, it was learned that Law had been fully aware of all this and somewhat casually assumed that "the geographic cure" would solve matters (see *Boston Globe*, 2002: 1; Belluck, 2002; Zoll, 2000a, 2000b).

A discredited Cardinal Law issued his *mea culpa* of contrition but too late to be effective in Boston. Ironically, the prelate who had sanctimoniously called down God's wrath on the *Boston Globe* reporters ten years earlier for exposing Father James Porter and others submitted his resignation in December 2002. It was immediately accepted by the pope who reassigned him to Vatican City, Italy (thereby providing Law diplomatic immunity from U.S. prosecutors).

While hundreds of victims began coming forward in 2002, the spark in the power keg this go-around of priestly malfeasance seems to have been the predatory actions of two priests in particular—Reverend John Goeghan and Reverend Paul Shanley. It was learned that sixty-eight year-old Geoghan had raped or fondled some two hundred boys over a thirty-year period and was only removed from the priesthood in 1993 and defrocked in 1998. Though many victims, now adults, had to settle for (or were forced by criminal statutes of limitation to settle for) civil suits, Geoghan was convicted in August of 2003 for groping a ten-year-old boy. While serving a nine to ten-year sentence, another convict named Joseph Druce—himself a victim of Geoghan's pedophilia in 1945—strangled Geoghan in his prison cell and is reported to have said (without remorse), "I killed the child molester . . . He won't touch any more kids (Lavole, 2006a)."

Shanley, aged seventy-one, retired when New England law enforcement officials caught up with him in California. He was also tried and convicted in 2005 for two counts of child rape and two counts of indecent assault and battery of a child. Once a guest speaker at a convention of the North American Man-Boy Love Association, Shanley was known to have advocated pedophilia as a priest. Cardinal Law knew Shanley's reputation and he reassigned Shanley to pastor a parish in 1985 (again with no forewarning to the next victim pool).

The legal repercussions were devastating to the Boston Archdiocese and in the ripple effect to other regions of the U.S. By summer, 2002 Cardinal Law had 118 lawsuits filed against him, 84 more were against Geoghan. Earlier in April, more than 45 persons already claimed to have been sexually violated in some way by Boston-area priests; by late June the alleged victim count had risen to 275 (which often happens once revelations of a scandal build a common awareness in previously silent victims). Three separate attorneys in Boston reported representing 250, 100, and 100 separate new clients, respectively. Lawsuits were inundating the archdiocese. Law's interim successor, former Auxiliary Bishop Richard G. Lennon, immediately confronted (in early 2003) 24 additional Boston abuse cases. The Reverend Sean O'Malley, the new permanent Boston Archbishop and a Capuchin Monk (He once wore his cassock to a press conference.) had previously taken a firm hand in settling the Father James Porter et al. scandals a decade ago and did so again, struggling to restore integrity to the archdiocese. He announced that at least 65 parishes would have to close due to declining finances in the collection plates and elsewhere, a shortage of priests, and the burgeoning costs of lawsuit settlements (Lindsay, 2004). These last costs reached $85 million to settle more than 500 claims. The archdiocese had to sell more than $189 million in church properties, including Cardinal Law's sumptuous personal residence. But then *another* 200 alleged victims stepped forward, and O'Malley offered only $7.5 million to almost 100 of these, averaging $75,000 apiece, and their attorneys howled with outrage.

O'Malley, who had graciously met personally with the first waves of victims in a spirit of reconciliation, was now resigned to dealing with this new batch solely through church attorneys, which had been Law's prior legalistic tactic. The scandal and attendant lawsuits were still going strong half a decade later (Lavole, 2006b, 2003a, 2003b).

The Boston mess served also as a nationwide catalyst for more exposure of scandal. During the first four months of 2002, 176 priests across the U.S. were implicated in sexual abuse (at least 1500 since the mid-1980s—*Boston Globe*, 2002: 8-9, 184). Dioceses and archdioceses in Dallas, Los Angeles, Cleveland, Albuquerque, West Palm Beach, Spokane, and Santa Fe were considering or actually filing for bankruptcy because of sexual abuse claims. Santa Fe alone had to borrow from individual parish savings accounts to pay out more than $45 million in settling 40 cases. New York City, Philadelphia, Indianapolis, Spokane, Milwaukee, and Hartford were also financially hit hard. Within a few years, the diocese/archdioceses of Tucson, Portland, San Diego, Davenport, and Spokane filed for bankruptcy (see, e.g., Ostling, 2006; Kusmer, 2005; Loviglio, 2005). In 2002 alone 350 of 46,000 Roman Catholic priests in the U.S. had either resigned or been dismissed for sexual malfeasance, and three nationally prominent bishops (in Palm Beach, Florida; Milwaukee, Wisconsin; and Lexington, Kentucky) resigned amid similar scandals.

The most stupendous victim-settlement case was that of the Los Angeles Archdiocese in 2007. There, amid last-minute backroom legal negotiations and tense courtroom scenes, it was announced on Monday, July 17, the day before trials began for more than 500 persons who claimed they had been abused by priests, that years of litigation were to result in a $660 million mass settlement. The previous Sunday, Cardinal Roger M. Mahony apologized to the victims, many of whom had fought the archdiocese for years to win even recognition of their grievances, but the apology was hollow. Perhaps of greater satisfaction to them was one further aspect of the settlement: the release of priests' confidential files after review by a judge (Flaccus, 2007a, 2007b).

This brief excursion into the Boston and Los Angeles priest misconduct debacles should not leave readers with the impression that clergy violations of layperson's safety and sexual integrity have been uniquely Catholic. There are a number of instances of mainline Protestant sexual malfeasance (though of very different groups, reflecting the non-central-ized nature of this ex-Roman Catholic break-away phenomenon) as well as others. Some cases represent "garden-variety" heterosexual immoral-ity, but others involve pedophilia and ephebophilia (sexual attraction for an adolescent or young teen as opposed to sexual attraction for a preteen child). Some examples:

- New York Rabbi Baruch Lemmer was convicted by a jury (equally composed of women and men) of abusing teenage girls, and it was reiterated in a 1998 issue of the Jewish women's magazine *Lilith* that there were many such reported accusations of sexual molestations by rabbis (Cooperman, 2000b). Such Jewish scandals occurred a decade earlier. (Bonavaglia [1992: 4] cited what she termed the "zipper fac-tor" in four cases in which Jewish congregations, including northern California's largest, witnessed rabbis who resigned after female members charged sexual harassment, seduction, and adultery.) One rabbinical court of Orthodox Judaism obfuscated its sealed findings on a rabbi accused of molesting more than twenty girls (Matthews, 2002). In Philadelphia Rabbi Fred J. Neulander, in one egregious case, was convicted in late November 2002 for hiring two men to beat his wife to death. At the same time he was having an affair with a woman he met when ministering to her dying husband (Associated Press, 2002c).
- Canadian Amerindians, or aboriginals (referred to by themselves as First Nations), were subjected to an ethnocentric effort started in the early 1800s by an alliance of Canadian federal authorities and The Anglican Church of Canada, the Presbyterian Church of Canada, the United Church of Canada (a merger of Methodist and Congregationist denominations), and the Roman Catholic Church. Their plan was to conscript whole generations of First Nations children and "assimilate" (i.e., denigrate native cultures and "Christianize") them into white society (First Nations, 1994). During the nineteenth and twentieth centuries, over 100,000 First Nations children were forcibly removed from their families, homes, and communities (siblings as well as tribal groups separated) by state authorities and placed in what were vari-ously called the religious denominations' homes, schools, dormitories, and campuses. These were in reality total institutions where the young persons experienced harsh monastic living conditions; psychologi-cal, physical, and sexual cruelties; virtual slave labor; and, of course, attempted genocide of their indigenous languages and traditions. Es-cape was harshly punished; escapees caught were not just beaten and humiliated but also "made examples" of to the others. It is estimated that thousands died in what were a cross between racist indoctrination centers and concentration camps. The last of the so-called "residential schools" was closed by the government in 1969. The First Nations

pressed for recognition, redress, and reparations starting in 1994. The Canadian government (and the participating denominations) has since received over 8,000 lawsuits, and experts believe the latter could ultimately cost over $1.26 billion to settle (Brown, 2002; Careless, 2002; Baglo, 2001; Ward, 2001).

- An alleged clergy sex-ring, led by at least one Episcopalian priest in the Diocese of Long Island, New York involved large quantities of money, cocaine, and young male immigrants brought to the U.S. for exploitation.

- The Church of Jesus Christ of Latter-day Saints (LDS— the Mormons) had one missionary receive a five-year jail sentence after pleading guilty to eighteen counts of "taking indecent liberties" with a minor in North Carolina (Associated Press, 2000). One former LDS bishop and past member of that church's main administration body, the Quorum of the Seventy, named George P. Lee, posed on the internet as a teenager to lure a seventeen year-old girl to Utah (Associated Press, 2000). He accepted a plea agreement in 1994 to plead guilty to attempted sexual abuse of a child (a third-degree felony) instead of standing trial (*Sunstone*, 1994). A former LDS bishop, Spencer Dixon, was charged in fall 2002 with first-degree felony aggravated sexual abuse of a child for allegedly fondling a thirteen-year-old girl's breasts and buttocks inside a church library. (He was subsequently "relieved of his ecclesiastical duties"—*Salt Lake Tribune*, 2002a, 2000b.) Pedophile Franklin Curtis, a LDS elder, apparently repeatedly molested Jeremiah Scott, then nine through eleven years-old, while Curtis was charitably taken into the Scott home as a guest during the early 1990s (Brady, 2001; Kramer, 2001; Moore, 2001). The Scott case lead a Portland, Oregon judge to order the LDS Church to release other internal records of sex abuse complaints and disciplinary actions (Associated Press, 2001).

- Two pastors in the Evangelical Lutheran Church (which has strict, clear policies on inappropriate clergy sexual behavior); one in Rosedale, New York and another in the North Carolina Synod; either were suspended or resigned for sexual misconduct with adult females (*The Lutheran*, 1996a, 1996b).

- In 2000 the Reverend Robert Eckert, an African-Methodist Episcopal minister in Grand Rapids, Michigan, was sentenced to jail for sexual involvement with a fifteen-year-old family babysitter (Ostling, 2002).

- The resignation of Dr. George Roche III from the presidency of the conservative Baptist-affiliated Hillsdale College in Michigan followed revelations that he had been conducting an affair with his daughter-in-law (who became the mother of his grandson) for fifteen years during which time he had divorced his first wife of forty-four years and remarried (LeBlanc, 2000).

- During a twenty-year period (1950-71), in Marmou, Guinea, West Africa, children of (mostly) Presbyterian missionaries whose parents were away in the field were students in a boarding school sponsored by the Christian and Missionary Alliance. There they faced a variety

of abuses ranging from belt whippings to rape (see www.mksafetynet.
cjb.net; Kennedy, 1995).

- The late Jeff Smith, host of public television's "Frugal Gourmet"
cooking show and an ordained United Methodist Minister, agreed
to pay an undisclosed sum of money to seven men who accused him
of molesting them when they were teenagers (*Fort Wayne Journal
Gazette*, 1998a).

- In early 2007 a Van Wert, Ohio judge passed sentence on twenty-eight
year-old Aaron D. Rediger, a youth pastor at Liberty Baptist Church,
after he admitted he had a year-long intimate sexual affair with an
underage parishioner. Rediger pleaded guilty to two of three felony
sexual battery charges (in return for the third being dropped) and
in addition to a two-year prison sentence was ordered thereafter to
register as a sex offender in whatever county he would reside for the
next ten years. After learning about the initial allegations, the church
fired Rediger and rescinded both his ministry license and ordination
certificate (*Fort Wayne Journal Gazette,* 2007).

- A website, www.reformation.com (maintained solely by a group of
Protestant volunteers), was active cataloging clergy sexual abuse in
the late spring/early summer of 2002. Since April 3, 1997, the group
cited as its own "sample" of scandals, 312 total cases: 59 Baptists, 150
fundamentalist/evangelical "Bible" church pastors, 31 Episcopalians,
22 Lutherans, 25 Methodists, 10 Presbyterians, and 13 others. There
have also been a large number of studies, both academic (See Jenkins,
2002; Stockton, 2000a; Seal, Trent, and Kim, 1993; Fortune, 1989) as
well as journalistic (see Ostling, 2002; Clayton, 2002; O'Brien, 2002;
Schreiner, 2002; Special Bulletin, 2002; Witham, 2002; Paulson,
2001; Woodward, 1997; Giles, 1993) detailing Southern Baptist to
Presbyterian to Jehovah's Witnesses' scandals.

- One Protestant victims' movement, virtually the product of one woman,
Southern Baptist Christa Brown, seeks to force that denomination's
officers to publicly address instances of clergy sexual abuse by its
pastors. Motivated by her own past victimization and terming the
scandals in the Southern Baptist Convention (the nation's largest
Protestant denomination) "Baptistgate." Brown has created a sophisticated website called "Voice to Stop Baptist Predators" which monitors
media coverage of cases of Baptist clerical sexual exploitation from
across the United States. She denounced what she terms Baptist male
leadership "blindness" and more than implies that it is the result of
collusion by leaders to protect pastors rather than laity. (See www.
takecourage.org and www.stopbaptistpredators.com/mission.)

Economic Exploitation

Just as white-collar/corporate secular crimes receive much less media
attention than street crimes, yet are responsible for more widespread
damage, the media pay more attention to sexual exploitation by clergy

than to clergy economic exploitation which affects a larger number of individuals and institutions (Shupe, 1998: 7).

During the 1980s and 1990s, not to mention the era of the twenty-first century, embezzlements, cons, schemes, and frauds have been endemic in Christian churches be these liberal or conservative, Catholic or Protestant, Mormon or otherwise. True, some have not been repeated. For example, the televangelist scandals of the late 1980s involving para-church mega-stars like the PTL Network's Jim and Tammy Faye Bakker or Dallas' Robert Tilton and W. V. Grant, Jr. inventing out of whole cloth phony foreign missions while literally scooping up tax-free cash sent in by purloined viewers and spending it on extravagant, hypocritical lifestyles. Perhaps they served as dramatic examples for deterrence: the Reverend Mr. Bakker and Reverend Mr. Grant went to prison for federal income tax evasion and both Tilton's enormous Dallas church and his television ministry were also ruined (Shupe, 1998: 57-61).

The other more "pedestrian" examples of looting church collection plates, coffers, and assets by treasurers and other fiduciaries continue to be recycled news with merely the names of particular groups changed. In 2007 one Indianapolis pastor, the Reverend Rochelle Johnson of Greater Faith Missionary Baptist, pleaded guilty to welfare fraud and agreed with prosecutors to reimburse $186,000 to the Social Security Administration (Associated Press, 2007a); another local clergyman, Jesse M. Beasley III, "misdirected" more than $12,000 from a state-funded social service program in his Living Word of God Ministries and was told to reimburse the state (Kelly, 2007); and in Mountainside, New Jersey, seventy-one year-old William J. Biunno, former trustee and choir member at Our Lady of Lourdes Roman Catholic Church, was caught on video tape literally stuffing his pockets with cash from the collection plate during mass. It is estimated by church officials that Biunno pocketed about $28,000 over an eleven-year period (Associated Press, 2007b). Some perpetrators continue to display remarkable greed and over-confidence in their secondary deviance. Some also can even be pathetic in their attempts to minimize the guilt of their offenses. The Episcopal Church's national treasurer, Ellen Cooke, for example, resigned from her job in January 1995 after serving eight years at an annual salary of $125,000. She pleaded guilty to transferring at least $1.5 million from church revenues to a private account as well as to income tax evasion. She treated the church as her private cash cow, spending the money on her tastes for travel, new houses, expensive jewelry, and private schooling for her children. She blamed her malfeasant behavior on "faulty memory"; her psychiatrist claimed it was the result of job stress and her lawyer explained it as due to a "bipolar mood disorder" (Fialka, 1995; *Christianity Today*, 1996a, 1966b).

Elsewhere (Shupe, 1998: 49-64) I have chronicled this sad litany of such peculating malfeasants of the 1990s who (it seems in retrospect) were mysteriously confident that they could get away with such thievery. They are still legion, as illustrated by the more recent case a decade later of Donato "Dan" Suffoletto. Suffoletto, business manager of a Roman Catholic parish in Buffalo Grove, Illinois helped himself to more than $600,000 from collection plates and charitable contributions over a five-year period to subsidize a gambling addiction that ultimately cost $1.8 million at Illinois casinos. When parish officials began investigating the lost money trail, they found opened offering envelops in his office wastebasket (Wronski, 2005).

Indeed, it appears that the American Catholic Church has a serious embezzlement problem. A survey released in January, 2007 by researchers at Villanova University found in a study of internal financial controls in the nation's 178 dioceses that of the 78 responding more than the majority (or 85 percent) had discovered embezzlement of church monies during the previous five years, with eleven percent of the dioceses reporting that a total of more than $500,000 had been stolen. Almost one-third of the Catholic dioceses reported thefts of less than $50,000 each. Commented one business ethicist: "Churches have a tendency to be in denial about the potential for this conduct in their midst" (Goodstein and Strom, 2007; see also Rendeaux, 2007).

In this volume it is more important to focus on *investment scams* which account for the most widespread serious financial (and devastating faith) damage within the economic malfeasance type. These are often "affinity crimes," the perpetrator using personal religious familiarity with, and/or purported background (or even authority) in a particular church or faith community to lull victims into ill-placed confidence and trust. Wrote one reporter in 2001:

> Securities investigators warned recently that faith-based investment scams have increased dramatically and urged clergy and lay people to demand documentation from anyone selling investments, including members of their own congregation. (Broadway, 2001)

Typically, schemes offer unrealistic, if not astronomical, returns on modest investments. The perpetrator's goal is to attract a large number of investors, only the first of whom actually do receive the promised returns but serve as bait for the later ones in this classic "Ponzi" pyramid hustle. The victims are vulnerable not only because they are investment naive but also because they often live on a financial margin, such as retirees, and have serious needs for more income. Some spectacular examples:

- Donald E. James, a Sunday school teacher at the Calvary Assembly of God church in Atlanta, Georgia and who was never registered as a commodity pool trader or trade advisor (required by federal law), raised $5 million from fellow church members over four years. James promised them an astonishing 18 percent return *per month* on their investments in commodity futures he was supposedly acquiring. The problem was that James invested less than $200,000 of the money (and lost $120,000 of that), spending the rest on a lavish lifestyle. Complaints began to mount, and in April 1999, a U.S. district court froze all of James' assets, forbidding him to do any more soliciting of investment monies. He subsequently went to jail on charges of theft (*Fort Wayne Journal Gazette*, 1999).
- Jonathan Strawder, who created a securities/missionary operation called Sovereign Ministries, took less than a year to raise $14 million from more than 2,100 fellow Christians. Later federal investigators learned that his bogus plan was to sell securities with part of the profit supposedly going to build churches in post-communist Poland and in Kenya. The churches, it turned out, were non-existent, and investors never saw their promised returns or their money back. Familiar elements composed this scam: Strawder purchased, among other things, two Porches, a Land Rover, a BMW, a yacht, a motorcycle, and two Chicago apartment buildings, yet most of the money went unaccounted for (*Fort Wayne Journal Gazette*, 1998b).
- Mark Hofmann, as a young man was a Mormon missionary overseas, but later in life became disillusioned and embittered against the LDS church. He became a master forger of pseudo-historical materials about the early (nineteenth-century) church. (He also developed into a sociopath serial bomber who ended up murdering several innocent persons to throw disgruntled investors in his pyramid scheme and police off his trail.) He conned a number of high LDS leaders out of tens of thousands of church dollars by selling them or their agents bogus letters and documents, playing on their fears that these materials would tell a history of church origins far different from the "official" story. Church officials authorized persons to quietly purchase them and donate the latter to the organization which would then "bury" them with minimal publicity in vaults inaccessible to most of the world (Shupe, 1991: 76-105; Lindsey, 1988; Naifeh and White, 1988; Sillitoe and Roberts, 1988).
- The founder of the Investment Research Management Corporation, John O. Van Hofwegen, as well as most of its investors, belonged to the Christian Reformed Church denomination in Grand Rapids, Michi-

gan. IRM raised approximately $400 million in a bogus real estate operation where yearly dividends of 9 to 11 percent were promised and actually paid to initial investors. But as the real estate market dipped dramatically during the late 1980s, the flood of new investors attracted by initial investors' endorsements could not be paid. Most of the later investors were retirees who lost their life savings. In addition, other Christian Reformed Church-related institutions, such as Calvin College and the *Back to God* radio ministry, lost altogether as much as $130 million (Herbert, 1998).

There have been other sensational affinity economic scandals, such as the Baptist Foundation of Arizona (associated with the Arizona Southern Baptist Convention) which fleeced more than 13,000 investors who thought they had purchased over $500 million worth of securities allegedly to be used to raise funds for Southern Baptist-affiliated charities. However, the BFA spent only about $1.3 million to that end, while lavishing $16 million on staff salaries and over $329,000 on perks such as staff automobiles (and squandering the bulk of the money on bad loans and dubious real estate deals—see Schroeder, 2001; Fager, 1999b). Or there was the Greater Ministries International Church, which operated a "gift-in, gift-out" gimmick supposedly taking investors' money (a total of over $500 million, similar to the BFA above, but in this case *from 18,000 victims*), investing in foreign trading of precious metals, and then distributing to investors *double their money back within eighteen months*. Most investors in this illegal, unregistered pyramid hustle never saw any money returned (Fager, 1999a, 1999d; Maxwell, 1995). Gerald Payne, unrepentant head of GMIC, was sentenced to a prison term of 27 years in March, 2001 on 19 counts of wire fraud and money laundering (among other crimes), while other officers—including Jonathan Strawder, whose $12 million Sovereign Ministries boondoggle (mentioned above) was a smaller spin-off of GMIC—received prison sentences of 5 years, 10 years, and longer (Fager, 2001).

A more comprehensive chronicle of the voluminous reports of such affinity frauds within both white and black churches would need its own volume—by now the numerous prosecutions and convictions have steadily accumulated. However, for a cynically audacious financial pyramid scheme that dragged down so many otherwise well respected and good-intentioned organizations and educational institutions as well as bilked so many victims, the Foundation for New Era Philanthropy scandal knows no peer. It was undoubtedly the most famous of the twentieth-century affinity frauds.

John G. Bennett, Jr., New Era's mastermind and chairman, was once described as an "inspiring and warm-hearted Christian philanthropist" (Giles, 1995: 40). Bennett created an immense pyramid scheme in which he falsely claimed to be able to tap a pool of "anonymous donors" willing to put up tens of millions of dollars to match funds invested by educational and charitable groups and all to be placed in the hands of sole recipient Bennett himself. Over one hundred colleges and missions believed the "anonymous donor" pitch and funneled large amounts of money to New Era. The foundation would then purportedly purchase the usual range of "high yield" stocks, and investors were assured of realizing their investments *doubled in just six months*. (Chapter 4 will take up the intriguing subject of religious believers' sometime gullibility and greed.)

Of course, there were no "anonymous donors." Later ministries and schools depositing funds in ongoing fashion were actually serving in lieu of those donors to match and pay returns on the investments of earlier investors. Meanwhile, Bennett (as the Securities and Exchange Commission came to discover) was diverting more than $4 million to his own personal businesses and paying himself a $26,000-plus salary *per week* (Neff, 1995; Giles, 1995: 40; Frame, 1995: 61).

In 1993, New Era took in $41.3 million from recently enrolled clients but earned only a dismal $33,788 from its real investments. New clients were eagerly sought, as they were needed to pay the old ones. In 1994, Bennett kept up his high-profile philanthropic reputation by contributing a total of $240 million to a number of institutions. Somewhat inexplicably, he even gave a total of $20 million to Planned Parenthood and Harvard University, neither of which had ever invested in New Era. At the peak of New Era's philanthropic frenzy, Bennett wrote $98 million in checks within a ninety-day period, averaging over $1 million per day in institutional pay-offs.

Bennett's extravagant and sometimes erratic largesse resulted in New Era's collapse, and he filed for bankruptcy, claiming $551 million in liabilities and only $80 million in assets (Giles, 1995: 40-1). Bennett tried to explain the situation as the result of "bad judgments" in managing funds but was eventually convicted of numerous types of fraud and sentenced to 12 years in prison.

Bennett also created ethical and moral dilemmas for those religious organizations which *had* received the promised returns versus those who were ripped off. For example, "winners" included prestigious evangelical Christian institutions like Lancaster Bible College ($16.9 million), Messiah College ($2 million), John Brown University ($2 million), Wheaton College ($4.6 million), and Gordon-Conwell Theological Seminary (49.8 million). Later investors, however, predictably lost large. A group calling itself United Response to New Era, made up of 150 Christian sister organizations (52 of which had received lucrative returns largely provided by the 61 later "losers"—Frame, 1995), formed to somehow deal fairly in sorting out the post-New Era mess.

By the early twenty-first century the prominent evangelical Christian publication *Christianity Today* observed that "between 1998 and 2001, at least 80,000 people lost $2 billion in religious scams" (Moll, 2005: 30) and ran as its January, 2005 cover/feature story "The Fraudbuster" about a convicted pyramid schemer-turned-born again pastor named Barry Minkow. *Christianity Today* had warned readers over the past several decades about affinity scam dangers and ran extensive coverage of Minkow and the Fraud Discovery Institute which he founded. The article was, of course, heavily laced with themes of redemption and amends, but it served as a testimony to an ongoing problem in churches. As one government regulator concluded, "Con artists try to make faith in God synonymous with faith in their investment scam" (Moll, 2005: 31).

Excessive Authoritative Control

The concept "excessive authoritarian control" by a clergy person might seem at first highly subjective. Could not one person's experience of alleged stifling control be another's spiritual growth-enhancing discipline? "This is admittedly the 'grayest' form of clergy malfeasance, which includes a continuum of behaviors from clearly identifiable to less easily discernible wrongdoing" (Shupe, 1995: 42). It would range from the coercive Catholic priest pederasty of the Reverends Mr. Porter, Mr. Geoghan, and Mr. Shanley to "control freak" pastors who claim religious justification to micromanage every aspect (employment, lifestyle, politics, leisure time, sex, appearance, and so forth) of group members' lives.

Before offering definitions of this abusive type, consider the extreme case of the Reverend Wilbert Thomas, Sr. The Reverend Mr. Thomas proclaimed himself a "bishop" though he was unaffiliated with any denomination. He pastored an independent black congregation, the Christian Alliance Holiness Church, with approximately three thousand members. The Mercer, New Jersey prosecutor's office conducted a seven-month investigation after word began to leak out of some of the Reverend Mr. Thomas' ministerial actions. Thomas and two other men in the church were eventually indicted on aggravated assault and criminal coercion. According to the indictment:

> Threats, sexual abuse, and beatings with tree limbs and rubber hoses were used to discipline congregation members and prevent them from leaving the group . . . Thomas forbade them from reading about People's Temple leader Jim Jones . . . [Thomas] used the violence to enforce his personal gospel of subservience and self-glorification. (Hoffman, 1983)

Thomas could be provoked easily and unpredictably. One woman told a journalist that Thomas had once had her whipped when she cut her hair without asking his permission, this after having had to provide him with sex on demand. Another member, Franklin Delano Adams, went to Thomas two weeks before Thanksgiving and asked him whether Adams should consider a career change to become a dental technician (in the context of asking Thomas' permission). Thomas became enraged at Adams "wasting Thomas' time" and had Adams beaten by a group of elders and senior members. They bent Adams naked over a table and each man whipped him at least five times until his thighs, hips, and back were severely lacerated.

Most excessive authoritative control is less violent and a bit more subtle. Clearly essential elements are that the fiduciary's actions are (1) grounded in the authority of pastoral authority, (2) leading to a loss of members' spiritual and physical autonomy, (3) in various ways beneficial to that fiduciary disproportionately at the member's expense.

It is possible, therefore, to reach a workable definition to allow recognizing this type of malfeasance. Aside from civil/criminal laws and ecclesiastical rules and standards, we can understand such behavior as *violating the voluntary exchange* of trust between a powerful fiduciary and vulnerable layperson. The violations of personhood brought about by rapacious sexual molesters and apparent sadists like the Reverend Mr. Thomas are at one extreme. On the other hand, "submitting onself to a rigid, spartan regimen of celibacy, poverty, periodic fasting, or pride-reducing rituals is not necessarily 'abusive' to psychologically healthy adults if such practices makeup part of a life-style voluntarily embraced" (Shupe, 1998: 8). Otherwise, to label all indoctrination centers that call for sharp conformity as abusive would not allow us to distinguish between concentration/prisoner of war camps and military academies or monasteries. (For examples of careless use of the "abusive" label by persons trying to account for their personally disastrous participation in a variety of new religious movements and other groups, see Bromley, 1988; Bromley and Shupe, 1981: 198-202).

Therefore, two similar, previously developed definitions are offered, and either can stand for the range of this third type of clergy misconduct. The first comes from two excommunicated Mormon writers using their former church as a prime example:

> Ecclesiastical abuse [excessive authoritative control] occurs when a Church officer acting in his official capacity and using the weight of his (less frequently her) office, coerces compliance, imposes his personal opinions of church doctrines of policy, or resorts to such power plays as threats, intimidation, and punishment to insure that his views prevail in a conflict of opinion. (Anderson and Allred, 1997: xvi) (Bracketed insert mine)

The second, slightly more brief and more inclusive definition is my own: "excessive authoritative control can be seen in a leader's 'excessive monitoring and controlling of members' livelihoods, resources, and lifestyles to enrich that leader, either in money or power" (Shupe, 1998: 8).

One well publicized Protestant example of flagrant (abusive) leadership hypocrisy and authority abuse occurred in November 2006. The Reverend Ted Haggard, pastor of Colorado Springs' 14,000-member New Life Church and president of the 30 million-member National Association of Evangelicals, was asked abruptly to resign from both posts after investigations confirmed that Haggard had been engaged in a multi-year affair with a gay body-builder escort and had purchased methamphetamine from a gay prostitute. The ruggedly handsome, photogenic Haggard, an outspoken opponent of same-sex unions, at first denied the drugs and trysts. (He was outed by his male partner on television.) Haggard eventually admitted it all on television no less in front of his wife and five children. Haggard betrayed his wife, his megachurch congregation, and those who believed in his moral leadership, including thousands of other pastors who endorsed or took pride in his NAE presidency and their financially contributing churches. Words of "love-the-sinner, hate-the-sin" may have lost their coinage for a time among conservative Christians with this revelation of scandal. However, the pastor who in 2005 was featured on the cover of *Christianity Today* (with the title: "Meet Ted Haggard the NAE's Optimistic Champion of Ecumenical Evangelism and Free Market Faith"), was back less than a year after the 2006 scandal and proclaimed "cured" of his homosexuality by a small workshop of pastors who took him on a secluded retreat for several weeks. His reception at his Colorado Springs church, however, was not so well assured (see, e.g., Stafford, 2005; Lemire, 2006; Simon, 2006; Webb, 2006; *Fort Wayne Journal Gazette*, 2007a).

Penultimately, I want to say something to readers of my theoretical "orientation" toward the clergy misconduct phenomenon and why it may, at times, seem harsh. My perspective here is one of the conflict paradigm.

There are a number of classical, neo-classical, and modern approaches (these last more resembling real theories) to conflict. Jonathan H. Turner's theoretical overview of conflict lists over a dozen theories alone if one includes gender stratification variations and other substantive emphases (1998: 153-245). My use of the conflict approach is more in the classical camp and within a group called "elitist theorists" (which Turner curiously skips altogether). These are predominantly the four European social scientists Vilfredo Pareto, Gaetano Mosca, Milovan Djilas, and Robert Michels, three of whom were in what is known as the "Franco-Italian" school. All four believed that the dialectical materialist Karl Marx (sometimes referred to as the "father" of conflict theory) was naive in believing that the evolving class conflict in industrial societies of his day would eventually result in a historical endpoint of classless (hence sociologically conflict-free) utopia called communism. All three believed also that Marx had made a faulty reading of the role of concentrated wealth and political power in modern industrial society. These elitist theorists held the following three assumptions:

1.   All social order, while ostensibly premised on the interdependence of institutions and various economic levels with the appearance of acceptance by most, is actually based on power and coercion of the masses by better-organized elites.
2.   All important social resources are scarce and unequally possessed; continuous competition and even conflict are the norm, not the unusual, with "haves" trying to keep and "have-nots" trying to get or take. Most groups in the middle of any hierarchy are striving to do both.
3.   Elites in any society or organization who benefit most from the disproportionate arrangement of scarce resources will always attempt to mask the conflict, insisting on some "natural," logical, or even "divine" apology or defense for this arrangement.

I am firmly in the camp of the elitist theorists, most especially with Mosca (1939), Djilas (1957, 1998) and Michels (1959). Indeed, the ideas of Michels (an avid Marxist activist as a young man, a disillusioned thoughtful scholar in his later years) and Djilas (a former communist imprisoned for his writings critical of a failed system) form much of my approach in Chapter 3. There I have used as a theme "the iron law of clergy elitism" taken from Michels' "iron law of oligarchy" in his classic and still timely book *Political Parties* (first published in 1915). Concepts like "the iron law of oligarchy" are used here to examine elite power and possible bureaucratic insulation from laity and elites'/laity's dealings with each other's reactions to clergy misconduct.

A final caveat for readers on the conceptual analysis of this book: no one faith tradition or group is singled out. When writing about the dark or unpleasant side of religion one is sometimes accused of being anti-religious, engaged in faith-bashing, or even just plain irreverent for the savage pleasure of lowering the venerated down a few notches. This criticism may be inevitable, but in this case it is untrue. Let me conclude this section with some words from my first book on the subject, published in 1995 when few sociologists were even paying attention to this social problem:

> Writing about malfeasance, or deviance, among persons in positions of religious authority is not different from reporting about elite deviance in corporations. (And sociologists have not been loath to deal with that subject.) . . . My goal in this study is to treat incidences of clergy malfeasance as embedded in a knowable web of inter-related events that are not as individualistic as they must seem to the victims who first experience them. Sociology looks for the unique in the familiar and the understandable in the bizarre. All that is present in the phenomenon of clergy malfeasance. (Shupe, 1995: 23)

Overview of the Rest of this Volume

Chapter 2 focuses on two primary questions: Why are we learning about such deviance *now*, as if the problem suddenly emerged with no precedent? How much of this misconduct really goes on, and how do we know? A constructionist approach to social problems is considered along with available studies, surveys, and observations to answer these questions.

Chapter 3 looks at the dynamics of exploitation, using the concepts of secondary deviance and Michel's elitist theory to examine elite deviance reaction strategies within different types of religious groups. I consider this chapter the heart of the book.

Chapter 4 shifts emphasis to *victims'* strategies as they mobilize countermovements and call for redress from church bodies. The logic of their tactics is considered using a major social movements approach known as resource mobilization.

Chapter 5 looks at the interplay (often negotiations) between elite spokespersons and their victim-advocacy counterparts. Condemnations from both sides of each other are noted along with denominations' own attempts to anticipate future such problems before they occur.

Chapter 6 looks at the true or larger meaning of the fallout from current scandals. Is it functional or dysfunctional, for whom, and at what time frames? How does it both help and undermine organized religion?

The Epilogue is just that in the subtle form of a warning. Clergy misconduct scandals, as I maintained on the first page, are not new, are ongoing as I write and you read, and will reappear indefinitely (even if the media stop monitoring them for a while). Why can we expect more scandals? What is it in the nature of religion as we know it that causes us to become so expectant?

2

Clergy Malfeasance as Secondary Deviance: Forms and Extent

If one wanted to find out the number of separate instances of clergy misconduct each year in the U.S., she would be hard pressed to find statistics at all either in the Federal Bureau of Investigation's annual Uniform Crime Reports or official tallies by any law enforcement agency at federal, state, or local levels. This is because the various sorts of criminal deviance committed by religious elites are not recorded in any categories as clergy offenses per se. *Affinity crimes*, for example, is a religious label, not a legal one. Rather, these offenses are simply folded over into the total number of non-clergy related crimes. Thus, if a priest sexually assaults a minor, if a denomination's treasurer embezzles, or a church officer bilks elderly members of a faith out of their life savings with a phony stock scheme, their deviant acts are mixed in with secular categories such as rape, juvenile/child molestation, sexual seduction, indecent or sexual assault, battery/endangerment of a child, child seduction, sexual confinement, general battery, premeditated assault, mail/wire/securities fraud, embezzlement, money laundering, federal licensing violations, income tax evasion, grand larceny, and so forth.

The American constitutional separation of church and state and this country's totally secular government agencies mean that the latter law enforcement personnel have to prosecute the actions just as they would the same committed by non-clergy. (There are even intimations that such agencies as the U.S. Justice Department are reluctant to tread on religious ground, as in the case of the Jim and Tammy Faye Bakker PTL televangelism scandal during the late 1980s—see Hadden and Shupe, 1988: 15ff). As a result, there are no official "numbers" nor any systematically collected by private religious groups, Protestant (such as the National Council of Churches) or Catholic (such as various victims' advocacy groups) beyond recent published instances. Social scientists (and a tiny minority of those) and a few journalists have been faced with four kinds of limited data sources: (1) anecdotal (qualitative) case studies and thumb-nail estimates based on clinical practice, (2) denominational surveys, (3) general or specific population victimization surveys, and (4) existing denominational policies addressing the clergy malfeasance problem. All methods in this quartet have their drawbacks. There are both pros and cons to each. At the end of this chapter, it will be possible to triangulate what we know and this will form a composite picture of the abuse problem.

Clinical-Anecdotal Studies

Clinical studies drawn from the private practices of psychotherapists and counselors who even take the additional effort to search for numbers and patterns within their patient files are a rarity. The most famous can be found in three books by A. W. Richard Sipe (2003, 1995, 1990). Sipe is an ordained Roman Catholic priest and, for forty years, a psychotherapist specializing in Catholic clergy sexual problems as well as a seminary faculty member. Here I will focus on just Sipe's longitudinal studies since they have been the most influential for scholars, mental health practitioners, and victims' advocacy groups. Sipe's admittedly non-random sub-sample of priests and other Catholic leaders in vocation (a Catholic term for clergy responsibilities) is now well over 1500. He found that one-third of his priest patients were sexually active (and simultaneously experienced emotional strain because of it). Another third had been witnesses to disturbing clergy abuse but were not counseled by him as patients. And a final third told Sipe they had been sexual partners, lovers, victims, or had had direct sexual experiences with priests, nuns, seminarians, and ex-priests.

Sipe's most often quoted estimates are that 20 percent of current Catholic priests are engaged in illicit *heterosexual* relationships, while another 8 to 10 percent are at some stage of (often-progressive) physical intimacies. Total that is close to one in three. Between 18 and 22 percent are involved in *homosexual* relationships (mostly but not always with others of their profession, including seminarians) or are attracted to homosexual involvements, or openly identify themselves as gay, or at least have serious questions about their own sexual orientations.

Only about 2 percent of Catholic priests, Sipe says, should be considered pedophiles, while another 4 percent are practicing or non-practicing ephebophiles (being attracted to adolescent boys and/or girls—see Sipe, 1990: 62). There are at this time around 49,000 to 50,000 active priests in the U.S. (the number is shrinking, many leaving the priesthood to marry and not all are American citizens). Simple math based on Sipe's tally—the best so far—yields a sub-sample of about 6 percent, or approximately 3,000 priests, who are sexually attracted to young persons. Overall, few of their cases have made the headlines.

Even Sipe's multi-decade data have significant limitations: they only represent those priests referred to him for counseling or who independently sought it. And, of course, his numbers apply only to Catholic clergy.

Denominational Surveys

Surveys on or by denominations give us a valuable if only partial internal picture of their clergy misconduct prevalence. For example, the Roman Catholic Church does conduct internally sponsored surveys on a variety of subjects, but most are not for public consumption. One exception is Hemrick and Hoge (1993) which found that a majority of seminary faculty agreed that the proportion of seminary students with dysfunctional backgrounds was greater at the time of their study than a decade earlier.

A much more publicized study during the early 1990s occurred when the Canadian Conference of Catholic Bishops created a special commission to deal with complaints against clergy sexual behavior in order to establish new abuse policies (Burkett and Bruni, 1993: 43; Berry, 1992: 314-6;; Nason-Clark, 1991). The U.S. equivalent came in the form of a 2004 study by the John Jay College of Criminal Justice in New York, commissioned by the U.S. Catholic Conference of Bishops. The aim of the John Jay criminologists was to determine, using diocesan data with the Church's permission (at first), characteristics of perpetrators, victims, and financial losses accrued through legal settlements of victim lawsuits against the Church.

This report claimed that around 4 percent of U.S. priests had been accused of abuse, studying 4,450 of the 110,000 priests who had served between 1950 and 2000. This proportion of cases was considerably higher than both the church's earlier estimate of 1 percent but not as high as ones put out by victims groups (though it was lower also compared to A. W. Richard Sipe's earlier estimate cited from his longitudinal clinical studies, mentioned above). One Santa Clara University psychology professor had predicted an estimate of 2 percent, while Dr. Reverend Andrew M. Greeley, an ordained Catholic priest and well-known sociologist, estimated between 2,000 to 4,000 minors to have been victimized by 4 percent of U.S. priests (Paulson, 2004). The report held that U.S.

bishops (across all dioceses) reported more than 11,000 accusations of clergy abuse, 6,700 of which were substantiated. Another 1,000 went unsubstantiated, and in the remainder of cases, the alleged perpetrators were deceased. (No statistics were broken down by diocese.)

Meanwhile, showing the political import of such numbers, William Donahue, President of the Catholic League for Religious Rights, issued through his organization its own special report in anticipation of the John Jay Report. CLRCR's data consisted of newspaper articles, not social science data, and dubious experts. It was also long on vague numbers and virtual "guesstimates" that basically sought to neutralize the bad publicity for the Roman Catholic Church by saying that there might be some abusive priests but that Catholic priests were no different (or worse) in amount of their deviance than Protestant and Jewish clergy or even school teachers! For example, a Jewish law professor/rabbi, with no evidence at hand, was quoted as saying he "believed" that sexual abuse by rabbis (which: Reformed, Conservative, or Orthodox? He did not say.) happened at approximately the same rate as with Protestant ministers, as if the Protestant denominations or anyone else had reliable unitary estimates for all their clergy. And, in this special report, actually an attempt to minimize the Church's embarrassment at the epidemic of priest sexual deviance, *pedophile* priests were illogically compared to other non-Catholic adult clergy and school teaching professionals committing adultery or having consensual sex only *with other adults* (CLRCR, 2004). The comparison did not really help CLRCR's case and only served to cloud the issue.

One usually does only a little better in having numbers of deviant Protestant clergy but never comprehensive statistics. Lebacq and Barton (1991: 68ff) found, in combining a number of smaller surveys to achieve a sample size of several hundreds of male and female Protestant clergy, that about one in ten had become sexually active with (adult) congregants who were not their spouses. The researchers also cited a survey in evangelical, Protestant *Christianity Today* magazine that discovered a much higher proportion of clergy—one in four—who admitted they had crossed the taboo sexual line with members of their congregations that they themselves judged "as wrong." Two years later Seal *et al.* (1993) published results of their study of a sample of 277 senior Southern Baptist pastors (1000 were initially contacted with requests to respond). In six southern states, six percent admitted that they had conducted sexual affairs with church lay members.

Conway and Conway (1993: 79) found higher rates of sex deviance: slightly over one-third (37 percent) of various denomination's pastors surveyed admitted to having had "inappropriate sexual contact" with congregants, and 12 percent confessed to having experienced sexual affairs with at least one person (male or female) in their churches during their years in the pulpit.

Finally, the United Methodist Church in 1990 issued an internal report in which it claimed that almost one in five lay women and as many as almost one in three (31 percent) of female clergy had been sexually harassed (from risqué innuendos to propositions) by fellow (male) pastors (United Methodist Church, 1990: 3-5). A little later, the Presbyterian Church U.S.A. (an amalgamation of previously smaller Presbyterian denominations) reported that during the early 1990s an estimated 10 to 23 percent of their clergy had engaged in sexual harassment or physical contact with either church employees or members in the pews (Bonavoglia, 1992: 41).

I have sketchily discussed the results of these studies by or on the Protestant denomination to show that during the years the American wing of the Roman Catholic Church's first wave of pedophile priest scandals were unfolding, Protestants were coming to grips with their own misbehaving clergy. The results of these surveys illustrate the contention that no single religious group or variation of Christianity possesses a monopoly on the sexual abuse dimension (though it is an undeniable fact that pedophilia incidents seem to more characteristic of Catholic clergy sexual malfeasance than in Protestantism where they are treated as a single entity or broken down by denominational groups. The "why?" question I will address a little later in this chapter.)

General or Specific Population Surveys

Research on the prevalence of clergy malfeasance within the general population is virtually non-existent. There are plenty of polls and surveys about public *reaction* to news of scandals but not much concerning actual *rates of victimization* as reported by the victims themselves within the general American population. (The continuing reason for this gap in information is baffling unless researchers of Protestantism are ignorant of the clergy malfeasance problem or simply find it to close to home and/or distasteful to pursue.) Large and otherwise comprehensive periodic surveys, like the GSS (General Sample Survey) conducted out of the University of Chicago by the National Opinion Research Center, have ignored the issue.

The only major study directly addressing this type of abusive experience was conducted in the *1996 Dallas-Fort Worth Victimization Survey* by the University of Texas at Arlington's Center for Social Research. This study provides some limited sense of how much clergy malfeasance across a variety of denominations actually goes on in a large, if not national, population. Researchers Stacey, Darnell, and Shupe (2000) drew a multi-stage, random sample (stratified by economic class into upper, middle, and low levels) of central Texas neighborhoods in what is known as the DFW Metroplex (with a total population as large as some states). They asked 1067 single-dwelling householder respondents about their own abuse experiences or about the experiences of persons close to them (family members, friends, co-workers).

The results dispelled the conventional wisdom of religious apologist defenders (and some academics—see Jenkins, 1996: 167) who have staunchly tried to minimize the extent of the abuse problem for whatever reason. The claim that public concern over clergy misconduct is a "moral panic," the result of media "hype" focused on essentially "a few bad apple" pastors did not hold up in the Texas findings. The victimization data startled the few criminologists who pay attention to religion at all. In this large Texas sample, about 5 percent of the respondents knew someone firsthand (not by rumor) who had experienced some type of ministerial abuse, from groping and sexual intimidation, to actual rape and pilfering of church finances. Another 3 percent had themselves experienced mental, economic, or physical abuse. Instances offered by respondents were vivid and detailed. Time had produced few foggy or ambivalent memories of being victimized here (a problem in some victimization studies). Separately detailed examinations of Protestants and Catholics and their various reactions to the victimization as played out in levels of altered financial giving, church attendance, heightened awareness of news of such scandals, and so forth were also examined (Stacey, Shupe, and Darnell, 2000). However, the basic prevalence of the findings stood out: nearly 8 percent of a general urban population, contacted door-to-door in randomly selected neighborhoods, reported being in some way affected by clergy malfeasance.

The conclusion to be reiterated from this limited data set is obvious: clergy malfeasance is neither regionally specific nor denominationally unique, nor does it involve only the highly publicized sexual cases, nor is it a flash in the pan phenomenon.

Denominational Policies

The fourth type of database on existing denominational policies concerning the clergy malfeasance problem is extremely cursory and disappointing. The very absence of such policies in many churches and denominations speaks to a number of possible reasons, from embarrassment to a more nonchalant optimism that "those kinds of things only happen in other churches, not ours," to sheer bureaucratic inertia.

The single attempt so far to provide a comprehensive tally of both Protestant and Catholic clergy sexual misconduct policies nationwide, was conducted in the late 1990s by myself, Simel, and Hamilton (2000). We adopted a pragmatic sampling frame: *all* Protestant denominations/institutes and Roman Catholic dioceses found in the 1998 edition of the *Yearbook of American and Canadian Churches* (Linder, 1998). We then contacted *all* 189 Protestant groups and every tenth Catholic diocese by telephone, email, and/or fax.

The results were disheartening in the sense that only a total of thirty-five Protestant groups and six Catholic dioceses (after follow-up contacts) sent to us the requested clergy misconduct policies (all on sexual matters). Otherwise, the majority of sampled groups either did not have written clergy policies (the majority) or would not send copies of their policies. The polite reasons given as to why there was no policy was typified by "oh, we don't have such a policy because our church doesn't have *that* problem." Refusals and counter-queries were provided over the telephone in wary tones—"Why would you need a copy?"—as if the researchers might be attorneys. Some more cooperative denominations requested formal written requests for such documents on university letterhead stationary, sometimes also asking about the study's purposes (which were always immediately explained). In short, the defensive posture even for many of those groups cooperating was the norm, not the exception. (To be fair to the non-responders, many smaller denominations had only part-time staffs to respond, as repeated callbacks to answering machines seemed to confirm.)

A second, more modest study along the same lines was conducted in Fort Wayne, Indiana, a city of approximately 300,000 persons, with a population of 190 churches and where requests for policies could more easily be followed up (Lutz, 2004). The study asked such questions on a fairly short questionnaire, such as: Was there a church policy, and was it in place? If no to either question, why not? If so, what situations would it cover? Has it been effective, and how aware of it are congregants/parishioners?

The list of churches was drawn from Fort Wayne's Ecumenical Associated Churches Clergy Directory. As in the national study, church administrators were contacted by telephone, email, and fax with follow-ups after ten days for initial non-respondents. Even though the questionnaire only took a few minutes to complete, it likely had low priority on administrators' "to do" lists. Lutz found that twenty churches in the city responded (not a much better return rate than the national sample above, 12 to 13 percent). Nineteen churches had abuse policies (the earliest maintained for over twenty years, the most recent less than four years). One major reason for having an abuse-harassment policy in place was due to the requirements of insurance companies. Many congregations, after all, offer day-care services, youth activities, and so forth. A few respondents said simply that having a policy was "the right thing to do." One said, "We've seen what happened to the Catholics without one." Responding administrators claimed that their members were definitely aware of such policies.

What can be concluded by such studies? at this point, not much. Certainly the comparative politics of policymaking that I urged be taken have not yet been adequately studied (Shupe, 1995: 145). Whatever non-respondents' motives, whether embarrassment, suspicion of researchers' intents, fear of exposure, lack of interest, and so forth, church policymakers need such information that so far is regrettably incomplete. It leaves a gaping hole in our understanding and constructive dealing with bad clergy behaviors and heading off potential problems. There is one final, positive note, however: every church in Fort Wayne that had a policy said it was very effective and that *there had not been any occurrences (or recurrences) since adopting it.*

Summary of Existing Data on Clergy Misconduct

Anecdotal case studies of sexual clergy misconduct, such as Protestant ones by Stockton (2000, 1998) and Fortune (1989) or Catholic ones by Berry and Renner (2004) and Burkett and Bruni (1993), can reveal the step-by-step dynamics of how abuse can start, gather momentum as secondary deviance, and then be resolved or dealt with ineffectively by hapless, if well-meaning, church administrators. While there are some academic writings on excessive authoritative abuse in Protestantism (e.g., Poling, 1991; Johnson and VanVonderen, 1991; and Yeakley, 1988), ironically, there is a fairly small but growing literature on the linkage of sectarian religious values to both authoritative and economic ("affinity") misconduct in one specific group, the Church of Jesus Christ of Latter-day Saints (e.g., Anderson and Allred, 1997; Knowlton, 1996; White and White, 1996; Shupe, 1991). Otherwise, few social scientists have analyzed economic or authoritarian clergy abuse except in the spectacular cases of cultic leaders, such as David Koresh's Branch Davidians (Wright, 1995), Jim Jones' Peoples Temple (Hall, 1989), or lesser luminaries like Love Israel (Balch, 1998, 1995) or even high-profile televangelists like the PTL network's Jim and Tammy Faye Bakker (Hadden and Shupe, 1988).

Denominational survey research, always selective and as a result incomplete for our purposes, nevertheless sheds some light on the fact that a variety of religious groups are finding problems (though usually considering only sexual ones) in clergy-staff/laity relations.

Regional (if not national) victimization surveys provide some indication of the scope of clergy malfeasance and whether it is "clustered" around specific clergy in specific churches or more widespread. (At this time it appears to be both.) The general disinterest of sociologists of deviance and criminologists in the religious institution as an enormous opportunity structure for crime has meant that virtually no one (except for the John Jay School of Criminal Justice mentioned above—and then only for one denomination and one type of clergy abuse) is doing any kind of comprehensive data collection.

Our state of knowledge about the political dynamics of groups formulating denominational abuse policies or not—and if not, why not—is abysmal. Without greater incentives, many denominations' national headquarters (much less local churches) do not even trouble to respond to social science inquiries.

However, given the persistence of religious scandals in American pluralist society and their constant parading through the mass media, the efforts by modern journalists, therapists, and social scientists reveal, through even the rudimentary information amassed so far, that we have only uncovered the tip of the malfeasance iceberg. There is likely more out of sight. We know now, for example, that clergy malfeasance concerns not only the sexual type of misconduct, that it is not exclusively Catholic or even Christian, and that it also involves blundering or consciously-cooperating bureaucratic *accessories after the fact* (accomplices) facilitating the secondary deviance by inaction or cover-up. Each new wave of victims coming forward, each new narrowly focused survey on one particular denominational sample, and each new announcement of the formation of a leadership watchdog policy gradually lower the waterline on the iceberg. Taken as an incompletely-known whole, clergy malfeasance appears to portend an immense, unexplored segment of the overall American crime and deviance problem.

Why Clergy Malfeasance Scandals Now?

A question many readers probably have is *why,* during only the last two decades, has the public been inundated with religious leadership scandals? Put another way, if such misconduct is perennial (as maintained in Chapter 1), then why has it been "kept under wraps" until recently or spoken about by religionists only *in sotto voce*? What is creating our sudden awareness of clergy malfeasance? And to be sure, this avalanche of malfeasance news is no illusion; hundreds of religious elites have already gone to prison and clergy victimization altogether has cost our society billions of dollars in just the past two decades.

The answer is that two factors have been at work, first to conceal clergy malfeasance, and then to hasten its revelations.

1. Clergy and the Media

One factor has been the "walk-on-water syndrome," a biblically based term coined by Southern Baptist minister Edward B. Bratcher (1984) for the tall pedestal upon which parishioners and congregants figuratively seem to want to place their pastors. Sinners want to believe that their religious leader does not partake of their own mortal foibles. For their parts, religious institutions often do not discourage this perception (or pastorolotry), whether Protestant, Catholic, or Mormon. Writes Bratcher (1984: 25):

> When the laity place the clergy on a pedestal, the clergy give a helping hand, enjoy the intoxication of the higher elevation, and strive to stay on the pedestal . . . . The paradox is that although the Bible teaches that pride and the desire to be like God are the sources of man's tragic fall, it is precisely at this point that we as ministers most often succumb.

Likewise, a parallel example of what I have termed elsewhere (Shupe, 2007) the "conceit of calling" can be found in an oft-quoted reference to Roman Catholic priests' holiness and charisma (Burkett and Bruni, 1993: 58):

> Many Catholics perceive priests as their conduits to God, men who work with one foot on earth, one in heaven . . . Minneapolis psychologist Gary Schoener, who has met or counseled many victims of molestation by priests, says it's not unusual for them to describe their child's eye view of the men as ethereal, almost other worldly. One victim told him she was taught that if she encountered both a priest and an angel of the street, she should walk toward the priest, because he is closer to God.

Also, from the Mormon Quorum of the Apostles when Elder Dallin Oaks (an attorney by profession) told an LDS Utah audience in 1981 that never, for whatever reason, should church members criticize any of their leaders because these have God's special "calling" and anointing. He added, "It does not matter that the criticism is true" (*Salt Lake Tribune*, 1985).

The mass media—particularly newspapers and motion pictures—have aided in this pedestal-placement by their reluctance to speak ill of religion at all. Before and after the Second World War, Hollywood turned out movies to appeal to a variety of denominational viewers that showed pastors uniformly as wholesome and heroic—from tough guy but with a heart-of-gold Spencer Tracy as Father Flangan in *Boys Town* to affable Bing Crosby as parish priest in *Going My Way* and *Bells of St. Mary's* to Frederick March as plain family man Protestant minister in *Heaven Can Wait*. Not until Burt Lancaster's 1960 academy award-winning portrayal of hard-drinking, womanizing, Bible-thumping hypocrite Elmer Gantry (based on Sinclair Lewis' 1927 best-selling novel of that name) did evangelists, as well as conniving community ministers, have a seedy dark side revealed. (At the time, the movie was rated "for adults only.")

Philip Jenkins (1998), writing of the gradual buying-up of local newspapers by larger syndicates, explains how "a culture of clergy deviance" was created. Local publishers and editors interested in running a story or even a feature series on a clergy scandal after having national ownership could no longer be intimidated as they once might have been by a bishop or pastor who threatened to meet such exposure with his flock's loud boycott of not just the newspaper but the advertisers as well. For instance, other than anti-Catholic potboiler books, like Emmet McLoughlin's *Crime and Immorality in the Catholic Church* (1962) or Paul Blanshard's *American Freedom and Catholic Power* (1949), newspaper editors and publishers previously had held a cautious attitude so much so that "even stories that today seem relatively trivial were quashed" (Jenkins, 1998: 118). Jenkins goes on to observe how such lack of reporting facilitated clergy secondary deviance:

> By far the most important consequence of the news blackout involved the clerical offenders themselves, who found themselves in an environment in which malfeasance was effectively removed from the possibility of sanction. This inevitably created a sense of invulnerability among real or potential wrongdoers, who knew that the most extreme actions could be undertaken in relative safety . . . . In reality, the Catholic church was by no means the only institution that enjoyed relative immunity from public scandal, whether in sexual or financial matters. Other churches and religious groups tended to be treated gently by police and editors, as much from a fear of undermining public confidence in the institutions as from fear of their economic power (1998: 119-20).

In fact, journalists Berry and Renner (2004: 80) speak of the cynical term "tight collar cases" used by big-city cops to refer to instances when a priest was caught in a vice squad raid or in a compromising situation with a minor but the news never reached the police blotter. Instead, the offender was quickly turned over to the bishop's discrete care. Worse, as Jenkins indicates, individual victims had little chance other than by word of mouth to learn that their personal experiences were not anomalous or isolated, hence, no consciousness of kind could as readily develop.

But, as Jenkins argues, things began to change as ownership of media ceased to be solely local. Scandals could not be contained so easily.

2. The Age of Victimization

Sociologist Andrew Karmen (1990: 38) once described the American penchant for individuals claiming exploitation and victimization by someone or some thing:

> There is no end in sight to the process of discovery and rediscovering victims. All kinds of victims are beginning to receive the attention, concern, care, and assistance they deserve. They are being rediscovered by investigative journalists who put together feature stories, entrepreneurs who put out new lines of personal safety products, social scientists who explore their plight at conferences, legislators who introduce new laws to benefit them, and self-help groups that organized support networks to overcome the isolation that has divided them.

Sociologist Armand L. Mauss (1975) wrote an influential textbook relevant to the "awakening" of victims. It was entitled *Social Problems as Social Movements*; the essential theme was that society only "recognizes" some behavior as problematic when some organized group (typically victims and/or their advocates) make loud-enough, persistent noises about it to put it over the public "radar" and gain sympathizers. Thus, "constructing" awareness of a social problem—now dealt with by the deviance approach, heavily grounded in symbolic interaction, appropriately called *constructionist* (ex., Adler and Adler, 1997)—is a process mobilized by protesting, labeling, angry activists. Examples include MADD (Mothers Against Drunk Driving), POMC (Parents of Murdered Children), and SNAP (Survivors Network of Those Abused by Priests).

Harvey Wallace (1998: 1-18) has documented the history of *victimology* (now an area of criminology). He found at least five modern theories of victimization (including that of Karmen quoted above). More importantly, Wallace traced the modern cultural wave of victims' movements to earlier versions in the 1960s and 1970s, such as the black (later brown also) civil rights movement, the feminist or women's liberation movement (which spun off rape crisis and family violence movements), and other causes—from protecting the environment to sounding the alarm over alleged dangerous, mind-controlling "cults," to obesity, and gay rights. In 1982, President Ronald Reagan appointed a Task Force on Victims of Crime, and it published a seminal report on victims' rights. The U.S. Department of Justice created OVC (the Office for Victims of Crime); the U.S. Congress, in 1984, passed VOCA (the Victims of Crime Act); and, by 1996, President Bill Clinton proposed a Victims' Rights Constitutional Amendment. Thus, a precedent or legacy of victims' movements was created.

Wallace's macro summary of the crime victims' rights movement fits well the micro movement of victims of clergy abuse (to be dealt with in Chapter 4):

> The victims' rights movement began as a small group of volunteers who themselves were crime victims and who had been victimized a second time as a result of their involvement with the criminal justice system. This small group of volunteers has grown and become a powerful force in America that continues to expand and change the way we view victimology (1998: 16).

Out of *this* cultural context, with Americans already "primed" with plenty of role models to be sensitive to all sorts of victimizing, it was only a matter of time before those injured, endangered, and intimidated by clergy misconduct challenged perpetrators and facilitators of this form of secondary deviance.

Homosexuality and the Roman Catholic Priesthood

The controversy over the alleged proportion of homosexuals in the Roman Catholic priesthood needs to be dealt with in concluding this chapter both because of the high profile of Catholics as America's largest denomination as well as the frequent attempts to link homosexuality in some way to the waves of pedophilia scandals since the late 1980s. To be sure, the church's canon law has had to deal with homosexuality (and sexual sin) throughout the history of Christendom (Heineman, 1990; Sipe, 1990: 50ff; Bullough, 1982), likewise for clergy sex with minors (Doyle, 2003; Isley, 1987). Same-sex erotic behavior has been a sin, hence deviant for its elites and laity, by Church standards in the U.S. at least since the mid-1970s (Berry and Renner, 2004: 34).

Earlier I presented Sipe's estimate, based on his longitudinal clinical data, that about 20 percent of the priesthood are homosexual (and possibly twice that proportion if active and inactive categories are combined).

Richard Wagner, driven out of the priesthood after his master's thesis was published as *Gay Priests* in 1981, interviewed fifty homosexual priests across the North American continent and concluded, "There is an informal network of gay priests operating in just about every section of [the U.S.]" (Wagner, 1980: 12). Journalist Jason Berry (1992: 183-6) has suggested that Catholic seminaries have become literal hotbeds of recruitment of gay men to a vocation where non-interest in women and constant outwardly fraternal contact with other men are virtues. This would turn the priesthood into what Tim Unsworth in *The Last Priests in America* (1993: 249) referred to as the "lavender rectory" and Donald Cozzens (2000: 107) said amounted to "a gay profession." The *Los Angeles Times,* in its own 2002 survey of 1854 priests, found Sipe's figure of 20 percent homosexual, half of whom were still celibate (or inactive – see the survey discussed in Berry and Renner, 2004: 35) to be accurate. Michael S. Rose published his potboiler *Goodbye, Good Men* in 2002 claiming that liberal Catholic theology, since the series of Vatican II councils held in Rome during the mid-1960s, was the cause of this homosexual conspiracy to recruit gay seminarians and drive out heterosexuals, thus preserving an increasingly homosexual clergy. (His book was ominously subtitled: *How Liberals Brought Corruption into the Catholic Church.*)

The homosexual issue is important for our purposes here only because some observers have superficially tried to link the Church's resolute refusal to rescind its ban of strict celibacy for persons in vocation as a direct cause of homosexuality *which in turn,* presumably, explains the much publicized pedophilia problem. In the wake of the 2002 Boston Archdiocese scandals, one could even turn to the Sunday morning television news-talk programs to hear pundit commentators like George Will and George Stephanopoulis debating the role of theological liberalism as somehow the root of all evil in the church's current problems. This simplistic "Rush Limbaughesque" tendency to always locate any form of liberalism as centrally problematic at any time misses the point in putting pedophilia abuse and homosexuality into Catholic or any other rational context of sexuality.

Evidence does exist that the Catholic Church's tradition of recruiting males to the priesthood as young as possible and committing them to lifetimes of celibacy is tied to sexual immaturity in adulthood. Ex-priest Gabriel Longo (1966: 40), for example, recalls how strict teachers in seminary prep school transformed gender differences into "a tantalizing mystery." Burkett and Bruni (1993: 52-3) also note:

Until the past two decades men who became priests frequently entered seminary in high school, at ages as young as twelve. Tracked early for the priesthood—and celibacy—they stopped dating as teenagers, if they even dated at all. Few went through the same process of psychosexual development as other men.

Likewise, Sipe (1990: 67-102) reports from his clinical data that some priests remained "immature, transient, exploitive, or essentially narcissistic," and other therapists have reported that priests in treatment were "grossly ignorant of sexuality," perhaps "regressive homosexuals" with narcissistic fixations on teenagers (Berry and Renner, 2004: 38, 59).

However, this is not the place to trace the origins of homosexuals in the Catholic priesthood. It is enough to state the salient points on the non-link between homosexuality and pedophilia in the Catholic priesthood:

First, homosexuality is not the same, either in sexual orientation or behavior, as pedophilia or ephebophilia. Most homosexual adult men are no more attracted to prepubescent boys than are heterosexual men. Whatever the Church's problems are with homosexuals in the rectory, they are largely irrelevant to pedophilic victimization.

Second, as an elaboration of the first point, pedophile priests, such as Father James Porter and many others, selected girls as victims as well as boys. The same-sex aspect of priest pedophilia has been over-emphasized by those seeking, for whatever reason, to draw a causal connection between homosexual priests and the enormous financial settlements for abuse now beleaguering the church.

Third, the growing proportion of gays in the Catholic priesthood *is* tied to the celibacy issue, *not* because celibacy leads lonely heterosexual men to turn to each other (and then to children for deviant sexual satisfaction), but because so many heterosexual priests, dissatisfied with the isolation and unreality of celibacy, are leaving to marry. Berry and Renner (2004: 33) explain:

Since Vatican II, the birth control letter and the antique celibacy law had driven off thousands of potential priests. The numbers of seminarians went into a steep slide, alongside a flood of men leaving clerical life . . . . In the 1970s as roughly one hundred Americans left the priesthood every month, most of them to marry, the proportion of homosexuals among men remaining in the ministry escalated. By the mid-eighties, the cultural dynamics of a gay world took hold in rectories, religious orders, and many seminaries.

Thus, the loss of heterosexuals in droves had increased the remaining proportion of homosexual seminarians and priests who, after all, had each other and could rationalize the sort of same-sex behavior that Michael S. Rose and others have criticized.

But that only explains the rising numbers of gay priests, not child molesters, in the church. Given a prevailing tolerance in larger society as well as pressures within all Christian churches for gays and lesbians to "exit the closet," it is only natural that now we would learn of more of "them" at the same time we learn of the other scandals. The pedophilia issue awaits another explanation, for which sociologists as yet can offer little.

Conclusion

The true extent of clergy malfeasance will likely never be known. It is a criminological truism that for most crimes, most victims never report their victimization; most perpetrators are never caught or prosecuted; and of those that are, many are never convicted. Even if the American government decided to suspend the separation of church and state and collected such religious statistics through the FBI, the bureau would miss a lot (as it does already).

What numbers we do possess from the case and anecdotal examples as seen in Chapters 1 and 2—involving thousands of victims and billions of dollars in costs—reinforce the impression that misbehaving religious leaders are many and causing a lot of harm. In that sense the Roman Catholic Church, despite all the criticism and embarrassment it has been subjected to of late, is to be commended for taking the bold step to commission the John Jay School of Criminal Justice to make a no holds barred review of clergy abuse allegations diocese by diocese.

The homosexuality issue in that Church's leadership ranks will not go away, whether it is perceived as tied to the pedophilia problem or not. We have been living in an age of social movements and their backlashes since the civil rights crusade of the 1960s. That liberation effort served as a template for a host of other rights causes. There will always be persons who resent this irreversible phenomenon.

3

Clergy Malfeasance as Secondary Deviance: Dynamics of Exploitation

Exploitation of followers by religious leaders in whose wisdom and benevolence they trust seems inevitable across faiths. Four brief examples illustrate this point:

Here is psychotherapist James S. Gordon, writing of the Bhagwan Shree Rajneesh from Poona, India whose followers (called *sannyasins*, including at one point Gordon himself) set up the Rancho Rajneesh near the town of The Dalles, Oregon. By money and sheer numbers, the Rajneeshees overwhelmed the area and through blatantly arrogant political domination totally alienated the town's original 750 residents. Meanwhile, the Bhagwan's group was falling apart internally from various lieutenants' petty (and sometimes deadly) feuding. The Bhagwan tried to flee the U.S. Immigration and Naturalization Service with much cash and jewelry and a 35-count indictment against him but was apprehended at an airport on the East Coast. Gordon reminisces about the collapse of the American wing of the movement *and* his disillusionment with the Enlightened One:

> More and more sannyasins were questioning . . . They felt abused by the organization Rajneesh had created, exhausted by the contortions through which its policies had put their lives. What they had accepted as devices sanctioned by their Master turned out to be derelictions he now disavowed . . . . the more I found out, the more I felt myself fighting a losing battle to give Rajneesh the benefit of the doubt . . . . In the end, Rajneesh became the kind of man, the kind of religious leader, he had always derided. If indeed, his ego had once dissolved and melted like a drop into the ocean, it seemed over the years to have renewed and enlarged and in his isolation it grew gross with his attachment to power and luxury and position. (Gordon, 1987: 221, 240, 245)

Here is sociologist Janet L. Jacobs, who interviewed forty male and female ex-members of Hindu-based, Buddhist-based, and charismatic

Christian groups, writing of an interesting (but by no means) unique trend in their recollections. Many had been physically and sexually/ emotionally hurt and exploited but blamed the second-echelon lieutenants rather than their first-echelon gurus or pastors. Instead of seeing accessories after the fact as working to facilitate the leaders' exploitive wishes and directions, these mid-level subordinates were regarded as subverting the otherwise benevolent leaders:

> Devotees would speak of the abuse, pain, and anguish they had suffered and yet these painful emotional experiences would be attributed to the corruption of the hierarchy or the mismanagement of the bureaucracy. It was not uncommon for a follower to report that he or she believed that the leader did not really know what was going on, or that in his holiness, the charismatic founder must have a plan in the abuse of his subjects. The willingness and the desire to exonerate the leader was perhaps the most consistent theme that appeared throughout the accounts of conversion and disaffection. Long after many of the devotees had moved out of the temples and the ashrams, long after they were no longer attending church, the connection to the God figure remained persistent in their consciousness. (Jacobs, 1989: 70)

Here is religious journalist Andrew Walsh reporting the situation in the Archdiocese of Philadelphia in September, 2005 when District Attorney Lynn Abraham released a 418-page grand jury report that took 40 months to conclude, with more than 100 witnesses testifying (including one cardinal ten times), 63 malfeasant priests identified and documented, and more than 30,000 pages of Archdiocesan records reviewed:

> The grand jury report's catalogue of charges and descriptions were brutally graphic, crafted explicitly to puncture bureaucratic posturing and denial: "We should begin by making one thing clear, when we say abuse, we don't mean just 'inappropriate touching' (as the Archdiocese often chooses to refer to it). We mean rape. Boys who were raped orally, boys who were raped anally, girls who were raped vaginally."

The church, for its part, went on a circle-the-wagons offensive, labeling the report "tabloid-like, a vile mean-spirited diatribe," and "anti-Catholic" in a style which Walsh minimally described as "truculent."

Finally, here is another journalist, the Associated Press' Shawn Pogatchnik, writing of 102 Dublin, Ireland priests (3.6 percent of Dublin's total pastorate) suspected of sexually abusing children in that city's 2005 scandals. This church disclosure seems to have been preemptive; that is, anticipating a forthcoming 2006 governmental investigation:

> The government probe, expected to run for at least 18 months, follows a similar inquiry into clerical abuse in the southeast diocese of Ferns. When the earlier report was published in October [2005], it exposed a catalog of abuse, including [a] priest who molested a group of First Communion girls on the altar but was never punished. While the Church has been on the legal and moral defensive in the United States in recent years, the sense of uproar and disillusionment has been more profound in Ireland,

a predominantly Catholic country that once exported priests worldwide. In Ireland, Church and State were intertwined until the 1970s—a breakup being accelerated by the abuse fallout. (Pogatchnik, 2006)

For an excellent account of an earlier 1990's wave of Irish priest sex abuse scandals—similar to one at the same time in North America see Sipe, 1998.

This book is not a psychology text about the perverse motives that lead individuals presumably committed to spirituality to take advantage of their authority over followers and fellow believers, sometimes the most vulnerable of these. Opportunity structures within power bases seem to provide so many such universal temptations that we really do not need to dwell on the types of personalities who surrender to them. Rather, the important sociological questions concern how such opportunity structures of inequality come to exist and how they are maintained. (Here the professional culture or social psychological mind-set of elites *is* relevant.)

In the following pages, some readers will be asked to reconceive religion along perhaps unfamiliar lines, but the goal is to shed analytical light on clergy deviance that otherwise remains bizarre and merely personally pathological.

Religion as Social Exchange

All social actors in every society or group are engaged in continuous exchanges of symbols (be these encoded vocal sounds, shared written etchings, gestures, body postures, insignias on clothing, and so forth) to give situations commonly shared meanings. In providing understanding, this pattern of symbol-meaning exchange lends predictability to our intentions. Exchanges also cover the bases for sociability when persons pursue the material and emotional stuffs of life—from bartering goods to trading symbolically valued currency for food, clothing, homes, and automobiles, to forming satisfying romantic/emotional commitments. Some exchanges have limits; some are purposefully left long-term and open-ended (more on both of these in the next section).

Sociologists Rodney Stark and William Sims Bainbridge have conceptualized religion as one institution (among others) dependent on such exchanges (see for their original statement, Stark and Bainbridge, 1980). Indeed, for these authors religion *is* social exchange. They argue straightforwardly that:

Rewards, those things humans will expend costs to obtain, often can be gained only from other humans; so people are forced into exchange relations. However, many rewards are very scarce and can be possessed by only some, not all. Having learned to seek rewards through exchanges with other persons, in their desperation humans turn to each other for these highly desired scarce and nonexistent rewards. And from each other humans often receive compensators for the rewards they seek.

When rewards are very scarce, or not available at all, humans create and exchange compensators – sets of beliefs and prescription for action that substitute for immediate achievement of the desired reward. Religion is one social enterprise whose primary purpose is to create, maintain, and exchange supernaturally based general compensators. (Stark and Bainbridge, 1985: 172)

In their view, the blessings of virtuous living (however defined) are spiritual intangibles: divine protection or intervention, serenity of the mind and soul, even salvation and immortality. These intangibles may or may not be realized in the here and now, but they are *promised* by religious elites in return for obedience to themselves and/or to spiritual tenets. These intangible benefits, say Stark and Bainbridge, are like IOU's, or promissory notes to be redeemed later for behavior now. And, like uranium's radioactivity, these IOU's have half-lives if not renewed. "Often people must make regular payments to keep a compensator valid, which makes it possible to bind them to long-term involvement in an organization that serves as a source of compensators" (Stark and Bainbridge, 1985: 6).

This basic exchange model—that people seek to maximize advantages and avoid disadvantages in all types of relationships and are more likely to try to readjust or even terminate relationships where imbalance threatens to continue—is one most sociologists accept. It is largely based on the work of George Homans (1967, 1961, 1958), who in turn had become enamored with B. F. Skinner's post-world War II operant conditioning psychology grounded in animal behavior studies. Both Homans and Skinner (famous for his stimulus-reinforcement scheme that "taught" pigeons to simulate playing ping-pong over a net as a series of learned responses) gave short shrift to the symbolic-cognitive sophistication of human beings. As a result, it placed them on essentially the same less ex- alted learning-produced level with other mammals and creatures capable of seeking pleasure/satisfaction and dodging pain (Ekeh, 1974: 895ff).

Elsewhere (Shupe, 2007) I have criticized this entire formulation as simplistic utilitarianism. It is in sore need of anthropological overhaul if it is to be of any use in accounting for why so often victims of clergy malfeasance do *not* discontinue their church memberships and faith al- legiances despite exchange imbalances but rather seek reform and may even become more ardent practitioners of their religion. However, for our purposes here it is useful to think of religion as an institution premised on the social exchange of laity obedience and deference to clergy in exchange for compensators, or future benefits taken on faith. Some further tinkering with the model can make it helpful to explain situations that Homans and Skinner could never have begun to imagine.

Now we will consider the role of elites in this exchange.

Religious Elites as Brokers

No one using the model of religion as a social exchange system has yet conceived of religious elites as brokers, but that is what they are. A dictionary definition of a fiduciary broker is "an agent who negotiates contracts, purchases, or sales in return for a fee." They are the "middlepersons" between the promised spiritual benefits, or IOUs, from supernatural sources (such as deities) and the buyers (such as supplicants or laity). The brokers negotiate between supplies of intangibles and demand by presenting/interpreting commandments, prescriptions and proscriptions, and scriptures/sacred writings with the help of prayers and rituals. The latter include confessions, marriage and burial rites, and communions and baptisms. Clergy are the agents of faith traditions. Thus, religious elites are special *trusted* fiduciaries in the go-between brokerage role.

David G. Bromley and Bruce C. Busching (1988) have distinguished between the social bonds created by *contracts* and *covenants*. Contracts in the secular business world hold specific terms and limitations, stipulated costs and/or rents, often with time-based warranties and conditions of default for buyers and sellers. Covenants, on the other hand, are deliberately more open-ended with less limited stipulations, more diffuse expectations among participants, and often made in an emotional or primary group context. For an example of the latter, the vows of a wedding covenant often mention such terms of the limits of the relationship ("in sickness and in health") and duration ("till death do us part"). (Pre-nuptial agreements seek some middle ground between the two types of agreements.)

Religious elite brokers deal with both contracts and covenants in their trusted elevated status. This gives them a certain amount of apparent power and real persuasion. On brokering contracts, just ask the thousands of victims who lost a total of billions of dollars in the past several decades to the likes of the trusted, religiously linked con artists mentioned as affinity criminals in Chapter 1. (An abbreviated list includes the Cookes; the Suffolettos; televangelist-style Grants, Lees, Tiltons, Bakkers; the Joneses; the Van Hofwegans; the Strawders; and the Bennetts.) Consider one illustrative, classic pastor-broker who financially fleeced his flocks, stole from charities, lied to the Internal Revenue Service, repeatedly betrayed his marriage vows, and cheated on his several mistresses, breaking both contracts and covenants. When he was found out, he played the "race card" with his African American followers by blaming his misconduct all on the white media; this was the Reverend Henry Lyons.

Lyons was a St. Petersburg, Florida Baptist pastor and president (1994-1999) of the National Baptist Church USA, one of this nation's largest black Protestant denominations. A brilliant, charismatic orator in the African American style, Lyons' hypocrisy, greed, and illegal brokering activities came to light while he was on an overseas visit to broker a deal with an African dictator (an illegal act in itself) with his traveling companion, his mistress Bernice V. Edwards. (Not only playing the role of accessory after the fact to Lyon's thefts from his own congregation and denomination, Edwards had been previously convicted of embezzling $60,000 from a school for at-risk students in a northern state.) At home during Lyons' absence, his wife just happened to be going through his briefcase and found a deed for a second, $700,000 waterfront home near St. Petersburg in the name of Henry Lyons and Ms. Edwards. (It turned out that Lyons and Edwards were also in the process of buying a $925,000 mansion in Charlotte, North Carolina.) Mrs. Lyons (also a victim of domestic violence by the reverend) drank heavily in response to the discovery of the second home, drove to this new domicile and set it on fire, then smashed her car into a tree as she tried to flee (Wilson, 1997).

Lyons had a broader pattern of affinity crime. Earlier he had personally pocketed at least $244,500 donated by the Jewish Anti-Defamation League and similar charitable groups which was collected to rebuild burned black churches in the South. It is true, as Hardett (1998) observes of the black religious subculture, that black parishioners often, and Lyons' congregation in particular, have been comfortable with their pastors as inspiring symbols maintaining well-heeled lifestyles with good homes and automobiles. Thus, Lyons' expenditures may not have seemed (at least on the surface) totally out of the ordinary despite his deviant brokerage of both contracts and covenants. Lyons, not surprisingly, tried to blame his felonious excesses on bad publicity from a racist media which did not like to see "one of them" prospering.

Despite the scandal, a majority of the denominational representatives at the National Baptist Church USA's 1998 convention ratified Lyons as president anyway. That same year Lyons pled guilty to five fraud charges as well as *forty-nine* other charges (the latter dropped through plea bargaining). He had failed to pay taxes on $1.3 million income, and he defrauded banks and other financial institutions. Soon into the same year as his denominational ratification, Lyons was convicted by a Florida court of, among other things, grand theft of at least $4 million from companies to which he had sold *bogus* membership lists of his denomination's membership (to companies for their own commercial purposes) and racketeering. Lyons was eventually sentenced to five and one-half years in prison and ordered to pay restitution of $2.5 million (Associated Press, 1998). By then prosecutors (and Lyons' church members) learned that he had been continuing purchases of several more homes, buying expensive cars, and supporting several *other* mistresses besides Edwards. Yet, in an incredible show of faith in Lyons as their fiduciary broker, the National Baptist Church USA voted to continue paying Lyons his $100,000 annual salary *for the next five years while he was incarcerated.*

Thus, if religion is thought of as a macro social exchange process made up of many micro exchanges, and elites serve as brokers between the benefits provided by the supernatural and the needs of average believers, then two questions about the *criminogenic potential* of the clergy emerge: Where do the solidifying tendencies of religious authority stem from? And how are these preserved, not just from generation to generation but also from persons to person?

Obtaining Religious Elite Authority

There is a rich tradition in sociological thought termed *elitist theory* on how power in any group starts out dispersed and fairly egalitarian but comes to be consolidated into the hands of a relative few. These few are the *oligarchs*, and their control of the many in organizations and societies is well nigh inevitable. Elitist theorist Robert Michels (1959: 11) referred to this tendency as "the iron law of oligarchy:"

> Thus the appearance of oligarchical bureaucracies in the very bosom of the revolutionary [democratic] parties is a conclusive proof of the existence of immanent oligarchic tendencies in every kind of human organization which strives for the attainment of definite ends.

The oligarchy duality of power is normal and predictable, however anti-democratic, unpopular, and even unpatriotic it sounds. "As a result of organization, every party or professional union becomes divided into a minority of directors and a majority of directed . . . As a general rule, the increase in the power of the leaders is directly proportional with the extension of the organization" (Michels, 1959: 32-33).

Similarly, elitist theorist Gaetano Mosca (1939: 50), himself once a legislator-politico in pre-Fascist Italy, wrote of this basic oligarchic separation:

> The first class, always the less numerous, performs all political functions, monopolizes power and employs the advantages that power brings, whereas the second, the more numerous class, is directed and controlled by the first... and supplies the first, in appearance at least, with means of subsistence and with the instrumentalities that are essential to the vitality of the political organization.

Milovan Djilas, once an ardent communist who fought the Nazis alongside Josip Broz Tito (later Marshal of the Yugoslavian dictatorship) and then was imprisoned for writing bluntly about the oppressive "new class" based on communist party membership, wrote about ideological oligarchs who used their monopoly of bureaucratic management of the state to enjoy exceptional privileges vis-à-vis the masses, including material advantages (Djilas, 1998: 174).

Substitute ecclesiastical brokers, or the clergy, for political and economic oligarchs in Michels/Mosca/Djilas, and the analysis moves closer to explaining the criminogenic infrastructure or power base that provides a fertile soil for clergy malfeasance to take root, incubate, and spread. Christianity, according to a consensus of scholars, began as a dispersed, egalitarian set of local churches during its first two centuries (see, for just a few examples, Frend, 1987; Rowland, 1985; Kee, 1980; Theissen, 1978; Frankforter, 1978; Johnson, 1976; and Carleton, 1970), so churches and denominations (thought of as social movements) have often developed along lines parallel to the oligarchies suggested by elitist writers. This is also true of some new religious movements already cited, such as Peoples Temple and Bhagwan Shree Rajneesh's cult, but also others, such as the AUM Shinrikyo of Tokyo subway-gassing infamy (Kisala, 1998; Kaplan and Marshall, 1996).

To answer the question of *why* Michels offers three cogent reasons, or causal components, of organizational development.

One primary reason—perhaps the lynchpin of the "iron law"—is the sheer size of evolving large organizations (or *population density*). Frequent, regular direct contact or dialogue with the emerging leadership becomes physically and mechanically impossible for most citizens (or in religion, believers). Says Michels (1959: 26-7):

It is obvious that such a gigantic number of persons belonging to a unitary organization cannot do any practical work upon a system of direct discussion. The regular holding of deliberative assemblies of a thousand members encounter the gravest difficulties in respect to room and distance; while from the topographical point of view such an assembly would become altogether impossible if the members numbered ten thousand . . . it is impossible for the collectivity to undertake the direct settlement of all the controversies that may arise. Hence the need for delegation.

Second, this delegation is the beginning of the end for democracy and the impetus for the growth of oligarchy. Transfer of authority from the masses to their representatives or directors elected or selected by some other method increases distance between the leaders and rank and file, and this renders the former functionally "invisible" much of the time to the latter. Again, Michels (1959: 34):

The members have to give up the idea of themselves conducting or even supervising the whole administration, and are compelled to turn these tasks over to trustworthy persons specially nominated for the purpose, to salaried officials . . . It is obvious that democratic control thus undergoes a progressive diminution.

Heinerman and Shupe (1985: 93), for instance, note the growth of the "palace guard" (their term) in the post-World War II LDS Church bureaucracy:

The First Presidency [the apex of the LDS Church power pyramid] was once much more accessible to the average member. It was not unusual for visitors simply to drop in unannounced on the Church president and maintain a first-name acquaintance with virtually all stake presidents. For instance, Henry A. Smith, retired *Church News* editor, recalled how during the 1930s he used to walk into the offices of the LDS president or any other General authority if he wanted to talk with him, without an appointment. . . . the average Mormon today has about as much chance of dropping in on the LDS First Presidency as the average citizen has of paying an impromptu visit to, say, a state governor or the chairman of the board of General Motors.

Elsewhere (1985: 87), after reviewing the many levels of administration in the Mormon Church, they conclude that "the elements of a theologically justified chain of command and the effective insulation of higher leaders from official dealings with most rank-and-file members (except when the leadership desires it) are all entrenched after 180 years of bureaucratic growth."

In terms of clergy malfeasance, this invisibility often results in how hierarchical opportunity structures can develop and shield abusive clergy by removing much of their accessibility from the laity, likewise, for the laity's chances to observe clergy at deliberations that affect them (for example, the closed door sessions of the U.S. Council of Catholic Bishops when clergy misconduct was discussed in 2006). Such lack of elite visibility is also abetted by lieutenants who, in deviant situations, act as "accessories after the fact," or accomplices (or, more kindly, buffers), benefiting in power and even financially by cloaking the behind the scenes reality of the brokerage. Cases such as those of televangelists Jim and Tammy Faye Bakker and Dallas' Robert Tilton and W. V. Grant, Jr., as well as the Reverend Jim Jones and depression-era Father Divine (after whom Jones modeled his own ministry) illustrate the important role of these upper-tier subordinates in deliberately promoting inaccessibility, hence invisibility (Shupe, 1995: 60-77, 104-5; Weisbrot, 1983; Burnham, 1979).

Invisibility also refers to how religious supervisors deal with accusations or revelations of abuse by lower clergy, how they may cloak their investigations of these with bureaucratic dodges and stalling tactics, and how they can use organizational protocol to restrict how laity can even authentically participate in investigations or reviews of allegations. Roman Catholic Church canon law, staggered in favor of clergy when lay accusations of malfeasance arise (not surprising because it was created over centuries for and by clergy), is a good example of the potential for obfuscation, according to Thomas Doyle (2003), a military chaplain and canon lawyer. When elites in the religious hierarchy can limit access to information on how accusations of clergy malfeasance are being processed administratively, they effectively contribute to keeping the deviant behavior further invisible and indirectly promote the secondary deviance and recidivism.

Marie Fortune's case study *Is Nothing Sacred?* (1987) shows how one abusive male clergy was knowingly able to play on this bureaucratic invisibility factor to his own benefit. Protestant denominational bureaucrats were terrified of scandal leaking out; as a result, the predatory pastor was able to bargain for reassignment to a new church with no penalties or publicity—as he had successfully done previously—in this ultimate cover-up of his sexual/physical abuse of several women in one congregation. For an example of the similar invisibility of bureaucratic procedures in the face of scandal, and their timid, clumsy handling by Presbyterian elders, see Stockton (2000, 1998). Catholic mother Jeanne Miller's own efforts to monitor justice being done in the case of her own adolescent son who had been molested by a priest quietly moved from parish to parish are instructive. Her frustration at the lack of information flowing down from an ostensibly "sympathetic" ecclesia that masked its decisions on family solace and priest discipline, reveals the same invisibility problems (see Miller, 1998).

I personally became involved as expert consultant to a plaintiff's attorney in a 1993 case in which a California Mormon lay-minister had fondled a young woman when he was chaperoning a group of adolescents and teenagers on an overnight camping trip. The teen female victim told her parents who then complained to their bishop (the equivalent of a local church pastor) *in writing*. The bishop assured them that he would investigate and "take care" of the matter so that there would be no repetitions. But the same male youth leader on another camping trip two years later tried to climb into a twelve-year-old girl's sleeping bag. Her parents also went to the bishop and learned of the previous written complaint. In the ensuing lawsuit it emerged that in actuality *nothing* had been done to punish or discourage the recidivist, nor was he removed from youth responsibilities—rather, the first family had simply been "cooled out" by the bishop. The parents of the second young lady sued the church and won, the LDS organization being found liable "with malice" for damages (and indirectly the invisibility of its lack of procedures, despite its assertions otherwise). However, the invisibility continued. As part of the "deal" for a sizeable financial settlement with the plaintiffs, the court records were sealed (and the attorney would not even tell me, the consultant, "off the record" exactly how much money was paid out (Harding, 1993).

The third reason for the inevitability of oligarchy in large organizations: early in the transition from direct member democracy to republic (with delegated proxies) to oligarchy in the internal political evolution of the organization, government, or religion, the delegates cease to be part-time or volunteers and become full-time and salaried. They are now professionals, with specific expertise in their roles, and the rank and file come to feel inadequate to evaluate them except in the most general and perfunctory terms. Observes Michels (1959: 31-2):

> The technical specialization that inevitably results from all extensive organizations renders necessary what is called expert leadership. Consequently . . . the leaders, who were at first no more than the executive organs of the collective will soon emancipate themselves from the mass and become independent of its control.

None of this type of organizational development is unfamiliar in the sociology of religion. Nineteenth-century German sociologist Max Weber recognized the important role of dynamic, charismatic, personalized leadership in the beginning phases of a new religious tradition, or cult, of holding together by sheer awe a precariously organized, incipient group of believers. However, within the process he termed "the routinization of charisma" the *prophetic* nature of leadership shifted to *priestly* as hierarchical authority and bureaucratic success developed in ecclesiastical oligarchies (Weber, 1964a, 1964b). Priestly authority was actually the end result of oligarchic tendencies that produced a "charisma of office" controlled by organizational elites. Joachim Wach (1967: 337) summarized this process where

> ... charisma of personal character appeals more to the emotions; official charisma is more "rational." Whereas the former claims complete loyalty, even personal surrender, the latter usually demands a circumscribed or "tempered" audience.

There is an accompanying professional culture of arrogance that, unless regularly and conscientiously checked, seems an almost certainty in the oligarchic transition. This can manifest itself, not just in the understandable elite reaction to scandal by protecting fellow elites and minimizing the damage to the organization's reputation, but also in attitudes regarding the church's ultimate mission and the clergy's role in this. These attitudes—again, unmonitored by modest self-reflection—can include a *sense of omniscience* ("We have the big, long range picture unlike those below/without access to our more complete understanding."), *conceit* ("We are not accountable for our actions and decisions to the same extent as are laity."), and *an exaggerated sense of confidence and righteousness* ("In the grand scheme of things it is for a greater good than our critics can imagine that we are justified in bypassing ordinary norms."). Examples of the consequences of this type of mind-set will be abundant in the following section in the excuses given in preserving religious elite authority. The result, however, is an inflated sense of importance, wisdom, and superior knowledge for religious elites. Adds Michaels (1959: 80), "With the appearance of professional leadership, there ensures a great accentuation of the cultural differences between the leaders and the led . . . *with the institution of leadership these simultaneously begin, owing to the long tenure of office, the transformation of the leaders into a closed caste"* [Italics mine].

For a final sense of the elitist message in how religious power is created and concentrated, contemporary Roman Catholic historian Garry Wills cites, in his book *Papal Sin* (2000: 2), the famous quote of nineteenth-century British Catholic historian Lord Acton, "Power tends to corrupt, and absolute power corrupts absolutely." What most persons who have heard that dictum do not realize is that Lord Acton was not merely writing of power generally. Rather, he was pointing specifically to Catholic ecclesiastical authority and the Vatican itself.

Or, as Michels concluded at the end of his classic *Political Parties* (1959: 373), "from a means, organization becomes an end."

Preserving Religious Elite Authority: I

Brokers of religious IOUs in exchange for here-and-now deference and obedience have to be engaged in ongoing authority maintenance. There are, however, several resources they possess through the charisma of office to help them preserve their status in the eyes of believers, often with minimal effort by virtue of how the church institution is set up.

One major resource is the most obvious: the omnipotent, mysterious, supernatural agency itself, particularly if personified in a deity for whom they are recognized spokespersons. Spiritual systems without the supernatural element are at a disadvantage, for their promised benefits lack the desired assurances on the most profound issues of existence, non-existence, and hoped-for continued existence. Rodney Stark, in his famous essay, "Must All Religions Be Supernatural?" (1981: 163) concludes that "not only is the notion of a non-supernatural or naturalistic religion a logical contradiction, but . . . in fact, efforts to create naturalistic religions will fail for want of that vital resource that has always been the *raison d'etre* of religion: *the gods*" [Italics mine].

Brokers unquestionably renew their authority by continuous association with the divine.

Thus, for example, the president of the Church of Jesus Christ of Latter-day Saints is not merely a chief ecclesiastical administrator. He *is* successor to Joseph Smith, God's prophet for His reformed Christian Church, with unique access to God's providence for humanity. Yet despite any personal qualities, Mormons are taught to believe that "there is an undeniable mystique surrounding this living link to God" (Heinerman and Shupe, 1985: 89).

Thomas P. Doyle, a Dominican priest and chaplain-lieutenant colonel in the U.S. Air Force, succinctly paints a parallel picture of Roman Catholic prelates:

> The bishops see their primary responsibility as preserving the visible institutional structure of the Roman Catholic church. . . . they are "organizational men" whose identity is dependent on the institutional Church. Furthermore the bishops themselves teach that their office is directly connected to God himself. (2001: 15, 21)

Doyle concludes that these elites identify *themselves* as essential to the life of the church and consider protecting the brokerage hierarchy tantamount to protecting the church itself. (Doyle was one of the original

Jeremiahs in a 1985 report to America's Catholic bishops alerting them to the growing emergence of the pedophile priest problem—for which he suffered hierarchical demotion and ultimately sought refuge as a military officer—see Berry and Renner, 2004: in particular, 31-71.)

Consider even non-theistic Zen Buddhism (both Chinese and Japanese versions), which essentially posits an all-inclusive plenitude or absolute of which everyone and everything are not only reflections but also are illusions if considered separate from it. Zen dispenses with saviors, forgiveness, resurrection, or deities but nonetheless maintains at a popular level the continuing Buddhist idea of bodhisattvas, or enlightened altruistic beings, who function similar to saints in Roman Catholicism (see, for Zen primers, Sukzuki, 1980, 1961; Linssen, 1958).

Another important preservation measure, which reaffirms clergy's and laity's continuous symbolic needs for a shared sense of legitimate authority, is the *socialization* of members to recognize the exalted status of their leaders. Earlier I referred to the "walk-on-water syndrome" that is not the monopoly of any one faith tradition. Elitist theorist Robert Michels even devoted an entire section of his book *Political Parties* (1959) to the respective psychologies of oligarchs and masses and how they reinforce each other. He titled one chapter "The Cult of Veneration Among the Masses" in which he observed (p. 67), "This need to pay adoring worship is often the sole permanent element which survives all the changes in the ideas of the masses."

Religious groups deliberately cultivate the special aura followers (want to) perceive in their leaders, as Bromley and Shupe (1979: 110-12) demonstrated concerning Unification Church followers' constructed legends of their charismatic prophet the Reverend Sun Myung Moon. (Charisma was regarded by these authors as a necessary resource to be mobilized in struggling social movements.)

Roman Catholic writer and editor Daniel Callahan (1965: 77) speaks of a "group think" lay conformity explicitly urged on students in this highly pyramidal church's parochial school system:

> [A Catholic student's] religious education is accompanied by a thoroughgoing indoctrination in the etiquette and demeanor required of the lay man in the presence of nuns and priests. He is taught to pay elaborate homage to the dignity and lofty status of those in the religious life. He will learn that normally it is not proper for him to challenge them, especially on religious matters. He will learn that deference to their religious authority, and the purported wisdom which goes with that authority, must be the norm to be followed at all times. What training cannot accomplish in this direction, the garb of nuns and the collar of the priest often can. These are signs of authority, signs that those so adorned are figures deserving of special respect.

Thus, a Catholic priest (or sister, brother, or other curate) is seen as a direct and indispensable broker between the believer and God. The consequences are that if he makes sexual advances toward a naive child or woman, and presents such actions as non-problematic or even somehow appropriate, he carries a certain leverage of credibility beyond that of, say, a school teacher, academic dean, or sports coach. As sociologist-priest Andrew M. Greeley (1992) once *a la Michels* cynically told an audience at a national conference of Catholic victims and their advocates, "The priesthood, gentle souls, is not a responsible profession. It is a privileged class, an immune class, protected *de facto* by its immunity through sanctions of both church and state."

Another example of official proclamations reminding followers of unquestioning homage due leaders can be found in the Church of Jesus Christ of Latter-day Saints, America's most famous home-grown religious success story. In its own way, the LDS Church is as pyramidal as the Catholic hierarchy, seeking uncompromising top-down obedience by reference to the sacred mission of its brokers. In the following brief selections from church-sponsored/endorsed publications and high-level representatives, General authorities refer to various top and mid-level administrators; prophets are the highest, such as the president and his immediate advisors and the Quorum [Council] of the Twelve Apostles. What can be seen is a direct identification of the church's current regime officers with the entire divinely ordained faith tradition:

In 1945: When our leaders speak, *the thinking has been done*. When they propose a plan—it is God's plan. When they point the way, there is no other which is safe. When they give direction, it should mark the end of controversy. God works in no other way. To think otherwise, without immediate repentance, may cost one his faith, may destroy his testimony, and leave him a stranger to the Kingdom of God. (WTM, 1945) [Italics in the original]

In 1972 (one LDS president to a president's first counselor): My boy, you always keep your eye on the President of the Church, and if he tells you to do something wrong, and you do it, the Lord will bless you for it. (Romney,1972)

In 1978: Christ and his prophets go together . . . it is not possible to believe in one without believing in the other . . . by rejecting the prophet we reject Christ himself. (McConkie, 1978)

In 1981: God will do nothing regarding His work except through His own duly anointed prophets! They are His servants . . . They will give us the Lord's word in no uncertain terms as God makes it known. That is why He has His prophets on earth. They are for edification of the Saints and to protect us from every wind of doctrine. Let us follow them and avoid being led astray." (Peterson, 1981)

LDS hierarchy attempts to control any scholarship of itself by its own historians, professors, and teachers act to preserve a unitary "official" narrative of origins and doctrines; it has been equally adamant on submission to official "correctness." (As one apostle, Bruce R. McConkie, told Brigham Young University students, "Please note that knowledge is gained by obedience" [Gottlieb and Wiley, 1982].) The LDS oligarchy has been particularly hard on social scientists if they forget or ignore demands to subordinate research findings to church theology. One case of leaders' strategy for conformity to protect both organizational reputation and their own broker status can be seen in 2002. Thomas W. Murphy, chair of the Anthropology Department at Edmonds Community College in Lynnwood, Washington (and a Mormon) had written an essay on DNA research for a predominantly Mormon edited volume. His research questioned the orthodox LDS belief that Lamanites (ancient Cannanites, according to the *Book of Mormon*, who migrated to North America more than 2,700 years ago at the time of the Israelites' arrival here) were related to historical and modern Native Americans. He reached this conclusion, using bioanthropological genetic evidence, and opined that the scripture's Lamanite claim should be regarded as "inspirational fiction" rather than scientifically backed revealed scripture. At first Murphy was threatened with ecclesiastical discipline, such as a church trial and possible disfellowship (i.e., to be placed on extended "probation" and denied participation in sacraments and so forth) or even excommunicated because he would not recant his findings. Only mass protests by friends, students, colleagues, and other sympathizers backed the LDS administrators down, at least for a time (Kennedy, 2002).

Heinermann and Shupe (1985: 202-15) have reported how scholars of various disciplines, including later anthropologist David Knowlton (1996), have had censorship of their research and publications or contracts not renewed when their intellectual products were not considered "faith-promoting." Such academic inquiry challenges the brokers' very claims to represent some supernatural agency's unique "account." For his part, after the publication of *The Mormon Corporate Empire* in 1985, John Heinerman was brought up before an LDS Stake High President's Council in spring, 1990 because he was "reported to have been guilty of conduct contrary to the laws and order of the church." (His co-author, myself, was not a Mormon and hence uninvolved.) The hearing procedure was an adversarial trial, with prosecution and defense sides to it and Heinerman unable to have identified or confront any of his accusers.

(Herinerman and I agreed beforehand that the former should blame any offensive parts of the historical/political/economic book on me, and that was done.) Heinerman was disfellowshipped for a minimum of eighteen months, which essentially meant that he could not speak in a Latter-day Saint meeting or enter any LDS temple or participate in LDS sacraments; he could not write concerning the church (for or against it) in newspapers, magazines, or books; he had to attend monthly counseling meetings with his bishop; and he had to tithe ten percent of his gross salary every month. Further, he was told this written decision and similar correspondence on his case would "go to church headquarters and be filed with your other records." Finally, Heinerman was never again to appear, or have further professional involvement, with me (which, to the church hierarchy's knowledge, was promised by Heinerman and fulfilled).

In such ways the existence of a definite supernatural power with which power brokers can identify themselves and can be seen as such by believers accomplishes in no small part one important socialization function for preservation of authority. Most of the time, its social control implications remain subtle, though occasionally blatant if only as deterrence to others. Space does not allow the many more examples easily gleaned from other faith groups. However, as will be seen in Chapter 4, and later here, one consequence of trying to preserve religious authority by brokers to followers, reminding them of divine association, are the catastrophic shattering of faith and irreparable sense of betrayal experienced by victims of clergy malfeasance. Followers and believers, in other words, can be set up for a harsh fall when the first two measures of preserving authority prove to have tragically misled them.

Preserving Religious Elite Authority: II

Everything in the subject matter of clergy malfeasance, from the consolidating shifts of power from laity to elites, to the presumptions of some elites that they are somehow free from the normal moral restraints of their offices, to the policies of other elites to cover-up or minimize scandal, deals with *power*. For the second part of this chapter's emphasis on the ways elites preserve their authority in churches, we turn to a modern theorist of power in sociology, Amitai Etzioni, particularly in his book *A Comparative Analysis of Complex Organizations* (1961).

First of all, Etzioni (p. xvi) defines power as "an actor's ability to induce or influence another actor to carry out his directions or any other norms he supports." This general definition implies a social exchange situation; it does *not* mean that other social actors do not have their own reserves of power, or that actor one's use of power over actor two does not cost actor one resources, only that in most cases actor one gets his way. What makes Etzioni's definition most useful for analyzing clergy misconduct are the various techniques (tactics) elites can employ in gaining compliance in one of two real contexts:

1.   to *maintain* deference and clergy authority during the ordinary routines of institutional affairs;
2.   to *retain*, even salvage deference and clergy authority in the event of possible lay disobedience and open scandal.

The previous two sections of this chapter dealt with the first context: the normal, regular social exchange situations between rank-and-file believers and their religious institution. The analysis in this third section is more interested in the second context, one where challenges to clergy authority arise or scandals have erupted. Both situations in this last section illustrate the dynamics of secondary clergy deviance.

For our purposes, Etzioni (pp. 4-39) identifies three principal techniques leaders use to obtain compliance or neutralize the reputational damage of scandal:

1.   the *normative* tactic involves the "allocation and manipulation of symbolic rewards and deprivations," often creating pressure on those "creating waves" over discovered internal wrong-doing or at least instilling guilt in outspoken victims and whistle-blowers;
2.   the *remunerative* (utilitarian-economic) tactic in which elites use "control over material resources and rewards through allocation of" such things as salaries and wages, pay off monies and compensations, services, and commodities;
3.   the *coercive* tactic, "the application, or the threat of application, of physical sanctions," more generally speaking injury, death, incarceration, and control of the satisfaction of basic physical needs, *religiously speaking*, the shunning, ostracism, this-worldly condemnation, future other-worldly spiritual damnation, access to sacred rituals and sacraments, or even formal excommunication.

Etzioni emphasizes that no one type of tactic has "an a priori superiority, nor is there one which, as a rule, is the most powerful." Many groups, including churches, employ all three forms of gaining compliance but tend to emphasize one more than the other two. Interestingly, should group elites try to use two different tactics simultaneously these will tend to mutually neutralize or cancel each other out. This is because, as an extension of Etzioni's thinking, these three tactics usually exist (to use a statistical analogy) in a *non-recursive* sequence, i.e., normative-to-utilitarian-to coercive, and not in reverse. Once normative and utilitarian (financial compensation) offers are made unsuccessfully, elites may try coercive measures. Once utilizing the latter, however, morale and attitudes of believers are irreparably hostile or damaged and more symbolic tactics lose their value.

Take the case of the Roman Catholic archdiocese of Hartford, Connecticut. Starting in the 1960s forty-three young persons claimed they had been sexually molested by a total of fourteen priests. In 1983, parents of the victims went to Archbishop John Francis Whealon to place the issue before him. The prelate, instead of adopting a conciliatory normative approach, immediately threatened the families with legal action if they pursued the issue further (the *coercive* tactic). One victim, now a middle-aged man, recalls: "There were times when I was driven to New York City and woke up in the back of the car, tied and being abused by men I didn't know." The fourty-three plaintiffs' attorney, Jason Tremont, upon news of the $22 million settlement finally awarded them (the *remunerative* tactic) said, "By giving victims a voice, we can change the behavior of the church and finally force the archdiocese to acknowledge responsibility for the past." Rather lamely, the spokesman-priest for the archdiocese said, "The archbishop wants to begin the healing process for those whose lives have been seriously harmed by sexual abuse, and for the church itself we must acknowledge and deal with what has been done with justice and compassion."

Thus, after unsuccessfully trying to coerce parishioners into silence, then paying them off after a nasty lawsuit which the archdiocese fought, the normative approach came somewhat too late (Eaton-Robb, 2005).

Moreover, as shall be shown in the following cases, each strategy has an ultimate cost attached to it for the religious organization. The goal with all three tactics, from elite brokers' perspectives, is to create a social exchange situation where for believers it is more costly to challenge or continue challenging the institution than to remain silent or back off into passive deference. In other words, it becomes in believers' immediate best interests to cease challenging the institution.

Now we can turn to the dynamics of Etzioni's three tactics in clergy attempts to obtain compliance and neutralize group stigma.

Normative Tactics

Etzioni states (p. 6), "From the viewpoint of the organization, pure normative power is more useful, since it can be exercised directly down the hierarchy." It is also the cheapest of the three tactics, costing brokers only symbolic "capital" and a little time (a point to be reiterated below).

Normative appeals are frequently used to *neutralize* the bad odor of deviance, one of the most important tools for preserving clergy authority. The concept of neutralization has a solid place in the labeling approach to deviance, first introduced by Sykes and Matza (1957) and since elaborated in its varieties by numerous sociologists. Thomson, Marolla, and Bromley (1998), for example, examined published "disclaimers" of deviance provided by Roman Catholic priest perpetrators that were little more than seduction lines professed by the predators to lull young victims. One notable Pentecostal evangelist, Mario Ivan "Tony" Leyva, intertwined an enormous post-World War II boy prostitution ring with his peculiar ministry. A published list of his homosexual, ephebophile exploits includes such classic "disclaimers" made to victims as "it has got to be a secret between just you and me and God," or that Leyva knew a "special way of loving each other" for "true Christians like us," or that "this *really* is God's special way for His people to love each other" (Echols, 1996: 40ff). Thomson and colleagues (1998) observed that other such justifications, or "accounts," provided after the fact by fellow Catholic elites were intended to excuse, minimize, or "normalize" priestly deviance in the eyes of victims and others.

Remember in the examples to follow that the whole point of the normative tactic considered here is two-fold: to *neutralize* the guilt, fear, and anger of victims/their advocates once the clergy misconduct has occurred and to *salvage* the good name of the particular religious institution. Several specific variations of the normative-neutralization tactic can be readily found in journalistic and other sources: to *protect* the organization and its leaders for the greater good of its humanitarian and divine mission; to *humanize* perpetrators and recast them in a more sympathetic light; to *redirect* blame toward the individual perpetrator and away from the system that sponsored or harbored him, or at least recast the victim as in some way complicit in the victimization; and to *blame* the whistle-blowers as malcontents and trouble-makers in the first place. Often these are not discreet, i.e, elements of different variations are encountered mixed together.

Emotional appeals to faith tradition loyalties and the larger goodness of its mission can serve as powerful symbolic forces acting to discourage victim complaints. This is what has happened during the past half-century in Utah, a state in which a number of law enforcement officials regard as the fraud, or affinity white-collar crime, capital of the U.S. According to Shupe (1991: 45):

> What is happening is that a remarkable number of persons who are or claim to be members of the LDS Church make their way to Utah or seek out Mormons elsewhere, to finance illegal quick-buck money-making schemes. Moreover, these grifters frequently try to win endorsements for their operations from LDS Church officials and then use these to reassure investors that the ventures have the approval of the LDS hierarchy and are thus "blessed" in some special way.

LDS church leaders as "celebrity" endorsers, or even themselves as corporate leaders, in schemes create unique religious fiduciary relations for many lay Mormon investors. "The con-artist's spiel can include a casual remark about a nephew on a Church mission, a high Church authority who is 'a good friend.'" Such subtle cues can be important to Mormons on deciding to trust someone whom would otherwise be a "stranger" (Shupe, 1991: 45). In the previous section of this chapter, the LDS church's encouragement to members to place absolute confidence in the hierarchy was highlighted. Indeed, according to one Salt Lake City attorney in that city's bankruptcy court trustee office, such schemes are "possible because the church has taught the members to have implicit faith in their leaders" (Shupe, 1991: 53).

The point is that when LDS Church members have been swindled in the same manner of other non-Catholic cases reviewed in Chapter 1, they feel themselves in an acute bind. To point fingers at their associates, friends, relatives, perhaps even at a bishop or stake president is more than embarrassing. It threatens to undermine the very essence of the ecclesiastical power structure's legitimacy, i.e., its special claim to leaders being "called" to authority by the Spirit of God. An average Mormon's admission of misplaced trust in leaders' financial advice challenges their presumed "gifts" of revelation and discernment. Hence, the victims are reluctant to turn in schemesters to police or to cooperate with investigators for fear the denunciation will reflect badly on their church.

Religious elites often fall back on normative appeals to church traditions or generalized loyalties that produce powerful emotions and attachments for laity and discourage the pursuit of redress. Marie Fortune's study of a clergy scandal in a Protestant congregation (and its bungled elite response) showed how the president of the congregation's lay board went so far as to collect testimonies on the minister's sexual exploitation of female congregants but then demurred at the prospect of setting up a confrontational meeting between the abusive pastor and his victims. The effort having lost its momentum, the official turned to sentimentality as a tactic for neutralizing the damage. He wrote in his decision:

> I believe that such a confrontation at this time would not result in any agreement, and would be a traumatic experience for all involved. There is no question in my mind that the Church would be severely damaged.
>
> It is my opinion that we should take steps to prevent any further indiscretions, but that we should also recognize and encourage the positive leadership for the betterment of the Church program. (Fortune, 1989: 50)

Concern for church reputation is also characteristic of the victims in the various Protestant economic affinity frauds mentioned earlier. More than a loss of person pride (at being so gullible) or financial loss (many victims in Protestant and Mormon scams are elderly and lose heavily, sometimes entire retirement savings), they also fear the faith implications.

Con-artist pseudo-fiduciaries are not loath to remind victims of the former's special roles as brokers representing God. With more than one government hot on his investigative trail, Gerald Payne, mastermind of the Greater Ministries Corporation (which bilked between 20,000 and 30,000 investors out of over $500 million across all 50 states) dissolved his fraudulent company in 1979. Payne declared it a "New Testament church" with Jesus Christ as sovereign head, no longer accountable to legal registration or tax/regulatory laws. (Payne termed these "unholy alliances with the state.") In court Payne issued an affidavit (as part of his attempt at a legal defense and to assuage his remaining followers) falling back on the First Amendment to shield himself and his collaborators from prosecution. He said, in part: ˙

> As Pastor, I cannot, by reason of my religious convictions regarding the Lordship of Jesus Christ over the Church, submit the ministries of the Church to government authorities. To do so would recognize a sovereign greater than Jesus Christ with authority over the Church and its ministries. (Fager, 1999: 21)

Televangelists, such as PTL's Jim and Tammy Faye Bakker and Dallas' W.V. Grant, Jr., were under fire during the late 1980s and early 1990s, respectively, from the Internal Revenue Service and the U.S. Justice Department. They likewise sought to reassure viewers in broadcasts that bad legal publicity was the result of a malicious officialdom motivated by, and in actual league with, Satanic forces (see, for example, Shupe, 1998: 57-60; 1995: 1, 17, 70-3, 139).

Even a Catholic parish's refusal to press charges against a priest who admitted in 2004 to the white-collar crime (no pun intended) of embezzling $226,000 from St. Mary Catholic Church in Edwardsville, Illinois was based on the need to normatively protect the organization. In what to parishioners and others must have seemed a magnanimous gesture of forgiveness, the bishop helped bury the fiduciary betrayal from public view in quick order. According to a diocesan communications director, "The bishop feels there's no advantage to prosecuting someone for that. . . . The bishop also didn't want the parish to suffer any hardships." The priest, having agreed to enter therapy (for gambling addiction) and repay the stolen money, was assigned to another parish in Jacksonville (Dettro, 2004).

Clergy are also people with ordinary weaknesses—a common neutralization disclaimer. Journalist Jason Berry, in his classic *Lead Us Not into Temptation* (1993: 17), relates how a Louisiana diocesan monsignor during the mid-1980s tried to downplay the indisputable pedophilia of serial abuser Father Gilbert Gauthe (whose case Jenkins [1996: 36] credits with shaping the "mode" of later reported Catholic Church scandals). The monsignor implored a father, Roy Robichaux, not to alert other parents about his son's molestation:

> Should anyone get hurt from this [Monsignor] Mouton admonished, the guilt would rest on Roy for making it public. Then Mouton said something that nearly knocked Robichaux out of his seat. "Imagine how Gauthe's mother would feel."

In other words, deviant priests have proud mothers sitting home too. Think of them.

A similarly manipulatively humanizing remark was made during a highly publicized Indiana case by Bishop John D'Arcy of the Fort Wayne-South Bend diocese in the late 1980s. A young man approached D'Arcy about being abused while an altar boy by a priest. The bishop advised the victim to keep that information under wraps, not even mentioning it to his parents. In a particularly insensitive example of *faux* concern for the young man's family, "He said there was no sense troubling them" (French, 1993). One is tempted to ask, No trouble for whom?

Interestingly, humanizing the perpetrator is a marked retreat from fostering any "walk-on-water" clerical aura as suddenly the charisma of office is overridden by ordinary foibles and personal defects. In 1992, when ABC's reporter Diane Sawyer drew together selected New England victims and their supporters from the emerging Father James Porter pedophile scandal for a *Prime Time* telecast, one father told of how years before he had approached his bishop about his son's molestation by Porter. The bishop cautioned him, "After all, you must remember, Father Porter is only human." (To which the parent replied, "No, Father, you have it wrong. You mean he is inhuman"—see ABC, 1992).

Some elites are downright preemptive to outside inquirers with a "none-of-your-business" attitude. One auxiliary bishop of the troubled Archdiocese of Hartford, Connecticut met with a pair of (female) reporters from the *Hartford Courant*. When they asked why a Central American clergyman, accused in October 2002 of sexual abuse, was still celebrating mass in a nearby parish following his termination, the bishop brusquely answered, "There is a very good explanation for that, but I'm not going to give it to you!" (Walsh, 2002: 5).

Other elites may portray themselves as victims or the actual abuse victims *as only apparent victims*, thus redirecting at least some of the blame away from the institution. This was the twin blame-reversal neutralization tactic in an ecclesiastical cover-up in Lafayette, Indiana in 1997. When Bishop William Higi learned that *The Indianapolis Star*, *The Indianapolis News*, and a local city newspaper were set to coordinate an exposé of a major priest abuse scandal involving at least forty victims and which had been taking place over a twenty-five-year period, he took the initiative by calling a press conference and dismissing the accusations as "old" and "sensationalized." Besides, he argued, a number of cases involved priest sex with teenagers and such cases were "different altogether" from priest sex with children. (One at first supposed he meant less heinous, but no. . .) Higi suggested these teens shared in the culpability in what has to be one of the most astonishing blame-the-victim attempts by clergy elite. He claimed that teenagers were, after all, capable of consent in sexual matters and "that sometimes a 14-year-old is not always a 14-year-old." Higi went so far as to take credit for his handling of this scandal as mostly "a success story" and felt that in the end he, if anyone, had become the victim due to all the press reporting (Caleca and Walton, 1997; Rahner, 1997a, 1997b).

Lastly, the victims and their whistle-blowing allies—indeed, anyone who refuses to let the topic just disappear—can be labeled a malcontent or troublemaker (if an insider) or an anti-fill-in-the-group (if an outsider) employing the sectarian hate card. In an analytical, quasi-autobiographical account of affiliation from a rigid Pentecostal sect, "T." had a final confrontation (one in an escalating tense series) in the church office with the pastor:

> When he attempted to discuss what he believed to be the two main issues of contention . . . he was immediately confronted with the rebuke. "We've heard that before from people on the outside." Offensive and defensive tactics abruptly switched hands. Suddenly the pastor began to challenge T.'s authority to question in the first place. He was asked: "What makes you an authority?" And he was told: "You haven't said

one positive thing tonight." "You're the only one in the congregation asking the kind of questions you're asking." (Darrand and Shupe, 1983: 184)

Following ostracization by congregant friends and a flood of rumors about his faith and personal behavior, T. was asked by a close friend not to participate in the latter's wedding ceremony, and finally:

> He was banned from yet another wedding, told that the word was spreading that "T. had a knife out for us." . . . Returning to the church to hear a visiting lecturer, T. was physically barred at the door from even entering (Darrand and Shupe, 1983: 186).

Or, after an Omaha Catholic priest with a penchant for child pornography had been quietly shifted from parish to parish by Archbishop Elden Curtiss, two laypersons—an eighty-year-old woman named Jeanne Bast and a fifty-eight-year-old man named Frank Myers—wrote separate letters to that city's *World-Herald* newspaper. Their common theme was church leaders' deceit and cover-up of clergy malfeasance. Not long after the letters' publication, an angry Archbishop Curtiss sent both writers letters of rebuke (as well as copies to their parish priests). To Myers he wrote, "Any Catholic who uses the secular media to air complaints against the leadership of the church, without dialogue with that leadership, is a disgrace to the church" (Silk, 2002: 2).

Apparently, the elderly Ms. Bast was considered an even greater disgrace. Noting her age, the Archbishop wrote to her:

> You should be ashamed of yourself! . . . The church has enough troubles defending herself against non-Catholic attacks without having to contend with disloyal Catholics. For your penance you say one Hail Mary for me.

Ms. Bast told reporters, "Nobody says that to an 80-year-old woman. And what does age have to do with it?" She called the bishop's suggested penance laughable, "I'm not seeking absolution" (Silk, 2002: 2).

Most attempts at normative control are not so heavy handed nor arrogant. The organizational imperative of most rational administrators with some knowledge of human relations, including clergy, is to minimize conflict and bad feelings with sugar, not vinegar, by seeking conciliatory resolution. Their professional worldview, grounded in an explicitly familial model, is to steer away from elite-lay tensions. This is the key motif in most tactics of reconciliation. Thus, elites talk forgiveness, restoration, healing, mediation, reconciliation, repentance, renewed covenants, and other rhetorical euphemisms of neutralization. To some critics they can be seen as merely dodges from accountability to the largest pool of potential victims—laypersons.

Protestant author Marie Fortune (herself an ordained minister) complains that church officials often "misname" clergy misconduct due to embarrassment and try to attach to it more familiar, biblical labels that downplay the fiduciary betrayal-power inequality dimensions:

> Evangelical churches, for example, don't hesitate to name a problem and deal with it openly, but they misname it. It's always adultery for them, and they go off on a tangent about the adulterous fallen pastor. All their energy goes into restoring the pastor. The victims never get acknowledged. So you have six or eight women in a congregation who, because we're only talking about *his* adultery with *his* wife, are never part of the picture, except as the scarlet women. (cited in Gordon, 1993: 23)

In the end, many calls for reconciliation between victims and institutions or even victims and perpetrator-brokers seek a maximal reduction of conflict, usually at the expense of the exploited victims. This is a symbolic "feel good" neutralization tactic for all which eases the public relations costs to the institution while avoiding the basic sociological issues of power imbalance and lay vulnerability. I have concluded previously (1995: 91):

> Reconciliation and reassurance thus become [if used cynically] a pseudo-balm to assuage victims without fundamentally altering power inequities or opportunity structures that further such abuse. Reconciliation is cheap short-run justice—to the advantage of ecclesiastical elites. [Bracketed insertion mine]

Remunerative (Utilitarian) Tactics

Remunerative tactics deal with brokers using money to preserve their personal legitimacy as well as that of the institution. There are two forms of spending such funds: paying hush money to victims for future silence about past secondary deviance or paying reparations (be they freely offered or as a result of court settlements in punitive lawsuits brought by victims).

The problem in determining how often the first payola economic tactic is used results from the secretive nature of most such payments. The latter are intended, after all, to discourage public knowledge of the clergy deviance. Sometimes we only learn of individually negotiated arrangements between clergy perpetrators and victims when payments are interrupted and/or victims still decide "to go public." This is what happened with the $250,000-plus to be paid to Praise the Lord Network secretary Jessica Hahn after she had sex (she claimed rape) with televangelist Jim Bakker and another Praise The Lord Network official (revealed when the payments stopped [see Hadden and Shupe, 1988: 9ff; Barnhart, 1988: 11]).

Other times it becomes revealed through later lawsuits. In 1993, New Mexico witnessed two hush payment scandals. In one, Father Robert J. Kirsch (one of several Albuquerque Catholic priests sued for alleged sexual exploitation) was alleged to have assaulted a female housekeeper when she discovered him in the rectory with an undressed young girl. The archbishop struck a deal with the housekeeper's family to provide both women involved with money in exchange for everyone's silence (Geiselman, 1993). In another case, the popular CBS-TV network investigative news magazine "60 Minutes" reported in the Spring of that same year that the Reverevd Robert Sanchez, Archbishop of the Santa Fe Archdiocese, had been confronted by a woman he had sexually assaulted earlier in 1978 and had been paying $25,000 supposedly to take care of her therapy costs as well as to obtain her silence (*Albuquerque Journal*, 1993).

Anecdotal cases from other churches, such as Utah's LDS organization and a myriad of smaller Protestant ones, suggest that the few instances the public eventually learn about are just that: the relatively few known but representing a presumably much larger iceberg, the bulk of which is mostly submerged. For example, over two decades ago, Heinerman and Shupe (1985: 235) estimated (based just on cases they learned of from informants) that the LDS Church's preeminent law firm *then* was handling around 3,000-plus legal cases in the U. S. and elsewhere, many settled with little or no publicity.

A better sense of what undoubtedly takes place in courtroom settlements where negotiations and results are sealed, and both plaintiffs and defendants are pledged to strict secrecy, can be gained from the many cases recently coming to light through publicly disclosed settlements. To be sure, not all involve Catholics. There are some spectacular Protestant examples (spectacular in the sense that the clergy involved are luminaries in their denominations even if the settlement amounts are not astronomical). The Reverend Barry Bailey, well-known senior pastor of Fort Worth, Texas' 10,500-member First Methodist Church, came under accusations of sexual malfeasance in 1994, 2 years after he had retired. A total of eight women accused the elderly pastor of having harassed them with unwanted advances during counseling sessions and lewd telephone calls during which he repeatedly discussed masturbation (and tried to touch himself in like manner when he was giving them "sexual education" lessons) over a three-year period. Bailey denied all, despite graphic charges by the outraged women. A jury, however, believed them to be victims.

Later a five-week trial awarded seven of the eight plaintiffs more than $3.7 million in damages for (among other things) the victims' loss of reputation, reckless infliction of emotional distress, invasion of privacy, and numerous psychological/medical bills following stress, trauma, and anguish (see, for example, Campbell, 1997a, 1997b, 1996a, 1996b).

But Protestantism represents a wide array of mainstream liberal-to-conservative denominations as well as a vast hodge-podge of decentralized small independent churches and splinter sects endorsing everything from snake handling to imminent arriving messiahs, radical faith healing, and Armageddon-battle preparations. There is no easy way, even with modern computer searches, to capture the sum of their abuse lawsuits. Most of the more visible ones involve the Roman Catholic Church. This is not surprising given both that it is the largest Christian denomination worldwide as well as in the U. S. and that a norm of strict celibacy and chastity for its entire clergy has been a Catholic hallmark for centuries. The Catholic cases, therefore, deserve special inspection below.

The first major modern case of child molestation in that denomination was that of Father Gilbert Gauthe in the Lafayette Diocese of Louisiana during the mid-1980s; this case is referred to elsewhere in this volume and meticulously documented by Berry (1992). Gauthe's victims were mostly prepubescent boys, involving literally hundreds of sexual acts, including anal and oral versions and Gauthe encouraging youths to engage in sex together while he photographed them. The cost for the church and insurers reached $10 million by 1987 and $22 million by 1990.

From that sensational case came an often cited report, delivered to America's Catholic bishops in 1985, *The Problem of Sexual Molestation by Roman Catholic Clergy: Meeting the Problem in a Comprehensive and Responsible Manner*, by Michael Peterson (a now deceased priest-counselor), priest-military chaplain Thomas P. Doyle (previously cited), and F. Ray Mouton, Jr. (ironically, Gauthe's defense attorney). The document, to put it mildly, was not received with great enthusiasm by the bishops. However, the report, aside from warning that sexual molestation was a long festering dirty secret that would eventually cause the church major image and membership morale damages, put forth the estimate that given what was known *then* of legal settlements the church would have paid off legal costs of $1 billion by 2000. (Berry [1992: 373] had independently estimated that by the time his book *Lead Us Not into Temptation* was published the church had already paid approximately $400 million to settle known lawsuits, covering victims' legal expenses as well as medical/counseling expenses for both victims and perpetrators.) This financial come-uppance was the result not of particularly bad years and a handful of bad-apple malfeasants but rather of the existence of a sexual subculture decades, even a half-century old.

How could what at the beginning of the first wave of Catholic priest pedophile scandals seemed like isolated cases begin to run such a tab? Berry's (1992: 23) report about the 1984 settlement in the Gauthe scandal, involving nine victims (from five families), and the legalist arrangement reached between lawyers for the latter camp and the church's insurance company, is instructive. It estimates what loss of innocence, trust, and feelings of remorse and guilt were worth in dollars:

> [The insurance agent] was offering a $19 million package. Less than $3 million would be paid up front; the rest would be paid out to each plaintiff in a structured annuity—long term, high-yielding accounts that provided an escalating payment shelf: say, $20,000 up front with $1500 a month until age eighteen; then $30,000 for college (or other uses) with a monthly hike to $2000; at age twenty-five, a $50,000, and so on.

Of course, in hindsight $1 billion total costs seems a gross low-ball estimate. It has escalated considerably since the first of this millennium. After all, Berry and Renner (2004: 7) could report three decades later that about 2,100 Catholic priests in the U. S. had been identified as being involved in legal proceedings involving sex abuse since the 1970s. By the 1990s, the criminogenic issue of the church hierarchy was becoming apparent. "Many cases *were* reported . . . sparking the realization among trial attorneys of a criminal dimension in ecclesiastical culture" (Berry and Renner, 2004: 74). For example, in 1993 Father James Porter's 25 victims in Minnesota and New Mexico received $48 million in an out-of-court settlement with the Archdiocese of Santa Fe (from when Porter was a patient at the Servants of the Paraclete Rehabilitation Ranch in New Mexico but was let out periodically to administer sacraments in rural parishes), while 68 original victims in the Fall River, Massachusetts Diocese received $5 million.

The settlements grew in size. The Reverend Rudolph "Rudy" Kos created a swath of victims in the Dallas, Texas Diocese and cost it $119.6 million (though the victims agreed to lower the settlement by ten million dollars or so to help preserve the diocese [Housewright and Egerton, 1997]). Reporting on more recent settlements, the publication *Religion in the News* (2006: 17, 24) noted that the Los Angeles Archdiocese could end up with the largest single judgment of any diocese in the U.S. with $250 million paid to victims so far, $100 million of that going to 90 persons just in Orange County. (The settlement was to become significantly bigger.) The Diocese of Covington, Kentucky meanwhile held the record by mid-twenty-first century with $85 million paid to 361 victims in such a smaller locale. Connecticut's Archdiocese of Hartford paid out $22 million in 2005, and the Spokane, Washington diocese (along with four others) had filed for bankruptcy.

The Roman Catholic Church also became involved in an enormous series of lawsuits brought by tribes of Amerindians (Aboriginals) lodged against it and other churches in Canada. The suits dealt with a politically expedient, sometimes brutal attempt by that country's federal government, starting in 1820 and ending as recently as 1996, to "assimilate" the children of First Nations (the indigenous Canadian inhabitants' self-description)—over 100,000 total—into white Canadian Franco-Anglo society through a series of forced conscriptions into so-called "residential schools." (Coercive measures used against the resisting young persons are described in the next section.) In recent years the Roman Catholic Church, the Anglican Church of Canada, the Presbyterian Church, and the United Church of Canada (a merged denomination made up of Methodists, Congregationalists, and other groups) have been sued by Aboriginal groups representing over 8,000 persons for sexual, physical, and cultural abuses. Some experts believe that over *$1.26 billion* will be eventually awarded, with the Canadian government and denominations sharing the costs (Fiegugh, 2003; Careless, 2002; Baglo, 2002).

How do things get so antagonistic, hostile, and ultimately expensive in churches where love and forgiveness are supposed to be part of a family model? One answer can be found in the initial defensive, legalistic stances taken by large corporate entities like the Catholic Church, a scenario repeated by church-paid attorneys across the U. S. This stance was best summarized by Chicago Archdiocesan lawyer James A. Serritella. At a closed conference of clergy at the Dominican priory in River Fall, Illinois in 1986, Serritella brashly told a priestly audience, "What you people have to remember is that when one of these situations develops, these people [the families] are the enemy, and I'm on your side" (Berry and Renner, 2004: 57).

For their part, the victims and their advocates who initially only sought justice and a realization of the ideals they had been taught by brokers, and perhaps at first "cooled down" by normative rhetoric, become outraged when they find they have been lied to and/or manipulated. Some were indeed, once bought off, as Berry and Renner (2004: 74) describe:

For survivors, the church that promised a path to salvation had betrayed them twice over—first as children, when they suffered sexual invasion; then, as adults, when they saw bishops or religious superiors acting like lawyers. Hush money silenced them. As canon law bound a priest never to reveal what people said in confession, sealed agreements muzzled victims from speaking about the cleric.

But revelation after revelation of scandal in an age of irrepressibly fast communications have created a giant snowball effect, the media collecting and exposing more and more instances of molestation and creating a consciousness of kind among victims that no church or denomination can possibly control. The normative tactics not only failed to preserve credibility, they incited victims to seek punishment of the brokers, eventually adopting the latter's same legalistic methods:

These [normative] tactics ultimately prove dysfunctional, for they alienate the laity. Perceiving their treatment to be the result of spiritual bankruptcy or insensitivity within the institution's leadership, the laity adopt mirror strategies: retaining attorneys, instituting lawsuits, and abandoning normative appeals in favor of remunerative or coercive strategies. (Shupe, 1995: 127)

Thus, normative tactics take on a self-defeating inertia if they are not sincerely intended and followed through. When victims of clergy malfeasance become mad, they want to get even, and nothing hurts corporations, even charitable benevolent non-for-profit ones, like expensive lawsuits.

Coercive Tactics

In Etzioni's scheme of the three tactics for preserving/obtaining compliance, or here elites' legitimacy and authority, the things he has in mind for coercive measures are literally physical, i.e., sanctions that entail injury, incarceration, or control of the satisfaction of basic needs. In religion, I have mentioned such measures as shunning and ostracization, pronouncements of damnation, denial of access to ritual and sacraments, and even excommunication.

To be sure, in religious institutions coercion may range from subtle (yet highly significant) pressure to blatant assault. There is a fine line between "subtle" coercion and normative pressure, perhaps little if any meaningful distinction in real instances. James T. Richardson, attorney and sociologist, examined through a qualitative study (1975) how a prominent, long-time member of a fundamentalist church became at odds with its pastor and was finally expelled. The study is interesting as an example of authoritative abuse because it demonstrates a step-wise process of ostracization and was conducted long before clergy malfeasance had become a front-page topic in the media. Basically, the church became entangled in a refinancing situation the parameters of which few members really understood, least of all the new, inexperienced minister. The lone dissident on the church board of fiduciaries was a knowledgeable real estate broker who formed the opinion that the refinancing deal was bad for the church and might even involve illegalities. Worse, if he were associated with it he could lose his real estate license, so he steadfastly opposed it.

After a church committee investigated and engaged in gross kangaroo court-style shenanigans, the man was placed on probationary status by the church deacons and gradually marginalized, with rumors and solicited testimonies from any previous church leaders with whom he ever disagreed mustered to "prove" he was a troublemaker. The deacons took votes on several recommendations, including one that the man "voluntarily refrain" from church attendance and another (that almost passed) that "all means possible (including arrest) be used to keep the man from attending." In their zeal to castigate and expel the dissident (who turned out to be correct about the refinancing deal's inadvisability) a letter denouncing the man as no longer a member of the congregation because of misdeeds was sent to various church-related individuals and agencies, including one that handled state licenses for real estate brokers. That undefined "misdeeds" suggestion prompted a state investigation of the church dissident (who *had* acted in a professionally ethical manner). Writes Richardson (p. 140), "The 'deviant' man involved was made dramatically into an 'instant outsider.' His previous valuable work for the church was discounted when the moral or fiscal entrepreneurs decided to define him as deviant and harmful to the group."

Richardson prophetically concluded (p. 141) that in business disagreements about financial policy, those with the most power maintain control and sometimes terminate the opposition:

> Less attention is usually paid to the morality of certain policies or decisions. When and if this becomes a major goal of some churches, a re-evaluation of priorities may be in order.

Was the tossing out of the real estate broker and his family from the church a coercive tactic? Attacking the source of a person's livelihood and professional reputation, as the deacons attempted to do, fits Etzioni's definition with regards to blocking "the satisfaction of essentials for life" criterion.

Normative pressure also relies heavily on religious loyalty and lay awarding of legitimacy to brokers for deterrence to work, the more pyramidal and ecclesiastical the organization, the firmer the social control. The Stake High Presidents trial of LDS author John Heinerman, mentioned earlier in this chapter, was a demonstration of a serious symbolic sanction (an eighteen-month period of disfellowship, or probation) but failure to acknowledge the church's right to stage such a degradation ceremony or to abide by its terms would result in excommunication, tantamount to a loss of personal salvation, which puts a coercive edge on theological social control.

There is another previous example, that of T. In the Pentecostal sect, he was physically barred—not merely symbolically condemned—from even entering the church building where he once had been able to worship. This physical aspect, then, designates coercive from extreme normative measures to seek compliance.

Iadicola and Shupe (2003: 174) observe that violence and religion often go hand-in-hand because "the truth-claims of various religions often inspire invidiousness, hostility, and intolerance." Here I would add, "and the need to assert authority, if not dominance, by brokers." Because the United States of America and most Western democracies are religious pluralities (and at most have only titular state churches, such as Great Britain or Sweden), physically coercive tactics by churches are usually rare. There have been, of course, some spectacular exceptions of violent coercive measures being taken to enforce obedience or even weed out troublemakers when the extreme symbolic sanctions of excommunication will not suffice. Most occur in marginal groups, some outside the law. For example, the Reverend Jim Jones routinely used incarceration, physical punishment, and fear to command compliance from his directives. Writes attorney-sociologist James T. Richardson (1982: 27):

> Jonestown was virtually a prison camp: no one was allowed contact with the outside world without permission and most outsiders were not welcome either, as Leo Ryan's party found out. Torture was employed as a way of maintaining control of members; adults were sometimes put for a week at a time in a wooden prison called "the box," 3 / 3 / 6 feet, and children were dropped into a water well for even small rule infractions. No other recent religious groups of which we are aware visited such terrorizing action on its members...

Likewise, there has been evidence of intersect extreme violence between various polygynist and renegade prophetic offshoots of Mormonism (see, for example, Sasse and Widder, 1991; LeBaron, 1981; Bradley and Van Atta, 1981) and within the splintering factions of the Hare

Krishna movement soon after the death of founder A. C. Bhaktivedanta Swami Prabhupada in 1977 (Hubner and Gruson, 1988; Franklin, 1987; Dart, 1986).

But more prosaic (by which is meant routine, non-murderous) coercion to maintain compliance and exercise authority can occur in more mainstream groups. Sometimes it merely takes the form of a threat. During the early 1980s Jeanne Miller, Chicago parent of an adolescent male sexually abused by a popular parish priest, along with her husband and other boys' aggrieved parents, fought the Chicago Archdiocese and its Cardinal Joseph Bernardin. It was slow going to press their complaints, particularly as her parish was split for and against the parents and the priest. In fact, the turmoil grew so intense and stressful that her marriage collapsed and some other parents backed out. In the meantime, Miller learned that persistent demands for ecclesiastical accountability do not go unpunished. Later becoming an attorney, she analyzed this situation for an academic volume:

> For two years, my husband and I and the remaining single mother who initially reported the abuse to us, fought through the courts to have Father restricted from his ministry with children. On March 30, 1983, we met with the archdiocesan chancellor, Fr. Richard Keating (now bishop of Arlington, Virginia) in the basement boiler room of St. Theresa's rectory, Palatine, Illinois, who told us that if we pursued the matter we could be excommunicated for violating canon law. It was a horrible threat. My belief system had been undermined, but my religion was still all-important to me. I was about to retreat until I realized that my beliefs belonged only to me and that this institution was powerless to deprive me of what was mine alone. (Miller, 1998: 157)

During this ordeal as she battled the archdiocese, Miller wanted to help raise the awareness over priest molestations in the manner of Jason Berry's *Lead Us Not into Temptation* and wrote her own book, *Assault on Innocence*. It was a thinly disguised "factionalized" autobiographical account of her family's experiences, written under the pen name Hillary Stiles to protect her family's status in the Catholic Church. In the episode below she describes a conversation based on fact between the smug, offending priest and the victim's mother where excommunication is not the most immediate threat:

> Meredith said, repeating, "Pete did not tell me what you claim you've heard spread around. In fact, Pete had a wonderful time and likes you very much. He actually defended you."
>
> "Well, I'm glad to hear he likes me. I have a lot of friends. Pete is going to be a freshman at Eagle Ridge High School next semester, right?"
>
> "Yes." She braced herself for what she sensed was coming.
>
> "I have a lot of friends on the varsity football team here. Having friends sometimes has disadvantages. Like, have you considered what my friends might do to your son when they find out what you're saying about me?" (Stiles, 1987: 80)

Or consider a more blatant coercive case and then a comment.

One black non-denominational church, the Atlanta-based House of Prayer, pastored by the Reverend Arthur Allen, Jr., seemed to have systematically subjected young persons to the violent whims of church leadership. Media reports in 2001 detailed accurately and graphically the physical coercion, apparently far out of proportion to any need for preserving authority. Nearly sixty children had been routinely struck or whipped with switches, belts, and sticks. Worse, the violence was church-sanctioned, the beatings administered by the children's parents in front of the congregation or while the parents held their children for others to strike.

The horror stories told in court, once the children were removed from their parents' control and placed for their own safety in foster care, stunned the city of Atlanta. It was not unusual for children as young as seven and ten to have visible welts, bruises, and open body wounds. One teenager told how she was forced to marry at age fifteen to a twenty-three-year-old man and then was beaten as punishment after she refused to have sex with him. A ten-year-old boy told police his arms had been held by one man, his legs held down by two other men, while a fourth struck him repeatedly on the back. The boy recalled the pastor standing over watching and directing members how long to beat him and when to stop.

The Reverend Mr. Allen acknowledged in court that he did indeed encourage corporal punishment for "unruly children," biblically justifying it as discipline. (In 1993, the Reverend Mr. Allen had been handed a thirty-day jail sentence for child abuse after he had "disciplined" a church member's young daughter.) The chief judge, Sanford Jones, finally decided not to release immediately forty-one children of church families from foster care. He had given those families the option to have their children return home *if* the parents agreed (1) to spank their offspring only with their hands, and (2) to not allow girls younger than sixteen to marry. *Those parents refused the conditions* (See, for a sample of Atlanta media coverage, Firestone, 2001; Judd, 2001; Martz, 2001; Wyatt, 2001).

Nothing in the media reports suggested that this behavior was part of a continuum of coercion; instead, it was thrown to readers as a freakish example of personal sadistic control, abetted by accessories after the fact in the congregation but still inspired by a rogue minister. The image of a church—any church—employing physically coercive resources to maintain compliance in a pluralistic society seemed (to put it kindly) medieval. Institutionalized coercion for purposes of authority preservation or even restoration is often treated by media as too bizarre to warrant coverage as anything but an exception that "proves" the nurturing model as the general rule. This is how most media reporting of the first wave of Catholic priest sexual abuse scandals during the late 1980s-early 1990s was handled and why the media suddenly had to "rediscover" the problem in Boston after the start of the millennium. The "few bad apples" approach suggests something psychologically aberrant with perpetrators but ignores anything sociologically criminogenic about religious institutions themselves. The latter possibility raises simply too threatening an image.

But the Atlanta case was seen as isolated and easily forgotten. The most systematic case of the coercive tactic which cannot be so dismissed has emerged in Canada spanning almost two centuries—a 176-year period from 1820 to 1996. It was that federal government's "assimilation" of aboriginal (First Nations) children initiative in cooperation with that nation's four largest denominations, including Catholic, Anglican, and mainline Protestants. Over 100,000 young persons were involuntarily removed from their indigenous tribal communities and placed in "residential schools," also variously termed campuses or homes. Not attempting here to second-guess the motivations of the originators of this plan, it soon evolved into a system of native youth resentment and sporadic resistance met with authoritarian control and sometimes harsh, stubborn punishment that crossed the line into abuse. The plan envisioned was actually, with no mincing of words, one of cultural genocide.

Conscripted students were forbidden to speak their native tongues, often discouraged from maintaining contact with their families, and often separated from siblings for years. Meanwhile, along with the essentials of Western European education being taught, their daily routines entailed forced labor and monastic lifestyles. At times the young persons considered themselves as convicts or prisoners of war, their white teachers and school administrators functioning as plantation overseers. First-hand stories from a compilation of residential school "graduates," published in 1994 by a First Nations assembly as *Breaking the Silence* (two years *before* the last residential school was closed down by the Canadian government) reveal routine beatings and whippings for trying to maintain native identities, heads shaved to shame and stigmatize run-aways, and small, fearful incalcitrant children locked in dark closets in the manner of child discipline at Jonestown. Food and water deprivation for days as punishment was not uncommon. Severe punishment of some children, others made to publicly witness, was intended to deter the latter from non-cooperation.

And, perhaps inevitably, with so many relatively powerless young persons, a sufficient opportunity structure was created to permit sexual predators into positions of authority. The litany of abuses later revealed included ritual fondling of genitals, forced intercourse, and (in consequence) mandated abortions (First Nations, 1994: 49-51; Brown, 2002). It was not the variety of personality inhibiting, fear and guilt internalizing, conformity-demanding tactics in the Canadian case that makes it unique, but rather the national scale of it all and length of time it continued.

Conclusions

The organization of materials in this chapter has relied on a reframing of religion and religious leaders perhaps unfamiliar to readers—first seeing the scared institution as grounded in *social exchanges* between mortals and the divine, with priests/rabbis/pastors/as the *power brokers* between the two parties. These brokers, who create elaborate hierarchies of authority as they professionalize their niches, serve literally as the expert go-betweens, a role which provides them with considerable influence over the laypersons dependent on their fiduciary wisdom.

Elitist theory from political sociology was employed to explain why in most religious institutions of any size all of the above occurs. Consolidation of power—sacred or secular—into the hands of oligarchs is a sociologically inevitable, or "iron," tendency. Likewise, maintaining or preserving authority by elites is an ongoing process to be reiterated just as individual elite authority must be continuously demonstrated and reinforced. Amitai Etzioni's three tactics of obtaining compliance, not developed by him with religious institutions and churches necessarily in mind, nevertheless present a useful background for interpreting how religious elites go about the business of shoring up their authority.

Thus, this chapter has illustrated the flow of the infrastructure of religious authority: how it is obtained; how it tends to crystallize into a special monopoly of elites with an accompanying subculture of self-confidence and even conceit; and how it is preserved on an ongoing basis. The social exchanges in religion do not always take place smoothly or equitably, hence the development of doubt, disillusionment, and resistance among believers—the topic of the next chapter.

In Chapter 1, I stated the axiomatic assumption that clergy malfeasance is inevitable and perennial. In the current chapter I have presented some sociological evidence why this is so. Human beings must combine their energies in groups to survive both during their own lives and for the long-term prospects of their families, tribes, and nations. For the same reason, they seek some common meaning larger than themselves to explain why they even exist, much less what they do (and should do) to survive. To paraphrase the concluding lines of psychologist Gordon W. Allport's classic *The Individual and His Religion* (1959: 161), Religion is the ultimate attempt of human beings to enlarge and complete their own personalities by finding the supreme context in which they rightly belong. Unfortunately, that search for meaning also inspires in emergent fashion an all-too flawed human enterprise that, like all institutions, invites abuses of privilege, which in turn also become patterned.

4

The Angry Activists: Victim Advocacy as Countermovement Mobilization

Why have a separate chapter on victims? What is the mystery about victims? Aren't they either simply unlucky and random or are they the predictable, vulnerable targets of exploitation by more powerful and/or unscrupulous religious leaders? On the face of it, consideration of victims ought to pose no problems for understanding.

But victimologists such as Wallace (1998) and Karmen (1990) suggest that sometimes the issue of who gets hurt and why is not so simple, even that in some instances there is a "shared responsibility" between perpetrator and victim, and that for any victim's part "the spectrum of [possible] responsibility extends from complete innocence to full responsibility" (Karmen, 1990: 114). This has been a hotly argued contention, beginning with the rape crisis movement of the 1970s (see Karmen, 1990: 125-41 for an in-depth discussion of this rape issue as well as the parallel crime of car theft from the victimology position).

Thus, according to such a perspective, *completely innocent* victims would be "crime-conscious people who tried not to be victimized. They did what they could within reason, to avoid trouble" (Karmen, 1990: 115). For example, Burkett and Bruni (1993: 6) dramatically describe the following frequent routine of frightened, potential young victims in a New England parochial school in which the famous sexual predator, Father James Porter, worked:

> "Father Porter's coming, Father Porter's coming." The warning flew down the quiet corridors of St. Mary's Grammar School whenever one of the girls saw the priest approaching. Then, as if on cue, dozens of girls in bobby socks and skirts that always covered their knees fled the center of the hallway for the walls, pressing their backs against the hard, cold tile. They knew that if you didn't turn your back to Porter, he couldn't sneak up and grab you from behind. If you didn't turn your back, he couldn't get his hands under your skirt.

Alternately, others—such as the numerous gullible (and often elderly) Bible-believing investors caught up in the myriad of Protestant and Mormon financial affinity scams cited in Chapters 1 and 3—could be said to play the role of *facilitators* in their own fleecing when they unknowingly, carelessly, negligently, foolishly, and unwittingly made it easier for the criminal to commit crime. Facilitating victims inadvertently assist the offender and therefore share a minor amount of blame. They increase the danger and open themselves up to trouble by their own thoughtless actions (Karmen, 1990: 110).

Of course, nobody wants to become a victim. It is truly an unwanted status. But in surveying all the possible types of victimization, or malfeasance, at the hands of sexually rapacious, financially amoral, and authoritarian religious elites, there *is* a need to address the issue of *possible* complicity. The important general characteristics of both victims as a group and the set of their fiduciaries in trusted spiritual relationships, as developed in Chapter 3, are displayed in Figure 1 below.

The trust and naiveté of the victims render them vulnerable and the presumed technical wisdom (or calling) and official higher (often revered) statuses of the religious elites (providing them unique opportunities for deviance) combine in an "arena" of power dependence where exploitation is possible and even probable in the long run. It is a safe truism that *any* power dependence arena will eventually suggest, or attract, malfeasant social actors. It could be noted further that this same mix of factors could hold as well for physicians/therapists, professors, and lawyers and their parallel set of patients, students, and clients.

Figure 1
Power-Dependence Arena of Victimization by Professionals

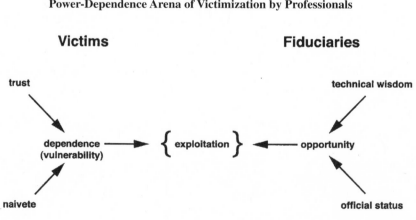

Likewise, victims who seek redress (justice) often do not act alone, particularly when they become aware that they have company. Individual anger morphs into reinforced collective outrage, but more importantly, sometimes organizes not just locally face-to-face but as larger social movements.

Victim complicity and victim advocacy, therefore, are the two themes to be explored in this chapter.

Victimization and the Issue of Complicity by Types of Malfeasance

Sexual

The examples of sexual abuse featured in this type have mostly been assaults against young persons: pedophilia and ephebophilia instigated by Catholic priests and Mormon elders; the mistreatment, again both pedophilia and ephebophilia, of missionaries' children left to the care of an African boarding school or committed on thousands of Canadian First Nations children taken from their tribal families and communities and virtually incarcerated in "residential schools." Then these have been the seemingly sadistic sexually related abuses heaped on young church congregants (sometimes with the direct approval of their very families, making the latter what criminologists and the courts refer to as *accessories after the fact*, or accomplices) as well as adults by rogue independent Protestant Church pastors.

These young persons in particular are, in victimologist Karmen's scheme of apportioning victim complicity, the "completely innocent" ones. No one could reasonably argue that these minors, many under extreme duress if not physically restrained, provoked/precipitated/invited their own abuse from adults. The few outright attempts to make the case implicating youths as somehow provocateurs in sexual exploitation rings has seemed almost laughably lame to outside observers. Recall Lafayette, Indiana's Bishop William Higi, mentioned in the previous chapter, seriously suggesting during the exposé of a twenty-five-year-old priest scandal in his diocese that victims such as a fourteen-year-old girl could in reality be a Lolita-style seductress, therefore a significant partner in the problem. Doyle, Sipe, and Wall (2006: 75) cite further a Catholic archbishop in the early 1990s who tried the same neutralization: that priests who became sexually entangled in affairs with minors have been the "naive victims of streetwise youngsters." (The archbishop's words are in quotes.)

Young victims' naiveté and sexual inexperience alone put them at risk with anyone older, much less a predator whom they trust because this person is a church leader they have been taught explicitly (and by example, implicitly) to be above suspicion. Nancy Nason-Clark, a Canadian sociologist at the University of New Brunswick, and her colleague Anne Stapleton have in several major conference papers (1992, 1991) and in publications (ex., 1998) explored the ramifications of one major Catholic priest scandal during the 1980s in the province of Newfoundland. They looked at levels of victimization that reverberated from the allegations of sexual abuse in St. John's Diocese. Nason-Clark notes (1998: 86), "When the reports of allegations and charges first surfaced, the media focused mostly on victims' recollections of abuse and on the long-run implications of an abusive past." The sociologists, however, conducted in-depth interviews with twenty-four women (many mothers) in the diocese to determine levels of victimization. While the media concentrated almost exclusively on the immediately physically affected victims, or the *primary* level, women who had trusted their children to supposedly benevolent hands of Church fiduciaries formed a *secondary* level. And there was a *tertiary* level of victims—members of the local faith community (of which more is said at the end of this chapter) who also feel betrayed and suffer lost trust and spiritual confusion. Concludes Nason-Clark (1998: 94):

> Almost all of the women we interviewed claimed that the Church in Newfoundland has not recovered from the scandal. Moreover, all save one reported dissatisfaction with the Roman Catholic Church's response to the scandal. While the women are adamant that their personal faith has suffered little (and perhaps even grown stronger) as a result of the clerical sexual abuse, they say they never again will trust priests as they once did. Catholic priests in Newfoundland have been collectively "struck from the pedestal. . . ."

To be sure, not all sexual malfeasance by clerical fiduciaries involves youth and thus sometimes is not as "completely innocent." This is suggested by Janet Jacobs in the excerpt from her study *Divine Disenchantment* (1989) at the beginning of Chapter 3. Usually these acts do not involve acts of rape or assault but rather are consensual (if opportunistic) due to pressure to engage in sex with leaders (they are told) in order "to grow spiritually." And retired Catholic priest-psychotherapist A. W. Richard Sipe (1995: 116), who has written extensively about allegedly celibate priests' affairs with women (single and married), writes: "Most priests' sexual relationships with women are not . . . complicated. Many are sequential involvements determined by the priest's opportunism, selfishness, immature exploitiveness, or character defects, which leave the women traumatized and confused." Such cases still fall within the arena described in Figure 1 but are covered under authoritarian clergy misconduct later in this chapter.

Economic

Sexual abuse by clergy receives the lion's share of the headlines, not only on account of its titillation value but also because at times many persons enjoy seeing the high and sanctimonious pulled down several notches. However, economic exploitation operating within the spiritual arena creates personal lifestyle losses, victim body counts, and the pandemonium of misery to a far greater extent. More persons overall are touched by this one type of malfeasance than by any other.

The most extensive type of economic malfeasance in the American spiritual realm, i.e., in our churches and faith communities, is (as argued in Chapter 1) affinity crime: pyramid schemes, bogus stock investment and insurance deals, and a host of small scams. While Chapter 1 featured some spectacular individual embezzlements, they involved relatively modest amounts of money. However, The Baptist Foundation of Arizona, the Greater Ministries International Church, and the Foundation for New Era Philanthropy each took in hundreds of millions of dollars. (Recall that the noted magazine *Christianity Today* estimated $2 *billion* in such losses for just the three-year period of 1998-2001.) Criminals refer to these mammoth schemes as "the big store" or "the big con," swindles that require elements of self-confidence and nerve as well as flamboyant talent that many small-time thieves like Episcopalian treasurer Ellen Cooke and Atlanta, Georgia Sunday School teacher Donald E. James lacked (Nash, 1976: 256).

The "big store" exploitations discussed earlier in this book manifest three important elements for complicit victimology.

First, these have been "affinity crimes." *Affinis* in Latin means *neighboring* or adjacent. Neighbors literally live next to one another, share similar lifestyles, and usually reside in an atmosphere of trust and reliability. In religion, affinity means persons sharing more than a mere physical locale. More importantly, they are co-believers, embracing a special bond stronger than the original meaning of affinity.

The Reverend Barry Minkow, the ex-white collar criminal turned Evangelical Protestant pastor of San Diego's 1,200-member Community Bible Church, who was interviewed by *Christianity Today* for his current other role as "fraud buster" of pyramid-style affinity hustles (Moll, 2005: 30), reiterates:

> [Perpetrators] learn the language and concerns of the group, build a sense of commonality, and then offer the "investment opportunity." By this point many Christians instinctively trust "their brother in the Lord" and don't think it necessary to investigate.

Because of this affinity factor, potential investors are more apt to let down their guard when presented with appearances or credentials related to their religion, when encountering persons seemingly knowledgeable, *and* when such persons possibly possess the endorsements and testimonials of revered leaders in their faith community. Potential investors are therefore more likely to fall into a vulnerable mode to an extent that never would occur if they encountered similar malfeasant individuals as non-members in a non-spiritual, non-power-dependent arena. As one regulator in the same Minkow interview article said, "Con artists try to make faith in God synonymous with faith in their investment scheme" (Moll, 2005: 30).

This is the background of numerous scandals in both black and white and Protestant and Mormon faith communities so often chronicled in publications as diverse as *The Wall Street Journal*, *Christianity Today*, and the Brigham Young University School of Management's *Exchange* magazine.

A second facilitating factor is victims' frequent sheer ignorance concerning the realities of investment returns. As seen earlier, when promoters like John O. Van Hofwegen of the Christian Reformed Church denomination promised investors yearly dividends of 9 to 11 percent, or when an Atlanta, Georgia Sunday School teacher assured his fellow believers of a whopping 18 percent return *per month* (and took them for $5 million), there does not appear to be *for some* an investment *too* good to be true. Gullibility rules the day for some believers.

But gullibility does not mean the same thing as stupidity. It has to be remembered that to investors who "want to believe" the scheme *in its context* often seems feasible and reasonable. For example, when housing prices across the U.S. began to rise dramatically at the end of the twentieth century (so much so that the average home in my own current modest cost-of-living Midwestern Indiana city of residence, Fort Wayne, costs $250,000—a pittance, I know, in some other regions) a lot of equity accrued in many homes. This yielded a tempting supply of ready cash. In ex-con-turned-pastor Minkow's experience perpetrators encouraged victims to take a second mortgage on their homes to invest money in the scam. Victims were promised that in no time they would receive a 100 percent return on their investment and soon be set for retirement. For many soon-to-retire boomers, investments guaranteeing 40 percent to 80 percent returns seem to be the financial solution for their golden years. (Moll, 2005: 30)

The second factor, thus, builds on the first. With such naiveté abroad in the population, it is no wonder that someone eventually shows up to take advantage of the situation. Such schemes can spread like a contagious disease in a host population of poorly discerning religious folks. As victimologist Karmen (1990: 110) observes, "Facilitating victims attract criminally induced people to them and thereby influence the distribution of crime."

A third factor rarely spoken about except in some particularly susceptible sectarian circles, such as Mormon parts of Utah, Idaho, Nevada, and California (where university conferences, official church warnings, and business publications agonize over the background reasons predisposing affinity crimes—Shupe, 1991: 44-75), is greed. Indeed, in the entire *Christianity Today* interview with Barry Minkow, after reviewing all the facilitating factors in evangelical Protestant affinity crimes, the only mention of this much rebuked human foible is the two-word motivation: "blind greed," mentioned only *once*. Religious folks—perhaps the more devout the more vulnerable—certainly are not insulated from the lure of quick sizeable profits.

Greed is an embarrassing facilitator for two reasons. First, affinity crimes rely on pools of religionists, people so integrated into their churches and faiths that the trust dimension can be assumed. For con artists, overcoming "the-one-more-dupe" hurdle becomes much easier when the dupes are co-religionists. In this way, religious virtues of faith and personal surrender backfire.

Second, greed, or avarice, for riches—particularly those not righteously earned by hard work—is a particularly old biblical sin. This is an ugly fact of many affinity cons.

Call it quick-buck thirst. Or as LDS historian Marden Clark a quarter of a century ago called it, "the easy money hunger:"

Our [LDS] emphasis on welfare, food storage, staying out of debt, and so forth has made many of us hyper-conscious of the role of money in our lives. We have placed a good deal of emphasis on success, both monetary and otherwise. It is no accident that some of the best known of the new breed of financial advisors are Mormons. . . . I can't help wondering if some of the things we glory in most don't get twisted to support the easy money hunger. (Cited in Shupe, 1991: 48)

Tithing, attending not just regular local religious services but also temple sacraments and general activity within one's local ward provide Mormons with a sense of spiritual protection or "insurance" and corresponding entitlement to material blessings. LDS author/historian Hugh Nibley warned Mormon readers of the danger of expecting material rewards for presumably righteous living. Nibley criticized this naiveté, "The Economy, once the most important thing in our materialist lives, has become the *only* thing. . . . like the massive mudslides of our Wasatch [Mountain] front, [it] is rapidly engulfing and suffocating everything" (Cited in Shupe, 1991: 48).

In sum, naiveté (or ignorance) coupled with the natural human inclination to want a fast, sure, lucrative return on an investment, then meeting up with pseudo-fiduciary scoundrels claiming investment expertise within the arena of a trusted affinity, eventuate in the exploitation outcome displayed in Figure 1. On the often unmentioned but understandably important facilitating greed issue, I need not rub it in further for victims. However, I quote the estimably renowned nineteenth/twentieth-century fraud investigator for the Chicago Police and sometime railroad detective Clifton R. Wooldbridge. Wooldbridge lent this cynical parting shot to readers at the end of his classic book *The Grafters of America*:

> If you have an atom of common sense you will avoid being "roped in" by these sawdust swindlers. If you are an honest man, there is no need to warn you. (Wooldbridge, 1908: 482)

Authoritarian

A religious elite using his or her sacred status to pressure or impose on believers courses of action otherwise unrelated to the latter's fiduciary role is guilty of authoritarian abuse. That formal definition, of course, is more slippery in real life. That point is that the elite making self-serving claims of the imposition as necessary for the well-being and even spiritual growth of the believer (or some other noble cause) may or may not be sincere. Recognizing this type of abuse calls for special discernment by both outside analysts and the believer himself/herself. Consider, for example, the encompassing lifestyle demands and sacrifices made by priors, abbots, and superiors of Roman Catholic, Orthodox, and Zen monasteries and convents as opposed to the capricious norms in the fiefdoms of David Koresh or Jim Jones.

The Mormons call unwarranted displays of ecclesiastical authority "unrighteous dominion," and its possible/probable/documented uses by leaders influencing believers' political attitudes and behaviors have become a contentious issue for some in that ecclesiastical institution which has also endorsed "free agency" (Heinerman and Shupe, 1985: 128-52). Liberal Roman Catholic scholars, such as Charles Curran and Hans Kung, have lost their academic positions in Catholic universities and received the wrath of conservative Church officials on account of their theological writings. This is despite the "openness" reforms of the mid-1960s Vatican II Council conferences and a pope's "Call to Action" initiative of the next decade (see, ex., Berry and Renner, 2004: 28, 208ff). (The same essential sanctions have occurred with Mormon scholars/professors at Brigham Young University and elsewhere, as mentioned earlier.)

Other conservative, mostly Protestant but some Catholic, groups call such extensive or "totalistic" authoritarian control *shepherding*, or *discipling*. This is a controversial practice at its extreme when a guru-disciple or experienced-member-novitiate mentoring relationship is established (in much the same ways that martial arts in Asia have been traditionally taught or that in Alcoholics Anonymous a newly sober person obtains a more mature volunteer "sponsor" to help strengthen an alcohol-free lifestyle).

This mentoring situation in religion is supposed to be limited to promoting specific skills or in cultivating spiritual growth, but it can at times get out of hand. Critics have pointed (with some justification) to two national sect groups, the Maranatha Christian Church and the Boston Church(es) of Christ, as illustrations. (In previous chapters I presented others.) In certain instances, spiritual power becomes excessive; the senior teacher/leader overrides the spiritual role and ends up intrusively dictating all sorts of behaviors to the junior member that have little to do with spirituality *per se* (Shupe, 1995: 65-7; Yeakley, 1988). Authoritarian abuses by "shepherds" can reach into the lives of their "sheep" to include arbitrary requirements on dress and appearance, choice of jobs or on-the-job demeanor, whom to date or marry, and even what books or movies can be read or seen. (Recall the case of T. in the previous chapter.) In one case I encountered, the shepherd even had his male sheep (or lamb) regularly mowing his lawn, washing his car, and performing routine house cleaning. (See, for a particularly outrageous case that ultimately culminated in a child's murder and police investigation, sexual hi-jinx and adultery, and a number of divorces, the now-defunct Seattle, Washington Community Chapel group—Shupe, 1995: 62-3.)

Authoritarian abuse is also one form of clergy malfeasance in which victim complicity is often inextricably involved if discussion is confined to adults. In a pluralistic society with non-state-enforced faith or denominational group hegemony, for example, fear of repercussions from Mormon or Catholic hierarchies for heresy or non-obedience only matter to persons who believe in the missions and legitimate authority of the respective groups' oligarchs. Some recently published autobiographical accounts of authors' lives in presumably high-demand, spiritually oriented groups, such as *I Can't Hear God Any More: Life in a Dallas Cult* (2006) or *Insane Therapy: Portrait of a Psychotherapy Cult* (1998), claim authoritarian abuse in the form of "mind control" and erosion of free will. These books are reminiscent of an earlier genre of "mental enslavement" potboiler exposés (some selling very well) going back to nineteenth-century ex-Mormons and ex-Catholics and then later to the post-World War II American "anticult" movement (Shupe and Bromley, 1980). However, the essential scientific validity of any "brainwashing" or "robotic control" argument for why people join and then conform to leadership demands in unconventional religious groups has been successfully debunked to the satisfaction of most behavioral scientists (Shupe and Darnell, 2006). Influencing individuals in the group context involve some social processes that indeed can be subtle but are hardly mysterious to social psychology.

The explanation for much adult victimization at the hands of clergy returns us to the social exchange underpinnings of religion itself. Leaders may vastly overextend their moral authority into the ordinarily private area of believers' lives, but they do so with at least the implicit acceptance and even eagerness of victims who *for their part* anticipate some return or trade-off. These rewards can be varied, depending on the specific group, its beliefs, and the character of the leader(s); they can include enhanced spiritual development, the promise of special favors or status, advancement in the organization, or even required love. A similar exchange mentality is supposed to exist between therapists and patients and professors and their students, hence the professional proscription against such liaisons (which are often honored in the breech—see Rutter, 1989; Dziech and Weiner, 1990).

For example, focusing just on young women in Eastern groups in American culture we can see this emotional social exchange at work. None of these women joined these groups as conscripts, but rather joined voluntarily as a spiritual quest. Write two non-social scientists in *The Guru Papers* (Kramer and Alstad, 1993: 96):

[Some] particular gurus depict what they are doing as modernizing ancient esoteric methodologies (sometimes referred to as "tantric") that attempted to bring self-realization through ritualistically breaking taboos. In the name of freeing people from their limitations and "hang-ups," this path is presented as the fastest track for contemporary Westerners to achieve spiritual goals, without undo austerity.

Sometimes what is demanded of women in particular is a self-surrendering form of love (or so they are told), and their ultimate realization that their leader has rejected this gift (usually after sex is consummated) is when the exchange contract becomes reneged on in their eyes.

Janet Jacobs in *Divine Disenchantment* (1989: 95-100) describes a woman in one group who was raped by three men thinking the act was somehow a test planned by her spiritual teacher. Afterward, however, she felt "unworthy" and shamed as her value to the group suddenly diminished. Writes Jacobs (P. 104):

That final acknowledgment, that the devotee will never be loved by the teacher, is perhaps the most hurtful realization of all, the turning point from hopefulness to disillusionment. In the case above, rape and degradation were perceived as a test of love and dedication, an ultimate act of faith that alienated this young woman even further from her teacher and left no doubt that he had, after all, rejected her for her weakness. For other converts, the betrayals were perhaps less harsh, repeated violation of faith by the leader who ignored his disciples, who abused them, and left them wanting more than he could possibly give to all those who sought his affection, protection, and knowledge.

This logic was promoted by the guru cult of the Bhagwan Shree Rajneesh during the 1980s when he discouraged conventional monogamous marriage among his followers as "the coffin of love" because it interferes with a person's spiritual self-development by ultimately inhibiting or restricting spontaneous sexual expression. For a time Rajneesh encouraged pluralistic and libertarian sex (Sharma and Palmer, 1993: 107; Gordon, 1987: 9). Psychotherapist James S. Gordon in *The Golden Guru* (1987) speaks of the *darshan*, an "energy-generating" mediation session to be held with the guru Rajneesh and sometimes others. In fact, *darshans* became a euphemism for trysts:

At night . . . a number of sannyasin women has "private darshans" with the Master. Many years later Rajneesh would claim that he had "had more women than any man in history. . . ." The women who had private darshans were told not to speak about this . . . (Gordon, 1987: 79)

One case of a highly educated professional Indian woman clearly illustrates her anticipation of a valuable exchange with Rajneesh:

"I was becoming a medium for Bhagwan's energy. I felt I was one of the chosen ones, very special . . ." She would kneel in front of Rajneesh at evening darshans, sometimes with other women at the same time. "When the lights were out, he sometimes touched our genitals, our breasts, stimulating our lower *chakras* [force channels]." (Gordon, 1987: 79)

But, given some distance of time, she came to doubt if the guru-follower bargain was equitable for both sides:

> At the time, she hoped that the energy would be illuminating, that the power and sexuality she felt would be transformed to love and wisdom. It was only some years later, after she became disillusioned with the organization around her Master, that she began to feel that his intimate attentions may have been a form of control, a means Rajneesh was coldly using to bind her and his other disciples to him. (Gordon, 1987: 80)

A particularly vivid example of such exchange where the authoritarian abuse is "normalized" in the eyes of both a primary victim *and* secondary victim can be found in Feurstein's (1991) study of Eastern religious sages who justify sex with followers in the name of breaking through sexual conventions to challenge and reshape the follower's social realities. During the 1970s Da Love-Ananda (formerly Da Free John, before that Franklin Jones), like Rajneesh, regarded marriage as a restraining worldly attachment. Like the Branch Davidians' David Koresh two decades later, Love-Ananda took his pick of female devotees, "leaving their husbands or lovers to sort out their wild emotions and confusion" (pp. 86-7). Consider this "testing" of not only a woman but her husband, he kept in conflicted anguish (and how he finally rationalized the adultery):

> In front of me, my wife was being sexually prepared for the guru. I coped with my violently irrational feelings by going into emotional numbness. Happily, I did not have to witness my teacher bedding my wife. We were all asked to leave the room. I was sent to a different building where I sat for several hours in the dark, dealing with the emotional hurricane that had been unleashed on me. Finally, I got a handle on my feelings. I realized that one of my attachments was to my wife, and that the guru was doing radical surgery on me for that. I had asked him, indirectly but loudly and clearly, to help me in my struggle for enlightenment. That night he was doing just that.

Even austere Zen Buddhism, once the largest Buddhist sect in both China and Japan during those countries' respective medieval ages, has had somewhat similar *roshi* (teacher)-pupil problems when it began to flourish in the U.S. Zen has Ten Precepts (similar to the Judeo-Christian Ten Commandments) which forbid the misuse of sex in promiscuity, rape, or adultery. Philosopher-ethicist and Zen follower Christopher Ives remarks in *Zen Awakening and Society* (1992: 111-3):

> In the past fifteen years several highly publicized crises in North American Zen centers have unfolded involved sexual relationships between Zen teachers and their students. This has triggered a set of questions. Is there something inherently wrong with a Zen *roshi* sleeping with a student? . . . Given the pain that has arisen for many individuals

involved in these incidents in North American and the apparent irresponsible abuse of power and authority on the part of the *roshis* involved, such contact can be seen as tragic. Further, it is contrary to Buddhist principles, for the precept on illicit sexual relations certainly makes no provision for sexual contact between teacher and student, and no prominent Zen figure has ever advanced a case for the *"upayic"* [teaching] value of such contact.

Thus, Christian pastors and shepherds, self-proclaimed messiahs, gurus, and Zen monks can be rogue fiduciaries on occasion, sexual and authoritarian opportunists in the power-dependence arena of Figure 1 along with the affinity criminals. It is important to reiterate, however, that victimology only claims that some extent of victim complicity means that many victims are at least partially responsible for the deviance successfully taking place. It does *not* claim that the victim deserves the harm from deviance or that the perpetrator is any less culpable for his or her actions.

Victims Seek Redress

Redress for victims of clergy misconduct is a synonym for *justice*. Justice, of course, can mean many things to different victims. For some it is the satisfaction of seeing hypocritical fiduciaries punished (removed, defrocked, jailed) or at least exposed, humiliated, and shamed. It is retribution. For others justice means compensation. After all, many more victims overall have been financially cheated than sexually abused, and the sexually abused ones often have their future lives seriously in need of expensive counseling and even medical repair. Nevertheless, probably all victims of any of the three distinct forms of abuse feel emotionally injured, distraught, and their overall trust in religion disturbed. For others still, justice may mean the blanket repayment of injury back to the entire religious institution, if only serving as a wake-up call to other fiduciaries that victims will not be content merely to nurse their wounds and go quietly away into the night.

The remainder of this chapter deals with victim advocacy groups that arise to advertise victims' existence, their hurt and outrage, and to expose crooked, unrighteous clerical brokers. One caveat: most of the organizations described below are made up either of Roman Catholics or members/ex-members of the Church of Jesus Christ of Latter-day Saints. This is because, as a sociological truism, the most hierarchical churches are (in the style of Robert Michels' "iron law" model) more likely to be entrenched oligarchies less permeable to criticism and review, their elites more insulated by their formal offices (See Shupe, 1995: 119-20). These churches are also more likely to be mirrored by more organized victim opposition "countermovements" whose leaders had to "cut their teeth" on learning how to develop strategies of seeking justice and penetrating the thick oligarchic hides.

These advocacy groups may be up against huge bureaucracies with deep financial pockets, but at least they can better take aim with their efforts, unlike victims in more decentralized Protestant congregations and denominations. There are smaller victims groups tailored to specific churches; for example, *Silent Lambs* is made up of Jehovah's Witnesses, while *The Awareness Center* has a Jewish constituency. However, the larger national groups which serve widespread victim pools will be emphasized in the following pages.

Why Are There Victims Advocacy Groups in a Growing Social Movement Industry?

When specific social movement organizations resemble each other in their goals, have similar memberships, share a common church/denomination of concern, and are not only aware of each other but even communicate and coordinate with one another, they are said to coalesce into a *social movement industry*. This particular victims movement industry has been a growing phenomenon in the U.S. for almost three decades. I term it the AAVM—the Anticlergy Abuse Victims Movement.

The AAVM in post-World War II America exists for three essential reasons.

First, American religious pluralism is remarkable compared to religious systems in many other countries because in the U.S. it operates in a relatively politically unrestricted marketplace. Therefore, with no official state religion nor any ministries or departments of religion at state and federal levels, victims' complaints against churches are mostly private (civil) affairs and take longer to resolve. When victims try to work through ecclesiastical channels for redress and find no satisfaction, they have two choices: hire attorneys, and/or locate fellow victims to combine resources in grass-roots advocacy movements. This is exactly what happened with many American citizens very unhappy with their experiences in a variety of post-World War II new religious movements (See Shupe and Darnell, 2006).

Second, as the iron law of oligarchy would predict, large ecclesiastical organizations—even independent "mega-to-moderate-sized" churches in metropolitan communities—are hierarchies of privilege and power. Lip service to laypersons aside, elites' fundamental sociological imperative is to protect the organization and, by extension, its agents—to "circle the wagons" when the latter are perceived under attack. (This is also to be expected from police, professors, doctors, and other professionals when they are criticized by the people they serve or service.) Thus, A. W. Richard Sipe, a former priest and psychotherapist writing in *Sex, Priests, and Power* (1995: 167, 6) analyzes the Roman Catholic Church's unsuccessful struggle with mandatory celibacy for clerics. He also notes that "control and power clearly become primary concerns" in the midst of current scandals and that as a result the church structure "is crumbling under the weight of its own hypertrophy, if not corruption."

Third, in social exchange terms, a contract between brokers and adherents has been broken. Worse, it occurred within the contexts of trust and dishonesty, for those are what any kind of abuse of power is about. The classical nineteenth-century French sociologist Marcel Mauss, a pupil and nephew of Emile Durkheim, wrote a book entitled *The Gift: Forms and Functions of Exchange in Archaic Societies* (1967) in which he dealt with the reciprocity expected in human exchanges *as a form of morality*. The function of any successful exchange is to reinforce and satisfy the morality of all exchanges. The gift (*le don*, from the French verb *donner*), however, is more than a physical present or personal favor. It can be a talent provided, a service lent, or an understandable pleasure or desire foregone by a leader for the good of a community. For clergy it can be the lengthy training and time of professional preparation, the loss of ordinary financial rewards, the endurance of minimally comfortable styles of living, and even the sacrifice of the physical joys and love of nuclear families in marriages. All these can be gifts to congregants when men and women answer a higher calling to form a sacred covenant in ministry in exchange for deference, special respect, and obedience by congregants.

When the "gift" has been given under apparently false pretenses, when the terms of the exchange have been reneged upon by one party at the other's expense, then all three reasons above exist for targets of clergy malfeasance to see a double-victimization: first, at the hands of individual religious perpetrators; then second, from the larger organizational sponsor that endorses and/or defends the latter. Conclude Doyle, Sipe, and Wall (2006: 75) in analyzing Roman Catholic Church responses to thousands of victims (most of sexual abuse):

There is much evidence to show that victims who complained were consistently seen as traitors and disloyal to their church. Many victims have reported feelings that they were viewed as seducers, seductresses, sinners, or, in some cases, opportunists and treated largely without sympathy. . . . Complaints were discouraged by the reception they received. Victims and their families were deceived, confused, ignored, not given credence, or discouraged. These families were inhibited by false, incomplete, and misleading information designed to serve the interests of the church hierarchy rather than those of the child victim. This pattern was consistent in dioceses and archdioceses across the United States.

Cultivating Consciousness of Kind

Originally, victims of clergy malfeasance had to learn about others' similar experiences from eye witnessing them, word of mouth at the local level, or media reports. Two creative "trollings" for victims illustrate the first avenue. Frank Fitzpatrick, as a boy a victim of Father James Porter in a New England parochial school, had adult flashbacks to sexual abuse by Porter; he found his first fellow victims years later through taking out a small classified advertisement in a regional newspaper that simply read, "Do You Remember Father Porter?" and gave a phone number to call. Lyn Toth accused a Catholic priest in 1992 of having sexually molested her when she was between the ages of ten and twelve. At the time her father confronted the priest who admitted it; the Reverend Carl Wernet died, however, in 1980 of cancer. When she approached the diocese as an adult, it claimed not to have any record of the abuse but nevertheless volunteered to pay for her counseling. Not satisfied, Toth created (what she termed) a "wanted poster" and tacked it up in public places, such as supermarket store bulletin boards, throughout the Cleveland Metropolitan area. Like Fitzpatrick's simple ad, it was blunt:

Wanted
Adult victims/survivors
of Acts of Molestations/Rape
by
Fr. Carl Wernet
Former Pastor
of St. Joseph Catholic Church
Avon Lake, Ohio during 1950-1960s
If you would like to share your pain
Please write to Lynn.

Toth provided her P.O. Box number and ended the note: "Let's heal together and stop the cover ups!" (See Shupe, 1995: 128-9 for further description.)

Such simple strategies characterized the first "wave" of Catholic priest scandals during the early 1990s, though of course they were soon picked up as newsworthy by newspapers and national television programs such as ABC's *Prime Time*. They worked to cultivate victim awareness.

Undoubtedly the most important consequence of such initial contacts has been the generating of victim counts, no matter how disparate or spread out geographically, and a corresponding *consciousness of kind*, or what Karl Marx referred to in economic terms as *class consciousness*, i.e., a sense of shared grievance. It has been an indispensable element in every major social movement of our time, from those of racial/ethnic/gender minorities to families of victims of drunk drivers, raped and battered women, homosexuals, and politicized Evangelical Christians.

In the beginning the AAVM organizations were fairly energetic but were still struggling "Mom-and-Pop" endeavors (See Shupe, 1995: 127-30 for a description of the shoe-string budgets and meager resources of several early efforts). But it was only a matter of time and technology before the AAVM world of U.S. mail/telephone/Xeroxing/faxing turned into the new millennium communications infrastructure of personal computers/email/the internet. The following six-step scenario has played out in local Catholic Churches and parishes as well as at the diocesan and archdiocesan levels. It illustrates how the largest Christian denomination in the U.S. unwittingly created the largest, most numerous social movement organizations in the AAVM:

1. A parent learns after growing suspicions that a priest, brother, or other cleric is misbehaving sexually with children, often boys, but sometimes both sexes.
2. The parent or family, perhaps in concern with similar families, complain to a church superior, such as a monsignor or bishop, and is assured that an investigation of the grievance will take place.
3. Later the higher elite official assures complainants that the "Father," or the offending priest/cleric, will be dealt with promptly and effectively.
4. Much later the aggrieved families learn that little to no remedy occurred. The "Father" was often merely transferred in low-key fashion to another parish (without forewarning the next locale of the perpetrator's past deviance).
5. History (or secondary deviance and recidivism) repeats itself.

6.   Now betrayed twice, the aggrieved families (and their victims who
      may be minors, if not already adults) are now angry and in no mood
      for pious normative appeals from elites. They begin to seek account-
      ability changes in the larger church administration and/or large financial
      settlements for damages (if not pressing for criminal prosecution).
      Now empowered, they also begin seeking allies and kindred spirits
      (victims) in other locales and within the larger public. With comput-
      ers they create and locate websites, publications, and other resources.
      In a short while they have generated a consciousness of kind that can
      be translated into conferences and face-to-face meetings, donations,
      grants, clearinghouses of information, and the resources necessary to
      sustain a formidable social movement (as well as ally for class-action
      lawsuits). Or these empowered laypersons can make unheard of de-
      mands for accountability from the clerical oligarchs.

This is the contemporary situation. Like their earlier counterparts in
the North American anticult movement, AAVM groups have chosen
expressive names: SCAR (Survivors of Clergy Abuse Reachout); SNAP
(Survivors Network of Those Abused by Priests); SWANS (Support for
Women Abused by Nuns); Survivor Connections; Justice and Peace,
Core Group of Concerned Laity; Mary's Hope; and Voice of the Faithful. These organizations have become clearinghouses of information for
self-help, referrals to mental health specialists and attorneys specializing
in victims of clergy malfeasance, bibliographic materials (including
books and copies of investigative reports), news of upcoming national
and regional chapter meetings and related conferences, city-by-city/state-
by-state/foreign reported scandals reprinted from newspaper articles,
links to related AAVM groups, editorials and case analyses, and even
"healing" poetry contributed by members (and, of course, appeals for
donations). All are non-profit. Some also respond with aid to Protestant
victims. Moreover, in this second wave of Catholic scandals in which
most of the first wave's victims groups are still operating, almost all
have websites as well as hard-copy newsletters. One only has to key in
the name for any of the groups mentioned here on the internet's Google
to receive a variety of sub-sites and voluminous pieces of information.
The groups keep growing in snowball fashion. Consciousness of kind is
being exponentially enlarged.

Since most readers are probably unfamiliar with such groups, below
is a sample of the largest AAVM organizations and some distinguishing
facts.

SNAP (Survivors Network of Those Abused by Priests)

Founded in 1989 by Chicagoan attorney Barbara Blaine, it is the oldest Roman Catholic victims' advocacy group in the U.S. It maintains a high national profile in protests against U.S. Catholic bishops' sometimes-tepid proclamations and demonstrates at their conferences. It is the quintessential national AAVM group and embodies all the characteristics and activities in the above paragraphs. Other later groups seemed to have mimicked SNAP's detailed, graphically elegant website. SNAP classically fits the general mobilization process I have outlined. Initially the "underdogs" in confrontations, groups like SNAP quickly set about cultivating resources that formed an emerging market of exchange with a victim/advocate clientele resulting from:

- sensational media reporting by mainstream television networks (ABC, NBC, HBO, and so forth) and large circulation newspapers (e.g., *Boston Globe, Los Angeles Times, New York Times, Chicago Tribune, Washington Post*);
- sheer enormity of the scope of response to such reports and word-of-mouth spreading in parishes and dioceses (a "He did that to me, too!" phenomenon);
- the immediate need of victims for information on similar cases, the subsequent "sociological imagination" at work as victims saw how their own case particulars fit into the "general pattern," victim reference groups were provided by SNAP so that victims developed consciousness of kind;
- a growing sense of having been victimized ultimately by ecclesiastical callousness or downright deception.

The Linkup (formally named VOCAL)

The Linkup was founded in 1991 by Chicagoan housewife/now attorney Jeanne M. Miller. (The Windy City's famously autocratic archdiocese during the 1970s and 1980s seems to have inspired such lay activism by legally minded persons.)

Miller, true to victim family form, had a teenage son molested by a serial priest perpetrator. She was initially "cooled out" by a bishop anxious to bury the scandal only to find she was lied to as the prelate moved the perpetrator to another parish where recidivism occurred. She fought her crusade for Catholic Church acknowledgment of the molestation problem all the way to the late Cardinal Bernardin's office (losing husband and friends in the process). Thanks to efforts such as hers the Chicago Archdiocese now has a Catholic abuse hotline 900-number and a review board made up of clerics and lay professionals. The Linkup's website and victim resources resemble those of SNAP, though SNAP has generally been more aggressive in protests. (Miller wrote up an account of her crusade in detail in an academic outlet—See Miller, 1998).

VOTF (Voice of the Faithful)

Headquartered in Newton Upper Falls, Massachusetts, VOTF is a lay Catholic victims group and on its website emphasizes that, aside from providing victims assistance and resources, it seeks more ambitious administrative reform within the Roman Catholic hierarchy in the direction of greater cleric/prelate accountability to laity. Lay input into selection of bishops is one example. VOTF's website lists as three broad goals:

1. to support survivors of clergy sexual abuses
2. to support priests of integrity
3. to shape structural change within the Catholic church

Its mission statement reads, "to provide a prayerful voice, attentive to the Spirit, through which the Faithful can actively participate in the governance and guidance of the Catholic Church." VOTF claims it is "centrist," not extremist, and narrowly Catholic, unlike The Linkup and SNAP which began with a focus on just Catholicism but expanded to assist non-Catholics with nowhere else to turn. (This also is similar to the anticult groups of earlier years which constantly found their umbrellas of concern over particular new religious movements expanding—see Shupe and Darnell, 2006).

Survivors First

Also a New England (Boston) AAVM group, Survivors First is addressed more to non-victim Catholics than are other groups. Its proclaimed four activities are healing, prevention, public awareness, and fundraising for survivor support groups. Interestingly, it has an extensive priest/bishop abuse database of newspaper, magazine, and other types of articles and reports (Most AAVM groups have one of sorts for current cases.) broken down into six categories:

1. criminal convictions
2. civil settlements of judgments
3. pending criminal actions
4. pending civil litigations
5. public allegation
6. private allegations

In addition, each case is designated by active ministry, on leave, resigned, suicide, admission (of culpability), and allegations in newspapers; *and then* further coded as diocesan or order (by name).

It is also worth mentioning a more modest AAVM-style organization (again, in response to an extremely hierarchical church) addressing allegations and perceptions of authoritarian abuse by leaders in the Church of Jesus Christ of Latter-day Saints. The group is named the Mormon Alliance and is made up of a mixture of ex-Mormons, excommunicated Mormons, and current active and inactive Mormons. Founded in 1992 and headquartered in Salt Lake City, the group publishes a newsletter, *By Common Consent* and holds a semi-annual "conference critique" at a public library or in similarly modest meeting places. This meeting follows the LDS Church's own semi-annual conference held with much publicity at Temple Square in downtown Salt Lake City.

The Mormon Alliance also publishes annual edited "Case Reports of the Mormon Alliance" volumes that report on criminal investigations involving Mormons, dilemmas of Mormon intellectuals, feminists, and other "marginalized" LDS members. It also reports on child abuse and offers such resources as a child abuse hotline and anecdotal stories and documentaries on spiritual faith and obedience "gone wrong." It presents discussions of various LDS church policies affecting the alliance's readers who live within the influence of LDS culture in Utah and other western states. Its publications, either offered by the alliance itself or Signature Books (of Salt Lake City), are compendiums of communications from commiserating people of faith alienated from their church's hierarchical leadership and seeking to keep their own consciousness of kind alive.

Conclusion

Victim complicity in instances of clergy misconduct is a range of possible involvement, and some kinds of abuse (economic and authoritarian) actually require some measure of it, with sexual abuse (at least concerning minors) likely relying on it the least. For adults engaging in intimate relations with clergy, either in adultery or simply in flings and affairs, the story would be different. Still, the issues raised by victimology in the "entire story" of any instance of clergy malfeasance, even if that complicity is of such a low order as ignorance or gullibility, rate consideration.

The emergence of the AAVM follows a fairly standard "value-added" pattern studied in other movements by sociologists. This pattern begins with individual grievances and discontents, suffered independently, and then awareness of others in similar situations. This leads to contact, sharing of stories, and an emerging consciousness of kind, which coalesces in organized determination to mount a campaign to broadcast members' grievances still further and to developing goals (redress in various forms) that perhaps culminate in a push for reforms in the offending institution.

This percolating of micro grievances, transmuting into the macro phenomenon of a social movement with resources to confront entire churches and denominations, is the result of breakdown in fundamental social exchange systems, of which religion is one form. Some sociologists see society as nothing but constantly emerging social exchanges—a collection of myriad transactions we reify into some stable structure. Certainly, analysis of clergy malfeasance reveals nothing to dispute such a model.

5

Counterreformation:
Redress or Neutralization?

On October 31, 1517, twenty-four-year-old Martin Luther, Roman Catholic friar and professor of Holy Scripture at the University of Wittenberg, nailed his famous "Ninety-five Theses upon Indulgences" to the castle door in the city of Wittenberg. He declared he was ready to enter into public debate on indulgences, i.e., *a priori* written notes of forgiveness from suffering in purgatory, obtainable by sinners for a price while on their way to sin. (The indulgences were one major way by which Pope Innocent VIII hoped to raise money to build the lavish St. Peter's in Rome.) Church-secular state relations in Europe were rife with the mood for reform (as had been some church leaders for decades) by the sixteenth century. Luther's audacious move was merely a catalytic one where otherwise "at the administrative level the quest for reform limped along like a lame man who does not know where he is going" (Chadwick, 1972: 12).

The Roman Catholic Church was to respond, internally as well as to state sovereigns, during the next two centuries with a "countermovement" to the Luther *et al.* Protestantism reformation movement. It was termed the Counter-Reformation. Yet, as British historian Owen Chadwick observed (1972: 351), it was really about much more in emerging European societies:

> There was a true sense in which the fight against Protestantism encouraged the reforming movement within the Roman Catholic Church. But it did not create it. The conflict with Protestantism gave to reform a new edge, to cut through the vested interests and administrative conservatism which everywhere frustrated reform. . . . [And] The vested interests were so powerful that no reformation, not even a Catholic reformation, was possible without an increase of the secular state.

The results were new nation building and the terrible Thirty Years War.

The thesis of this chapter is that clergy scandals of the 1980s, 1990s, and the early years of the Third Millennium (the spectacle of unabashed self-importance and financial irresponsibility by celebrity televangelists; the comeuppance to Christianity's oldest and largest denomination for initially denying, down-playing, or trying to outright quash whistle-blowing on its own epidemic of clergy sexual malfeasance; the gradual awareness by various Protestant and other groups that they likewise lacked a significant portion of discernment regarding their leadership prevarications and abuses of lay naiveté) have provoked a general renewal of lay inspection toward clerics. It has stimulated a rethinking of clergy's prior privileged role in ministry and prompted demands for leadership accountability. It has encouraged a more Missourian "show me" wariness in lieu of always confidently assuming total leadership benevolence. It has consequently spawned a new healing or "recovery" ministry involving professionals far beyond the clergy.

This new outlook on religious elites has been also filtered somewhat through the type of religious *polity*, or political structure, in which laypersons find themselves. It has been a counterreformation (note the lowercase c with no hyphen to differentiate it from the older parallel movement), sometimes calling for resignation or reforms more structural. The new counterreformation has been not only Roman Catholic and, thanks to modern communications technology, now thoroughly democratized. It has required only several decades, not centuries, to mature.

This chapter is an essay in what genuine redress, as opposed to mere neutralization, the counterreformation has had to offer. *Redress*, as defined in Chapter 4, means justice. *Neutralization*, as used by most labeling theory sociologists, refers to a deviant (or a deviant's spokesperson) admitting he or she has committed a disapproved act, but:

- there was actually a good (or higher) reason for doing it;
- not as much harm was done as people might think;
- the person (victim) to whom it was done had it coming or was complicit or, alternately, is simply delusional;
- or the action in the long run might possibly be beneficial (that is, have a latent function).

Here I employ neutralization beyond its rationalization use to mean also an elite strategy by which a church's brokers try to contain (stifle or minimize) damage and embarrassment caused by a rogue cleric's malfeasance.

These two outcomes of redress and neutralization need not be mutually exclusive. Indeed, when some scandals are still in their infancies, some redress may actually achieve the other.

Denial and Neutralization

Chapters 3 and 4 showed normative techniques employed by religious elites to "cool out" potentially angered victims or redirect blame away from the perpetrating agents/brokers of the particular church or denomination. Outright denial of wrong-doing is typically a stopgap exercise used only at the outbreak of scandal by otherwise hapless spokespersons. For example, this was a ploy of various televangelists when journalistic investigations were first made. During the early days of the Jim and Tammy Faye Bakker PTL scandal, the Bakkers and their lieutenants characterized (on and off the airwaves) the investigative *Charlotte Observer* as "an agent of Satan" for smearing their ministry and as "demonic" (Barnhart, 1988: 235; Martz and Carroll, 1988: 7, 118). Similarly, after the ABC *Prime Time* news magazine had skewered Dallas charismatic preacher/televangelist W. V. Grant, Jr. for his slight-of-hand faith-healing practices and fund-raising campaigns for bogus charities, Grant told television viewers "They actually ask you to believe this old anti-Christ yellow journalism." He condemned that earlier ABC exposé and in a following report by ABC blamed many of his subsequent problems with the Justice Department and Internal Revenue service on a conspiracy of "the media and the Devil" (ABC, 1996).

Geographic isolation of blame for undeniable scandal, most often a reliable tactic in "mature" widespread ones, can be plausible for a time for some believers. During the first wave of Catholic priest pedophile revelations during the early 1990s, Pope John Paul II made a triumphant worldwide tour aimed especially at reinvigorating young Catholics. During his much-publicized 1993 visit to the U.S., a World Youth Day rally was held at Denver, Colorado. While not dwelling on the embarrassing scandals, the pontiff did briefly acknowledge the growing problem (Raby, 1993); he blamed the whole thing on American pluralism and its cultural relativism:

In a culture which holds that no universally valid truths are possible, nothing is absolute. Therefore, in the end . . . objective goodness and evil no longer really matter. Good comes to mean what is pleasing and useful at a particular moment. Evil means what contradicts our subjective wishes. Each person can build a private system of values. (Mattingly, 1993)

Likewise, according to Canadian sociologist Theresea Krebs (1998: 15):

> In 1993 the highest governing official in the Roman Catholic Church revealed his position regarding the sexual abuse of children by clergy and religious in the North American Catholic Church. As reported in the *Edmonton Journal* on January 24, under the headline "Permissive Society to Blame for Abusive Priests—Vatican," the chief Vatican spokesperson, Joaquin Navarro-Vallis, identified pedophilic clergy in the Roman Catholic Church as a uniquely North American phenomenon: "One would have to ask if the real culprit is not a society that is irresponsibly permissive, hyper-inflated with sexuality capable of creating circumstances that induce even people who have received a solid moral formation to commit grave moral acts."

This single-nation admonition flew in the face of considerable evidence (See Stacey, Darnell, and Shupe, 2000: 190-95) that the scandal was in fact on an international scale in the church. (In fact, an entire book has been written on that pope's seeming willful ignoring of the priest sex scandal among his agents—see Berry and Renner, 2004). Likewise, Cardinal Oscar Andreas Rodriguez Maradiaga, Archbishop of Teguchigalpa, Honduras, became for a time Pope John Paul II's lightning rod on the purportedly "unique" American scandals. Previously a leading advocate for human rights as well as head of the Conference of Latin American Bishops during the late 1990s, he once obscurely compared U.S. media coverage of the Catholic Church's sex abuse crisis to Stalin and Hitler (Kusmer, 2006).

Denials, however brusquely dismissive, offer only brief respite if there is indeed fire beyond the smoke. This is particularly true in our media-consumed age with a premium placed on highlighting whistle-blowers for immediate (if brief) celebrity status. It is well nigh impossible for any large church, much less huge ecclesiastical denominations, to contain awareness of secondary elite deviance and perpetrator recidivism for very long. And denials, while cheap and easy to deliver, usually arouse more suspicion than they dispel. A cynical public has come to accept denial of every wrong-doing from political, corporate, and now religious elites as merely the expected first salvo at the onset of an unfolding scandal, in the same way a judge anticipates as a matter of course a "not guilty" plea proffered by an apprehended hands-down serial burglar.

Neutralization is often a more complicated resource-intensive business than denial. It relies more on a longitudinal faith tradition that inspires respect and provides brokers with the charisma of office. In addition, as a strategy, it is operated within bureaucratic machinery that can by sheer density of offices and levels obfuscate disclosure, stall information flow, and delay timely processing of grievances and their adjudication. Thus, neutralization is more often the strategy of choice for elites in groups with *hierarchical* polities (ones in which the polity, or political structure, holds a clear chain of command throughout various levels of ordination, where the pastor of a local congregation is answerable to higher elites further up the hierarchy). There are considerably fewer options for elites in churches with *congregational* polities (where clerical authority is more grounded in non-rational, consciously anti-bureaucratic, laity-ratified criterion of direct divine, or charismatic, "calling" to leadership.) "Normalizing" deviance from its inception, rather than neutralizing it later, is the norm here. In hierarchical groups, elites are better insulated by traditional bureaucratic privileges. For congregational polities, on the other hand, just as in the Protestant-Roman Catholic parallel, there are fewer intermediaries between the elites and laity (see Shupe, 1995: 35-40 for an elaboration of this distinction).

Consider two cases—one in the hierarchical Roman Catholic denomination, the other in a congregational independent Protestant Church—and how their separate polities influenced how scandal could or could not be ultimately neutralized.

The Philadelphia Archdiocese

The "great Philadelphia cover-up" is now a matter of legal record, investigated meticulously by two grand juries through more than 30,000 pages of Philadelphia Archdiocese records and testimonies from more than 100 witnesses over a 40-month period beginning in 2002. These juries found that recent prelates had neutralized long-standing complaints against clergy with deliberate evasion crossing the line into obstruction of justice. Cardinal Anthony J. Bevilacqua, archbishop during 1988-2002, had even been called to testify at least ten times. Despite his and his lawyers' claims that the grand juries' reports were biased, anti-Catholic, and part of a "witch hunt" (Shupe, 2005), it was evident that "during the 1990s, long after priestly sexual abuse became a public issue, the hierarchy was crafting more sophisticated strategies to prevent external scrutiny of their policies for investigating and resolving charges against priests" (Walsh, 2006: 17).

Bevilacqua, like his predecessor, had an elite's preoccupation about public relations and his institution's image. Bevilacqua also had possessed a lawyer's orientation. After all, he graduated in civil law from St. John's University and held a doctorate in canon law from Rome's Gregorian University. During Bevilacqua's tenure, when an accused priest was questioned by a superior and simply denied an impropriety or malfeasance, church officials in the archdiocese abruptly considered the matter satisfactorily "resolved." Routinely, neither victims nor church staff members were then interviewed (if they had ever been), and further investigation was functionally "crippled." Worse, "under Bevilacqua, the archdiocese's approach to the investigation of charges against priests was to restrict investigations and to mislead complainants" (Walsh, 2006: 18).

As in the other scandals involving long-term priest recidivism, perpetrators were repeatedly "recycled" (the "geographic solution"). Church spokespersons, in their harsh rebuttal, railed against the grand juries (whose members, it might charitably be remembered, were hardly volunteers for the arduous trial work that took them away from their regular lives *for more than three years*). Official apologists consistently tried to neutralize the facts that Bevilacqua had repeatedly encouraged archdiocesan underlings who did their apparent best to minimize or "truculently" squelch numerous complaints and whistle blowing about clergy misconduct (Walsh, 2006: 24).

To be critical, this sort of evasiveness is not inevitable in a hierarchical, ecclesiastical bureaucracy *if it genuinely offers accountability and takes lay grievances authentically.* In contrast, consider secular parallels in the more customer-friendly attitudes and public relations sensitivity of larger corporations from Ford, Toyota, and Saturn, to Target and your local national supermarket chain stores. Brokers between such companies' top management corps and consumers demonstrate an appreciation that marketplace competition and choice exists. Large hierarchical churches, with their historical grandeur, insulation of often "invisible" elites, and subsequent distance from laity, at least initially lacked that realization.

To be sympathetic, elites of large churches—Catholic, Protestant, and Mormon—likely do not deliberately set out in some social pathological sense to continue the hurt of victims or to engage in a secondary deviant pattern of reactionary deception. Some of this neutralization can be by default rather than intentional callousness. Catholic scholar John P. Beal (1992: 642), for example, observed during the first wave of Catholic priest sex scandals the mundane dynamics of elite "distance" and insulation:

> Despite all good intentions, most diocesan bishops are not as immediately accessible as is needed if there is to be a prompt response to a denunciation. Details about clerical sexual misconduct are not the sort of information most people want to leave on a telephone answering machine or relate to the bishop's secretary.

Remember that ordinary persons are caught up in a sociological reality with its own dynamic influencing individual thought, self-interests, and policy decisions: the iron law of oligarchy and the roles it demands of actors, as discussed in Chapter 3.

Community Chapel of Seattle, Washington

Community Chapel was a classic congregational entity inspired by the charismatic (but never ordained) Donald Barnett, an employee of the Boeing Aircraft Corporation, and his wife, a Welcome Wagon hostess. The eventual mega-church began in the Barnetts' Seattle home, gradually attracting a growing coterie of followers with Barnett's emphasis on Bible millennialism and Jesus Christ's imminent return. It had grown enough by 1969 to construct a church, then later a small Bible college. In its heyday, Community Chapel had over three thousand members in its central congregation and twenty-two satellite "chapels." It also owned and controlled a kindergarten through twelfth-grade academy, the Bible College, and a 44-acre, $10 million estate where the group's main sanctuary was located (Overland, 1988a).

Barnett's church had a board of deacons who managed mundane daily matters, but it was clear his charismatic visions drove the increasingly deviant direction of Community Chapel's theology and practices. Those activities Barnett was able (for some time) to "normalize" without much check on his mystical inspiration included (what Barnett termed) "moves of God," such as:

- unique revelations from God to the pastor that, according to Barnett, put him in unparalleled contact with God and made him one with Jesus Christ (Enroth, 1992: 35-6);
- proclamations that men should not wear beards, traditional Christian holidays such as Christmas and Easter should not be observed due to their pagan origins, and only sacred music composed by the church's members could be played or sung during services (Overland, 1988b);
- In addition to traditional Pentecostal-style emotional tongue-speaking and prophecy, God told Barnett to encourage "spiritual dancing" between the sexes and physical touching/stroking during services; and to endorse "spiritual connections," i.e., forming pairs of married and single persons of opposite sexes and heterosexual pairs of married spouses to other members (Enroth, 1992: 12ff).

The erotic orientation of these latter practices erupted into full-fledged kissing and fondling during chapel services and rampant liaisons of spiritual partners outside their homes. Adultery began to anger spouses and split families, and some even charged their mates with parental child neglect. While certain segments of Community Chapel seemed to be in a persistent state of charged libido, Barnett was personally linked to repeated seductions of female congregants and was believed to have had "spiritual connections" with over thirty women.

For some participating members this consensual behavior was "normalized" by broker Barnett's claims of divine revelation. But the misgivings mounted, particularly as families began to fall apart and the adultery ranged out of control. With no one beyond the congregation to check Barnett or assist him in containing his fragmenting central congregation, and with even his otherwise generally passive board of deacons in revolt, worse precipitating events occurred. In March, 1988, a Community Chapel mother, understandably distraught by the entire Chapel subculture, drove her five-year-old daughter to a local motel and drowned her in a bathtub to spare the child (the mother said) the eventual demonic possession of puberty. Two years later, when the deacons finally bolted and formed an alternative congregation free of Barnett's mystical influence amid a number of bitter lawsuits against the pastor, it became public that in 1975 he had earned a police record for exhibitionism. Barnett had pleaded guilty at that time to masturbating in front of four maids in a hallway of the Circus Circus Casino Hotel in Las Vegas.

In congregational style, Barnett had no supervisors or ecclesiastical allies to mount any effective neutralization of the scandals. Soon Barnett's mega-church of several thousand souls shrank to a remnant of several hundred.

It is unthinkable that a mystical Barnett-type or his radical revelations could even initially permeate into, much less purchase influence over, a mainline hierarchical group like the United Methodists or Missouri Synod Lutherans. Such groups have built-in social controls for gross heresies. Some congregation-type leaders, like Barnett, Jim Jones, or David Koresh, can normalize deviance for a while, thus avoiding the need of denial in response to criticism. But they also lack support outside their local groups, hence no invisibility or distance from angry laypersons protect them.

This polity dimension, broadly designated, can mediate (*not* cause) how deviance is received within and without the group. In the next section we see how it affects the search for redress.

Redress: The Justice of Healing

Once past denial and the variations on elites trying to neutralize fellow broker-fiduciaries' (or their own) deviance, the full measure of the modern counterreformation can be understood as healing. A dictionary definition of healing is to restore or return to health, to set right or amend. Healing for all the actors in the clergy malfeasance drama, however, does not mean simply a reconciliation where it is agreed to amicably bury unpleasantness and hurt and then revert to some earlier, presumably more harmonious state. Rather, as Figure 2 suggests as a beginning agenda for the process, authentic healing requires movement forward, not backward, premised on sincere atonement for abuses, honest communications, and genuine reform of the asymmetrical power relationship between brokers and laity.

Figure 2
The Agenda for Justice

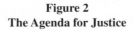

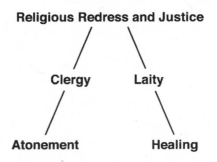

The last alternative dictionary definition above is amendment, and it is the key to healing here. Healing is not a return; it is growth. It does not dispense with the past, but rather recasts the past. As forecasted over a decade ago, a counterreformation will seek answers

> explaining why churches and other religious groups adopt internal reforms; how victims and organizations deal with elite scandals; and how we can turn clergy malfeasance into a constructive process of lay education, improved professional socialization, and organizational growth. Hopefully, it will occur in more proactive, less defensive organizations. ...churches and denominations are unequal hierarchies of power that provide the context for all the malfeasance. That is our given. Thus, are we not going to need some internal realignments of power? (Shupe, 1995: 146)

Polity has to be a major consideration in this growth, particularly as we exam what has been analyzed, suggested, and enacted (admittedly a very unfinished work in progress) for three discreet levels of healing: the immediate victims and their families; local church congregations and denominations; and broker-perpetrators themselves.

Immediate Victims and Their Families

The immediate victims (or *survivors*, as they now prefer to be called) and their families represent the first tier of clergy malfeasance victimology. They are the natural beginning focus for attention and intervention, given our highly psychologized, individualistic culture. They personify the humanity within the larger sociological problem. Most sources written about them either raise public alarm about religious elite misconduct (particularly the earlier ones, such as Rosetti, 1990; Berry, 1992; or Burkett and Bruni, 1993 that did much to publicize the Catholic priest pedophile problem just as Sipe's 1990 work did for more general priest sexuality) or directly address issues of victim healing. It is with these second sources that this section is concerned.

Some of their considerations of clergy malfeasance victims, particularly sexual abuse, are folded into the victimology of other professions and/or overlap with a variety of other problems, such as sexual harassment and addiction, rape, and incest. There has been a "generation" of such reports emerging during the late 1980s and early 1990s (coinciding with the first wave of North American Catholic priest sex scandals), such as Pellauer, Chester, and Boyajian's 1987 *Sexual Assault and Abuse: A Handbook for Clergy and Religious Professionals*, Rutter's highly influential 1989 *Sex in the Forbidden Zone: When Men in Power—Therapists, Doctors, Clergy, Teachers, and Others—Betray Women's Trust*, Feldmeth and Finley's 1990 *We Weep for Ourselves and Our Children: A Christian Guide for Survivors of Childhood Abuse*, Carnes' 1991 *Don't Call It Love: Recovering from Sexual Addiction*, Conway and Conway's 1993 *Sexual Harassment No More*, Brown's 1994 *Victims No More: Ministry to Survivors of Sexual Abuse*, or Kroeger and Beck's 1996 *Women, Abuse, and the Bible* (see full references at the end of the book).

However, in the "mature" victim-oriented literature—dealing as it does with issues of stages of healing, confrontation and reconciliation, and agenda for reform—a noticeable Protestant-Catholic division emerges. Protestant (particularly evangelical) sources almost uniformly treat authoritarian, manipulative, even predatory clergy as individual brokers gone biblically astray. The level of their deviance is pictured as going no further than those "bad pastors" *in their local congregations.* Healing for victims consists of getting their "heads and hearts" back on a biblical course and getting on with their sadder-but-wiser Protestant Christian lives.

Ecclesiastical-Hierarchical sources, largely Roman Catholic but some on Mormonism as well, read more like social movement manifestos for consciousness-raising among victims and their sympathizers, sometimes with an angry reformist bite. The sphere within which victim justice and healing occurs, in others words, is much narrower and congregational for Protestants than for hierarchical groups. Some examples will illustrate this difference.

Congregational (Protestant) Church Healing for Immediate Victims

Congregational (Protestant) victimology casts both perpetrators and victims in roles of having strayed from a knowable, biblically sound path in which submission, service, and headship (leadership) have been forgotten, ignored, or distorted. Leaders in particular have misinterpreted or exaggerated portions of the Bible to suit their own egos and power needs in the extreme modes of Jim Jones or David Koresh. Ken Blue, in *Healing Spiritual Abuse*, admonishes about leadership errors, "Most false doctrines result from overemphasizing a biblical truth, thus making it an untruth, or taking a biblical truth out of context and twisting it to a purpose the Holy Spirit did not intend" (1993: 30). Pastors forget the humility of their calling: "Jesus stated clearly that the only legitimate spiritual authority is servant authority" (Blue, 1993: 31). It is this servant authority that is so often abused (Blue and other authors use this abuse term to include economic, sexual, and authoritarian forms). Blue (1993: 33) further observes:

> Positional authority carries with it the power to be coercive, to compel. Servant authority, however, cheerfully forfeits this power, so that those who submit to it can only do so freely and voluntarily.

Characteristics and tactics of abusive leaders (ritual degradation of members, claims of infallibility or biblically unverifiable "special" discernment, isolation of members, squelching of discussion of leader criticism, and so forth) are standard in such writings (for example, see Porterfield, 1993; Enroth, 1992; Burks and Burks, 1992; White and Blue, 1985; Johnson and VanVonderen, 1991). Most authors refer eventually to Jesus Christ's vigorous rebukes of Pharisees, particularly to Matthew

23 where Jesus warns people against clergy hypocrites of their day. Because so many Protestant religious experts cite this passage as the archetype of criticism on spiritual abuse and inauthentic leadership, key elements follow:

> you must do what they tell you [on the authority of Moses] and follow their instructions. But you must not imitate their lives! For they preach but do not practice. They pile up back-breaking burdens and lay them on other men's shoulders—yet they themselves will not raise a finger to move them. They increase the size of their phylacteries and lengthen the tassels of their robes; they love seats of honour at dinner parties and front place in the synagogues. They love to be greeted with respect in public places and to have men call them "rabbi!" [Brackets mine.]

Jesus warns against the hubris of leaders using titles such as "Father" or "Leader" and continues:

> The only "Superior" among you is the one who serves the others. For every man who promotes himself will be humbled, and every man who learns to be humble will find promotion.

Jesus rails against "blind leaders" and "blind fools" who dishonor the Temple, and says in the most damning terms:

> What miserable frauds you are, you scribes and Pharisees! You clean the outsides of the cup and the dish, while the inside is full of greed and self-indulgence. Can't you see, Pharisees? First wash the inside of the cup, and then you clean the outside.

> Alas, for you, you hypocritical scribes and Pharisees! You are like white-washed tombs, which look fine on the outside but inside are full of dead men's bones and all kinds of rottenness. For you appear like good men on the outside—but inside you are a mass of pretense and wickedness. (Phillips, 1972)

There are numerous references to other passages in apostles' letters where bishops are stewards and fiduciary brokers (such as "For a bishop, as God's steward, must be blameless" [Titus 1: 7], or "Moreover, it is required of stewards that they be found trustworthy" [1 Corinthians 4: 20-21]), but it is clear that (evangelical) Protestant-congregational victimology regards abusive clergy, no matter how beguiling, as only one side of the coin.

Victim complicity, in particular lack of discernment of "unrighteous dominion" or forewarnings of non-biblical abuse, is the other side. The injuries of laypersons are numerous, such as loss of faith and general distrust of religious leadership or even the Bible, as well as physical damages (rape and incest trauma and battery) and psychosomatic problems (depression, free-floating anxiety and fearfulness, feelings of alienation and isolation, loss of self-esteem, anger, suicidal tendencies, sleeplessness and loss of appetite, and nightmares/flashbacks). Remedies for healing are prescribed accordingly.

The healing procedures offered by many Protestant authors involve step-progressions laced with supporting biblical references. Maris (1996: 11-26) writes of fourteen options for victims to pursue, from seeking psychological support to prosecuting via criminal, civil, professional, and ecclesiastical legal avenues. Willerscheidt (1995: 26-9) advocates phases of healing that she admits resemble thanatologist Elizabeth Kubler-Ross's stages of dying (anger, denial, depression, bargaining, acceptance). Willerscheidt's "predictable stages of recovery" (her phrase) start with working through anger or even sensitizing victims to feel it; then to addressing self-esteem issues; empowerment; restoration of spirituality and faith in God and the religious institution; eventual confrontation with the perpetrator (with a supportive intermediary present) to finally returning "feelings of guilt and shame" to him or her. Somewhat similar techniques can be applied to family members who may have experienced parallel injuries; she adds:

> Family members often have a particularly hard time dealing with the emotional fallout. . . . Family members are secondary victims of the exploitation, and they need to be helped through their own anger, disgust, and frustration. (1995: 29)

Marie Fortune (1989) presents seven points of healing in her classic study *Is Nothing Sacred?* while Elisabeth A. Horst maintains in *Recovering the Lost Self* (1958: 19) five almost identical step mandates for victims:

1. Identify and learn to recognize shame in your life;
2. Get out of shame-producing situations;
3. Take responsibility for your own healing;
4. Act as if you have a right to be here ("Hold your head up. State an opinion.");
5. Seek genuine help and support.

Seminar facilitator-therapist Kay Marie Porterfield (1993: 133-43), who more than most authors links childhood trauma to adult susceptibility to clergy exploitation, in *Blind Faith: Recognizing and Recovering from Dysfunctional Religious Groups* lists familiar steps: acknowledging pain, coming to grips with pain, learning to trust, breaking free from perfectionism, integrating the experience, finding a new frame of reference, and finding the courage to continue. Similarly, Johnson and VanVonderen (1991: 53-60) point out the early life "pre-abuse set up" in adult Protestant victims and observe that "People learn to be or to act powerless by experiencing relationships that have either prepared them to be abused, or *not* prepared them to *not* be abused." These authors call this remarkable interpersonal umbrella (one that would include us all) as constituting "shame-based relationships" (p. 55). Their step-by-step recovery solution is a mix of mostly getting "right-headed" concerning biblical injunctions about authentic leadership along with reaffixing blame, shame, and guilt onto those who actually deserve it (i.e., the perpetrators).

Here and there are also a few tantalizing hints by authors of moving beyond the individual lay victim/perpetrator roles to considering some larger institutional or sociological context of unequal power. Porterfield (1993: 27) acknowledges:

> In any religious organization, tension is bound to exist between the sacred or vertical dimension and the social or horizontal dimension of the group . . . when the balance tips too far toward maintaining the social structure, though, a group risks failing to meet its primary stated function—to foster the individual's opportunity to connect with the Higher Power.

And Johnson and VanVonderen (1991: 232) conclude *The Subtle Power of Spiritual Abuse* with three final admonitions, the third a precursor to the AAVM described in Chapter 4:

1. You may have to leave the church or group because of unresolved issues;
2. [Predictably] ". . . listen to God and do what He tells you";
3. [anticipating the more Catholic consciousness-raising victim response as Horst (1998: 19) advised in her fifth step] "When you experience spiritual abuse, find your own friends who understand and tell them about it. Get some support."

These sources are replete with case studies and anecdotal evidence of successful recovery for the abused. To date, however, there has been little systematic collection of data on survivors in the general population, recovered or not, except for the 1996 regional survey conducted in Dallas-Fort worth by Stacey, Darnell, and Shupe (2000). The data remain almost entirely clinical.

Ecclesiastical-Hierarchical (Roman Catholic-Mormon) Church Healing for Immediate Victims

Unlike more congregational groups, ecclesiastical-hierarchical denominations often place more levels of ordained leadership between the laypersons and the deviants. The price paid for enjoying the rich majesty of tradition and elaborate theology is greater constraint on interpretations of scriptures and idiosyncratic lay beliefs. As a result, in this second type of group laypersons are not as much thrown back on their own devices of personal discernment and individual scriptural interpretation. Moreover, given all the factors previously discussed concerning such oligarchic groups' clergy invisibility and elite insulation, not to mention the considerable bureaucracy through which redress must be sought, it is not surprising that *perpetrators are more readily perceived by victims as extensions of the entire faith tradition as well as of the operating institution.* Thus, the level of healing perceived by consciousness-sharing victims becomes intervention in the group of unequal power and privilege itself rather than toward the individual's reliance on personal scriptural knowledge.

To be sure, as in the Protestant mode, scriptural references can be brought to bear justifying and rationalizing whatever form of healing is sought by either brokers or victims. AAVM groups described in the previous chapter make that an integral part of their task (or minister to the abused). Victims' personal healing with perpetrators can also sometimes be desired, with mixed results. Frank Fitzpatrick, private insurance investigator and victim of Father James Porter when Fitzpatrick was a boy, tracked down Porter years later (by then an ex-priest and married) in part just for that reason (ABC, 1992). The result was one major catalyst in the first wave of Catholic priest pedophile revelations and the AAVM.

Likewise, in 2006 Michael Donovan, a sixty-three-year-old Vietnam veteran retired and living in California, sought out Roman Catholic priest Thomas Schaefer, who had sexually abused him thirty years prior at a Washington, DC parochial school. (Schaefer, it turns out, had molested at least twenty other boys in the Washington Archdiocese and pleaded guilty in 1975 to five such cases. Along with one other priest, the pair accounted for about one-third of 123 sexual abuse reports in that archdiocese.) Donovan contacted archdiocese officials, learning that he had been Schaefer's earliest victim. The archdiocese paid for Donovan and his wife to travel to Washington and for psychological counseling (and, in 2006, they negotiated a financial settlement). Donovan made his way to his old school, then to the Vianney Renewal Center in Dittmer, Missouri (a facility for troubled—often aged—priests) where Schaefer, by then eighty, was a resident. Donovan confronted Schaefer, but their meeting did not produce a spectacular display of fireworks or even venom. Schaefer did not admit nor even claimed to remember doing anything inappropriate with Donovan but apologized anyway. For Donovan's part, he achieved a level of healing and closure. He claimed, "I feel very good about being here. . . . It completes what I had to do. I've got what I needed out of it" (Murphy, 2006).

Not so for the Reverend James Moran, a sixty-year-old Catholic chaplain at Washington Hospital Center in Schaeffer's and Donovan's old archdiocese of Washington. Sexually abused in 1970 by an older priest while he was a seminarian, Maron decided to make years of personal pain and guilt public during Holy Week, 2006. In a pastor training class made up of approximately twenty hospital staff members and patients' relatives, Moran shared his abuse experience, "railing against church leaders who protect abusers and care more about money than victims." Soon after an archdiocesan official called to chastise him and inform him that his active priest credentials were being pulled immediately. Moran commented, "My gut feeling is that I have been raped again" (Boorstein, 2006).

As shown repeatedly, broker perpetrators can continue to be sanctified, protected, or at least provided the benefit of the doubt over laity within a dense hierarchy in the event of scandal. Laity reared in an ecclesiastical tradition with strong emotional ties to it may revere that hierarchy, but as victims, even if they are quiescent for a time, they do not thereby become reliably conditioned "groupthink" lemmings in the mode of the "citizens" in George Orwell's fictitious authoritarian regime in *1984*. Explain Doyle, Sipe, and Wall (2006: 265-6):

> Clinicians who interview and treat victims of clerical abuse discover that one of the most common consequences of abuse by a Catholic priest is the complete loss of comfort, support, and spiritual sustenance. That loss includes a sense of meaning of life that they had experienced and were entitled to get from their religious faith. Those who do not understand the nature and depth of this deprivation think that the victim can merely "forget about it," "move on," or "find another religion." . . . People who have been grounded since childhood in one faith, in which their self-worth, acceptance, spiritual identity, and salvation were vested, cannot simply forget that faith and join another. Victims betrayed and abused by a priest can "get on" with their lives, but the past that is missing cannot be restored. Something is dead; something has been truly killed.

And the *structure* of that institution within which its agents are inextricably embedded becomes the larger perceived target for reform.

Several cases professionally or journalistically described illustrate the structurally induced tense mood established at one point or another between laity and clergy, even if rapprochement is sought by both sides. Indeed, even if more accountability rather than structural reform is the victim advocates' goal, participants are aware of sociological issues (if only lurking in the background) beyond individual levels of forgiveness and atonement.

Krebs (1998) discusses how the Canadian Conference of Catholic Bishops (CCCB) learned from the (then called) U.S.' National Conference of Catholic Bishops (NCCB) how *not* to respond to revelations of priest sexual abuse and hierarchical cover-up. When two active priests and an attorney (the latter also a Catholic) submitted a report to the NCCB warning of the church's looming problem in both widespread priestly deviance and coming scandals/financial liabilities (see Doyle, Sipe, and Wall, 2006: 99-174 for the complete text of this report, entitled *The Problem of Sexual Molestation by Roman Catholic Clergy: Meeting the Problem in a Comprehensive and Responsible Manner*), they were coldly rebuffed. Their warnings, projections, and suggestions were ignored. The bishops' meeting at which it was presented did not even make copies for distribution to prelates; the authors were stonewalled as to an official acknowledgment; and no later NCCB meetings took up the matter of the report.

Krebs observes that the CCCB, faced with its own national priest abuse crisis, established in 1989 an Ad Hoc Committee on Child Abuse to study the matter and create guidelines for anticipating/preventing future recurrences, both at levels of supporting victims/their families and for dealing with perpetrators. The ad hoc committee issued a report in 1992, entitled *From Pain to Hope*, with *the final fifty chapters ostensibly taking up issues of reform in the church in Canada,* from delegation of authority to advisory committees, to setting procedures for adjudicating abuse allegations. The asymmetry of broker privilege, however, actually was deflected when it was not addressed in practice. Krebs (p. 27) comments:

> The recommendations also support that authority take the form of community service rather than power and damnation. Church Structure, however, receives scant reference.

For that matter, Krebs recounts that during the same time as the report was much touted by the CCCB, some bishops were still active in neutralization of victims' complaints by offering financial settlements for silence and cessation of any civil or criminal legal actions.

Like Krebs, Jean-guy Vaillancourt, in his book almost two decades earlier entitled *Papal Power: A Study of Vatican Control over Lay Catholic Elites* (1980), remarks how Catholic prelates have so often "cooled out" lay complainants with "commission politics" (i.e., forming feel-good cathartic committees of investigation whose earnestly crafted reports are effusively received and then ignored) and awarded lay elites token (if temporarily gratifying) consultations without serious intent to make use of them.

Krebs (1998: 27) pessimistically concludes that:

> with regard to priestly sexual abuse, officials retain the right to make formal decisions while appearing to demonstrate open and receptive concern for victims and their allegations against clergy. The church effectively can still neutralize criticism and absorb scandal by involving the laity in a facade of change.

As evidence, Krebs cites the CCCB's document's advocacy of a five-session format to facilitate workshop discussion groups to which lay Catholic persons would be encouraged to attend. The first workshop alone zeroes in on sexual abuse in the church ("Our church" in the title, widening the ownership umbrella of the problem arena—or complicity—to include laity as well as the offenders). Victims and other parishioners in this workshop are encouraged to share experiences, to emote, and so forth. After that, however, the remaining four sessions shift the topic to dynamics of child sexual abuse generally, both in society and the church as well as personal and community responsibility (complicity again) for such abuse. Krebs' final critical observation (p.29):

> Many members of the hierarchy, however, are proficient rhetoricians who continue to deflect institutional responsibility for the sexual activities of some of its personnel. . . . Rather than admit its own Culpability, the Church points to the prevalence of all forms of abuse in other institutions and society at large and encourages its members to do the same.

(Recall in Chapter 2 that this was the same "clouding the issue" tactic employed by the Catholic League for Religious Rights in 2004 in response to the massive study of U.S. Catholic priest abusers by the John Jay College of Criminal Justice in New York.)

In another, more detailed case—that of Elizabeth Pullen's (1998) sociological study of the St. Anthony Seminary scandal in Santa Barbara, California during the late 1980s and early 1990s—victims' limitations in pursuing redress and accountability through structural reform from hierarchy elites is even more pronounced. Revelations at St. Anthony's Seminary (a Franciscan seminary with high school student boarding and noted boys' choir having educated hundreds of men from western states and Mexico) emerged in 1989 with accusations by two former students against a priest. (The latter was eventually arrested, arraigned, and convicted of having orally copulated with a person under the age of eighteen; the statute of limitations had run out for the second victim.) Other accusations sprung up and, by 1992, a wider investigation was planned. First, early that year letters were mailed to approximately 350 former seminarians asking about possible inappropriate physical contact and abuse. Then, a second mailing went out in 1993 to families of approximately six hundred *more* former seminary students to include some who withdrew before graduating. Altogether, thirty-four students (covering a twenty-three-year period) said they had been subjected to a wide variety of priestly sexual behavior, from fondling and mutual masturbation, to oral and anal intercourse. These replies from the surveys resulted in eleven of forty-four friars working at St. Anthony's during that time as being identified abusers "with reasonable certainty."

The scandal reverberated beyond the seminary into the larger community due to the nature of its high-profile ministry. Despite St. Anthony's strict quasi-monastic limiting of students' personal interactions with "outsiders" to close friends and family, its music, drama, and athletic programs and its unique worship services involved many faithful in Santa Barbara. As Pullen describes this larger ministry:

> In the liturgical renewal following Vatican II, Sunday worship services at the seminary became known throughout the Santa Barbara area for their innovation and experimentation. . . . By 1968, eucharistic services incorporated outdoor settings, electric guitars and drums, fluorescent vestments, pop art banners, and sculptures. . . . At the same time, the Franciscans had decided to open Sunday liturgies not only to the families of the seminarians but to all in the neighboring community. Services began to attract hundreds of local Catholics. . . Community members still refer to this period in the late 1960s and 1970s as a primary reference-point in their identity as a self-created, non-parish congregation. Members enjoy both the autonomy and participation that is possible for communities outside the traditional parish structure, as well as the association with a large, dynamic religious order. Friars teaching at the seminary or just passing through Santa Barbara often worshiped with the greater community, among them academic scholars, social activists, and gifted artists. (p. 70)

The scandal shook Santa Barbara Catholics in many ways and drew in varieties of concerned citizens and families linked to St. Anthony's. By the end of 1993 the St. Anthony's Seminary Support Group for Sexual Abuse Survivors was formed. (Pullen conducted interviews and participant observation in the group.) In addition, a church-related Independent Response Team (IRT) was developed. The support group made contact with survivors-victims and their families; monitored their therapy and health concerns as well as treatment by the Franciscans and the IRT; and monitored how legal settlements in pending lawsuits were progressing. The support group as a mini-AAVM, not the church, also became a conduit for inter-victim news and communications. Also, (as referred to in the next section) were the activities of the support group as it reached out to the non-seminary community with professionally led therapeutic and educational sessions using (in some instances) the CCCB's *From Pain to Hope* materials.

Beyond immediate (primary), family (secondary), and congregational-community (tertiary) needs, the support group became the main healing agent that interfaced with both the Franciscans and the IRT, monitoring the latter two groups' implementations recommended by the initial lay-dominated board of inquiry that had conducted the two waves of victimization surveys. Holding the Friars/IRT's feet to the fire on realizing recommended changes afforded some ongoing optimism but also eventual frustration. For example, issues that the support group sought some decisive action on included the possibility of imposed limits on victims' various therapies, greater celerity in processing victims' financial claims, openness about the HIV statuses of accused perpetrators, and disclosure of identities and locations of all perpetrators.

The bottom-line for our purposes of polity consideration has been provided by Pullen on the St. Anthony's scandal aftermath almost a decade after the first abuse revelations:

> many members recognize that its [the support group's] efforts have had only a limited effect upon the policy decisions of the institutional church. . . . the group's major demands about disclosing and disseminating information as to the identity, location, and HIV status of the perpetrators have met with consistent refusals on the grounds of confidentiality. (p. 79)

Support group activists found, to their chagrin, that the IRT (as a hierarchical agent) had centered its efforts more on monitoring treatment of perpetrators than on adjudicating claims of the victims. While the support group did enter into a multifaceted effort of lobbying for changes in child abuse legislation, seeking establishment of regional educational programs, and continuing to address community confusion/anger/disillusionment, it ran into a bureaucratic brick wall when pursuing accountability policy changes from the church. The oligarchs rejected that dimension of redress altogether. In fact, the bulk of the victim redress was ultimately instigated, ramrodded, and achieved thanks alone to the community-supported, victim-driven local social movement called the support group. The entire episode of St. Anthony's scandal, said Pullen, can be summarized in the support group's lack of sustained institutionalized influence on church policy and procedure. In the current environment of the U.S. Catholic Church, as long as the Support Group focuses its efforts upon structural changes, it remains dependent on the institution to acknowledge its existence and legitimacy. (pp. 81-82)

Such power-dependent relations in the twenty-first century can foster militancy in a better educated and easily mobilized laity—more so than past church hierarchies were accustomed to. The prime example is the experience of Roman Catholic bishops and the AAVM during a two-year period: 2002-2003. Briefly, here is how it unfolded.

The Doyle-Mouton-Peterson report of 1985 purchased little attention from Roman Catholic ecclesiastical elites who basically dismissed its unpleasant importance and kept most U.S. bishops blissfully unaware of the efforts of these three prescient professionals. Just as a decade before, the periodically emerging local scandals involving wayward clerics were largely assumed to be grotesque anomalies, like the earlier Father James Porter and David Holley. To be sure, bishops knew of such pedophile cases, but these could usually be dealt with discreetly and *sub rosa* by diocesan lawyers to preserve what many observers now call the "clerical culture of secrecy and deference."

Not so in 2002, when, thanks in large part to unrelenting journalists at places like *The Boston Globe* (which won a Pulitzer Prize for its scandal coverage), *The National Catholic Reporter*, and *The Hartford Courant*, the crisis of the Boston Archdiocese struck the Roman Catholic Church and the larger American religious scene like a bugle call. The city of Boston, with a population of almost four million souls, roughly half of whom are Catholic, was understandably devastated. "In no other major American city are Catholics more represented in police precincts, in courtrooms, in boardrooms" (*Boston Globe*, 2002: 7). Its favorite Catholic son, Cardinal Bernard F. Law, at first defensive and evasive, ultimately left this city and country to bury his career ignominiously in the Vatican City bureaucracy (see Chapter 1).

Nothing demonstrates how Catholic victims seek personal healing through structural reform than the meeting of the United States Conference of Catholic Bishops in Dallas, Texas in June 2002. They met to discuss the managerial affairs of that 66.4 million-member North American denomination, particularly to cope with the embarrassment of media-saturated scandals, the growing damage of punitive lawsuits by victims, and some forward-moving national policy to dig them out of the mess.

Not only the 195 bishops and reporters but also the major AAVM groups attended, and not just a few spokespersons of the latter. There were street protesters and demonstrators. Placards on sidewalks read, "Take back our church!"; "Jesus wept!"; "Change the church!"; "Married priests now!"; and "Let laymen elect bishops!" To bishops inside the Fairmount Hotel ballroom, such sentiments were unnerving, not to mention smacking of mutiny. Along with the major AAVM organizations like SNAP, Voice of the Faithful, The Linkup, Survivors First, and Call to Action (the mandate of which, among other things, calls for international justice and democracy in the church), there were also causes and their spokespersons representing long-simmering grievances, such as the Gay and Lesbian Alliance Against Defamation, and Dignity/USA with planned 12-hour-long vigils. These grievances included desires for lay input in electing and reviewing bishops; approval for priests to marry; ordination of women and of homosexuals; and recognizing gay or same-sex marriages in the church. Even one group of gay Catholics who took a visible white van as close to bishops' meeting hotel as possible protested popular linkage of homosexuals in the clergy to the pedophilia problem (Cava, 2002).

From the four-day conference's inception, bishops nervously sensed the lay mood for radical reform. According to one newspaper account, Bishop Wilton D. Gregory of Belleville, Illinois, president of the United States Conference of Catholic Bishops, reinforced a contrary conservative fear in his address to his peers:

> [Referring to outside AAVM groups but not any by name] Bishop Wilton Gregory took a firm stand against lay Catholic groups that are pushing for major changes, such as ordaining women and allowing married priests: "As bishops, we should have no illusion about the intent of some people who have shown more than a casual interest in the discord we have experienced within the Church this year." (Cooperman, 2002)

Bishop Gregory threw some jibes at unnamed non-Catholics he said were exacerbating the tension, then he criticized dissenters in the church: "Sadly, even among the baptized, there are those at extremes within the church who have chosen to exploit the vulnerability of the bishops in this moment to advance their own agenda" (Cooperman, 2002). Curiously, now the bishops (according to Gregory's lead) had shifted themselves to the victim role, and the victims' advocates outside were recast as agents of discord, even persecutors.

Meanwhile, for the first time victims were not all outside. Some relatively few were given the floor literally in front of the rows of assembled prelates; they provided graphic details of horror in uninterrupted stories and tragic personal testimonies, complete with tears and obvious suffering to which hithertofore only the diocesan lawyers and secular jurors—not usually bishops—had to listen. The atmosphere was punctuated with accounts about the legalistic insensitivity and inapproachability of shepherds when their flocks were hurting.

Clearly, the main task in the bishops' docket was creating a two-fold future policy: how to deal with past and current priest abusers, and how to build future safeguards against such wolves finding their way into the fold. By now, the bishops were believers in the Doyle-Mouton-Peterson scenario; by January of that same year already at least three hundred new lawsuits alleging priest abuse had been filed against bishops and dioceses (Zoll, 2002c, 2002d). The culmination was the bishops' much touted "zero tolerance" policy for abusers in which they pledged accountability to laity (and by that, to secular law) and created a Charter for the Protection of Children and Young People. The latter would permanently bar any priest who was found to have been an abuser from performing ministerial duties (from conducting mass and giving sacraments, to teaching in Catholic schools, to presenting themselves in public as priests, and even down to passing out rolls in a Catholic-funded soup kitchen). Moreover, each of the U.S.' approximately 195 dioceses would have to create committees composed mostly of lay Catholics—*independent of the bishop*—to review not only any questioned priest's fitness to remain in active ministry but also the diocese's handling of sex abuse cases.

It was a cleansing moment of seeming atonement; a pledge for a more open hierarchy; a feel-good reconciliation between vulnerable laity and their spiritual fiduciaries. But almost immediately the AAVM's spokespersons claimed the charter had been merely a "toothless sop," or an "inadequate gesture" without muscle to enforce it. The bishops had actually deferred the details of how exactly they were to be accountable, and with what consequences, what was to be done with bona fide *criminal* priests, or what to do with bishops who had acted as accessories after the fact by lying and/or covering up predators' previous activities. In a word, the Dallas meeting was silent as to fellow prelates' responsibility for prolonging the whole ugly scandalous mess.

Three were three major reasons for hierarchical elites not so easily ceding authority over to non-elites:

First, the Charter for the Protection of Children and Young People called for an Office for Child and Youth Protection with a director and professional staff housed at the Bishops Conference headquarters in Washington, DC. This office was to issue an annual report on how effectively the nation's dioceses *are* actually protecting children. (Examples of such data are mentioned in Chapter 2.) The bishops named lay Catholic Kathleen McChesney, former number three administrator at the F.B.I., to head the office. However, while she was supposed to supervise how well the bishops enacted charter policies in their dioceses, she admitted she was not able personally to investigate individual allegations, nor was she privy to secret canonical court proceedings.

Worse, McChesney's office was to be under the National Review Board set up by the bishops. The latter picked lay Catholic Frank Keating, former law-and-order Republican governor of Oklahoma, former F.B.I. agent, and past associate attorney general. Keating was known for his outspoken, independent, off-the-cuff style. Before becoming the board's head, for example, Keating had once advocated that disgruntled lay Catholics could consider exercising "the power of the purse" if bishops would not authentically police their own ranks. He said, "it's time for the lay community of that diocese to say we're not writing another check until things change" (Ostling, 2002).

Keating soon clashed with the bishops, a number of whose hearts did not seem to be in the charter after all. The problem Keating discovered was that the same people whose lax attention and compulsion for hierarchical secrecy allowed the scandals to multiply were also to be in charge of administering processes of discovery and discipline. Keating was not able to take the lead in proposing or determining "corrective action" for either direct perpetrators or their cover-up supervisors. One year after his appointment, Keating ended his tenure on the National Review Board, "issuing a final, unrepentant blast in which he compared uncooperative bishops to a criminal organization," specifically La Cosa Nostra, "trying to conceal information and hide cases of wrong-doing by priests." Keating went out in scathing detail:

> My remarks, which some bishops found offensive, were decidedly accurate. I make no apology. To resist grand jury subpoenas, to suppress the names of offending clerics, to deny, to obfuscate, to explain away—that is the model of a criminal organization, not my church." (Stammer, 2003a, 2003b)

Keating quashed the bishop's hopes that the National Review Board would effect a public posture of accountability, atonement, and internal reform. But after a flurry of bishops' complaints via telephone, email, and fax, a split board finally requested his resignation. At the end, Bishop Wilton Gregory ironically praised Keating for his "enormous contribution" to the church's "house-cleaning" efforts (Stammer, 2002a, 2003b).

In the aftermath David Clohessy, national director of SNAP, commented:

> I'm absolutely stunned that a few blunt comments from a concerned, conservative Catholic lay person could be so harshly received by America's bishops. I think it casts enormous doubts on the credibility of the board and the bishops. From our [SNAP's] perspective, the board's work has barely begun" (Stammer, 2003b).

That same year, SNAP held its own annual convention. With two hundred delegates mindful of Keating's fate and the same bishops' apparent second thoughts at cooperating, SNAP founder Barbara Blaine reaffirmed the entire AAVM's continuing role in victim healing in spite of the hierarchy.

> My faith is in God, not the men in leadership. We are being the church to one another. We are doing what the bishops should have done. (Ostling, 2003)

Meanwhile, Pittsburgh's Bishop Donald Wuerl issued a statement of neutralization that blamed the victim advocates' disgruntlement and the continuing controversy on American Catholic laypersons' "religious illiteracy" within an "aggressively secular" culture.

Second, the Vatican, which already had mixed feelings for its large, independent American Catholic wing, announced that the zero tolerance policy could not so easily be implemented. The Vatican was particularly afraid of false accusations against clergy and their canonical rights of due process. Five months after Dallas, the bishops reconvened in Washington, DC to adopt a compromise policy because of their own concerns and those of many bishops. For example, the Dean of Canon Law at Pontifical Gregorian University in Rome said that U.S. bishops should avoid telling congregations that priests had sexually abused someone if the bishops believed the priests would not abuse again (Associated Press, 2003).

Philadelphia's Cardinal (formally Archbishop) Bevilacqua emphasized a "Christ-like" compassion for abusing priests be paramount, while others felt that rather than defrocking all such priests (as the charter originally called for) exceptions should be made for elderly priests whose accusations concerned deeds decades old—since the accusers were now adults anyway (Associated Press, 2003). Journalist Rachel Zoll (2002c) reported in a newspaper article entitled "Bishops' Plan to Oust Priests Coming Apart" *one month* after the ballyhooed Dallas conference:

Parishioners are rallying behind accused priests. Clergy are suing alleged victims and complaining to the Vatican. Experts in church law are questioning whether the plan violates priests' rights. Leaders of religious orders have accused the bishops of ignoring Catholic teaching on redemption and are allowing some abusers to continue their church away from children.

Commented one theologian at the University of Notre Dame about the charter: "It is unraveling" (Zoll, 2002c). Truly only the pope in Rome—neither other bishops nor even Cardinals—can demand a bishop's resignation. The hierarchy had its own built-in safeguards that could not so smoothly be democratized. And in the end, the Vatican made clear, bishops—not lay people in the pews—had the authority to oversee clergy.

Third, again *one month* after the bishops' proud promulgation of the Charter for the Protection of Children and Young People at the Dallas conference, *nine* dioceses discovered new scandals, rendering the heady promise of zero tolerance a bit unrealistic. It was announced by SNAP that the archdioceses of Louisville, Chicago, and Milwaukee, and the dioceses of Richmond (VA), Tulsa, Kalamazoo, Lexington (KY), Albany (NY), and San Diego had new major abuse revelations (Watkin, 2002).

The Church of Jesus Christ of Latter-day Saints, founded in Fayette, New York in 1830, naturally possesses less of an ecclesiastical legacy than the two-millennia-old Roman Catholic Church. But in less than two hundred years it has managed to create a considerable international corporate bureaucracy, with the apex of its pyramidal polity centered in Salt Lake City, Utah. Personal charisma and a folklore of lay interaction within a spirit realm used to play more of a role in nineteenth-century members' lives (Quinn, 1987; Shepherd and Shepherd, 1984), but these elements have been muted in the same way German sociologist Max Weber (1964a) described how priestly authority inevitably edges out the prophetic.

Mormonism has had its claims of sexual, economic, and especially authoritarian victimization by elites, but without nearly as much publicity as the Catholics. (Some examples were mentioned in Chapters 1 and 2.) Yet LDS victims, due to their unique legacy of American persecution/re-imaging and their subcultural and geographical traditions, face the exact dilemmas in seeking redress and/or living with their victimization that Doyle, Sipe, and Wall (2006: 265-6) wrote about (cited earlier in this chapter). Such victims cannot "just get over it" or simply "move on" when embedded in an all-encompassing faith tradition which is at the same time a cultural *worldview*. Such victims, religiously speaking, are not simply mainline Protestants who can shrug off emotional and other injuries and switch to some other denomination.

What is of interest here, then, is how personal healing of perceived wrongs to LDS laypersons by brokers is achieved in *dissent* from those leaders' official policies (whether these be over homosexuals, women's roles at home or at work, other lifestyle precepts, or relations with other faiths) and *defiance* of elites' oracular pronouncements on matters of theological obedience and intellectual groupthink.

On dissent and defiance, which here are meant *public* behaviors, one could easily imagine the costs to "bucking" leadership admonishments in tight-knit majoritarian LDS communities. From where would the personal healing come when one risks discord and strain within families, among friends and co-workers, and possibly ostracization and even excommunication? Why risk having the label "apostate" attached, surely the worst stigma that can be laid on a Mormon? Particularly when the odds of making more than a dent in the vast ecclesia, run by men believed by the devout to have divinely awarded apostolic credentials, are negligible? At least the Catholic victims have had the advantage of well-publicized, undeniable national scandals to provide leverage to call for structural, power-based reforms.

Three post-World War II examples of dissidents will provide the materials pointing to answers. Before considering them, however, the internal socio-political climate of the LDS Church during those years must be briefly addressed. In modern post-war times (the forties, fifties, and sixties), according to many observers of Mormondom, the LDS Church has been in danger of its success, i.e., acceptance and assimilation or absorption into larger Protestant American culture. Noted LDS sociologist Armand L. Mauss in *The Angel and the Beehive* calls this realization the basis of a reaction, a "retrenchment," or conservative, attempt by church leaders to reassert the distinctiveness of Mormon culture and especially its ecclesiastical-style religion for members:

> At the grass-roots level, the reaction has not been so clearly focused, but it has included a kind of "fundamentalism," an effort to demonstrate to themselves and to others that Mormons can and ought to exemplify a special posture and life-style of austerity, scriptural literalness, and unquestioning obedience to leaders. (Mauss, 1994: x-xi)

It is in that era of reasserting obedience that the leaders' quotes in the first section of Chapter 3 become relevant, for they were setting part of the "retrenchment" agenda. O. Kendall White, Jr. (1987: xi), also a Mormon sociologist, terms this "retrenchment" effort a product of *Mormon neo-*

orthodoxy, "a response to the expansion of modernity—the secularization of society and culture."

Mauss sees five responses in the subcultural retrenchment or realignment affecting the grass-roots members: renewed emphasis on the principle of continuous revelation through contemporary prophets, renewed emphasis on genealogy and temple sacraments (including vicarious baptisms of ancestors), the missionary program, family renewal, and religious education. This last response overlaps with the intellectual life of church members, and it is from there that three examples have been selected. They offer illustrations of LDS dissent and personal healing *efforts*. (No victim would likely say healing is complete.) And like the Catholic lay renewal movement spearheaded by sexual abuse victims point toward the elements of an emerging counterreformation. Mauss (1994: 171) observes about the mobilization of defiant intellectuals and their tense reception by church brokers:

> During the past twenty-five years, these intellectuals and their publications have become increasingly worrisome to church leaders and especially irritating to those general authorities of a fundamentalist bent. . . . the writings and conferences of today's Mormon intellectuals have elicited an unusually public critical response from certain quarters of the church leadership.

The dissenters to be briefly sketched are Sonia Johnson, D. Michael Quinn, and Lavina Fielding Anderson.

Sonia Johnson

The twentieth-century prototype for dissident Mormon female intellectuals was the late Fawn M. Brodie, historian-author of *No Man Knows My History: The Life of Joseph Smith, The Mormon Prophet* (1995). She wryly and carefully dodged the issues of Smith's authenticity as a prophet or his sincerity as a populist leader, also considering aspects of Smith's humanity (such as, by her reckoning, his forty-eight wives, some secretly married to Smith while their first husbands were still alive) at a time (the mid-1940s) when the LDS church leaders were trying to play down certain still-controversial aspects of the founder's life. Her book was non-apologetic and balanced. One award-winning author, Jon Krakauer (2003: 214) has observed, "every post-1946 treatment of the Mormons under Joseph Smith was written in the immense shadow cast by Fawn Brodie's masterpiece *No Man Knows My Name*."

But she was excommunicated for it.

Sonia Johnson was a scholar-activist one generation removed from Fawn Brodie. Johnson was a mother of four, had a PhD, and been a college instructor. In her ward, she had served as an organist and taught women's classes. But she developed conflicts as the ill-fated Equal Rights Amendment (targeting women) passed congress and was sent to the states for ratification.

Two journalists, Robert Gottlieb and Peter Wiley, in *American's Saints: The Rise of Mormon Power*, describe her dilemma:

> Sonia Johnson was by the late 1970s at once a practicing Mormon and representative of a new type of professional Mormon woman. . . . holding down three church positions, paying her full tithing, and regularly attending ward meetings. By the late 1970s, she increasingly experienced a sense of contradiction between her church status on the one hand, and her beliefs and attitudes, particularly regarding the ERA, on the other hand, Johnson and other professional Mormon women, many of whom lived much of their adult lives outside Utah, were strongly committed to the ERA as a symbol of the need to develop more equal roles for women both in Gentile society and in their church. (1984: 206)

Conservative religious leaders across the U.S. railed against the ERA as having the potential to encourage Wicca worship, unisex public bathrooms, women conscripted into the military, and lesbianism. The amendment was particularly anathema to the LDS patriarchy in Utah. (On the LDS leadership's mobilization and funding of anti-ERA groups as far-flung as Virginia and Florida, see Heinerman and Shupe, 1985: 144-52.) Failing to break through the unresponsiveness of top LDS hierarchy members, Johnson became an impassioned, militant lecture circuit speaker and knew how to cultivate media attention for what to many seemed like an oxymoron: Mormon feminists. Undoubtedly, Johnson's outspoken, occasionally outrageous style contributed to the abrupt demise of her church membership in late 1979. (She once rented a plane to fly a "Mormons for ERA" banner over Salt Lake City during one of the church's semi-annual General Conferences at which representatives of the worldwide LDS Church gather.) She had gone from merely being (as Gottlieb and Wiley, 1984: 207 termed her) "a vocal nuisance" to a serious problem.

Unlike a male as in the trial of Mormon author-anthropologist John Heinerman mentioned in Chapter 2, LDS women (who cannot hold priesthood offices) are entitled only to a closed-door hearing consisting of their ward's bishopric (the bishop and his two counselors) without being told the accusation(s) or the accusers, much less having an advocate or the right to cross-examine anyone. In 1979 she was excommunicated, theologically unable to join her husband and children in the afterlife (since they were "sealed" in a temple) unless she would publicly repent and ask to be re-baptized. An appeal above the bishopric level failed. Of her life's tail-spin as a Mormon, her later U.S. presidential candidacy, and other aspect of her post-LDS career, one can turn to her autobiographical *From Housewife to Heretic* (1981).

D. Michael Quinn

A respected historian by any standard and an expert on early Mormonism, with all its blemishes modern LDS leaders would rather ignore, D. Michael Quinn has also been a prolific author—virtually no works of which have endeared him to promoters of "retrenchment." Private doubts and minor heresies are one thing; a man who commands enough peer respect to authorize his own *de facto* history of the faith can be a threat worth marking. Quinn is a prime example of individual general authorities in the LDS Church trying to assert control over intellectuals' speaking and writing so as to insure their sole product of the latter is "faith-promoting" socio-historical reality.

Quinn's work on polygamy or on folk magic in early Mormonism, the latter buttressing early and later critics' contentions that Joseph Smith was a treasurer-hunter and dabbler in popular spiritualism to enrich himself until he struck gold in founding a new religion, stirred fury among the elites. Worse from their viewpoint, Quinn has gone on to thoughtfully reflect and write about pressures on him from the ecclesiastical top to sanitize his conclusions during his professorship at Brigham Young University (the church's flagship school). He claims they violated his academic freedom and intimidated other more timid social scientists. For example, Quinn's two better-known works as an essayist (whose titles give a flavor for their contents), are entitled "On Being a Mormon Historian and Its Aftermath" (1992a) and "One Hundred Fifty Years of Truth and Consequences about Mormon History" (1992b).

Quinn's contention is that honest differences of opinion and interpretation, including carelessly neglecting certain pertinent evidence, is one thing; deliberate ignoring or concealing it is another. For such a research philosophy, Quinn during the 1980s and 1990s was a persistent target of church leader opprobrium and of steps to discourage his defiance of Mormon subculture's subtle norms of "political correctness." Mauss (1994: 183) writes:

> D. Michael Quinn . . . has published a particularly detailed account of such initiatives taken against him by church leaders for some of his controversial publications while he was a member of the BYU faculty. Such a move through the university board or administration to punish or constrain a professor for his legitimate scholarly work,

would certainly jeopardize the accreditation of any university. In fact, Quinn claims his critics in the hierarchy (some of whom, in fact, serve on the BYU governing board) instead used ecclesiastical channels to discipline him, demanding (for example) that his local stake president revoke his access to the temple.

Mauss charitably refers to this last type of unsubtle pressure on an intellectual "particularly irregular."

Quinn ultimately resigned his position at BYU and was excommunicated in 1993 as much for his writings about LDS elites' heavy-handed treatment of intellectuals as for any of his specialty historical research. He was one of the so-called "September Six" writers and thinkers excommunicated that same year. The group included: an independent, conservative (in LDS terms) scriptural scholar whose work kept in focus Joseph Smith's original millennial bent, which the church now soft-peddles; the president of the Mormon Women's Forum, for speaking in public about ordination of women and the "Mother in Heaven" (God's consort) concept; a Salt Lake City attorney who outspokenly criticized Mormon elites "unrighteous dominion" and helped organized the one truly LDS AAVM, The Mormon Alliance, in 1992; another LDS feminist author who advocated making the priesthood co-educational; and a women writer who regularly began criticizing the LDS ecclesiastical judiciary for authoritarian abuse (see below) and also helped found The Mormon Alliance. A number of others are described in Ostling and Ostling (1999: 351-71), but Quinn has been probably the best known among contemporary Mormon historians.

Lavina Fielding Anderson

Referring to the entire clampdown on dissenting Mormon intellectuals by the Elders of the New Zion, sociologist Mauss (1994: 183) comments: "Many of other Mormon scholars and intellectuals, including recent and current editors of *Dialogue* and *Sunstone*, have had similar experiences." *Dialogue: A Journal of Mormon Thought* is a journal presenting liberal-to-maverick LDS topics and views in an academic style; *Sunstone* offers its pages, as it does time at its annual symposium held at Salt Lake City since 1979, to liberals, free-thinkers, and contrarians in modern Mormondom. Lavina Fielding Anderson is well known and comfortable in both overlapping publications. Indeed, "Anderson is an extremely potent symbol of church discipline because she is involved with several important Latter-day institutions that persist in examining religious questions apart from hierarchical control" (Ostling and Ostling, 1991: 352).

Anderson, with a PhD in English, has been an associate editor of *Dialogue* and continues to attend the Sunstone Symposium and writes for *Sunstone*. She had edited the quarterly publication of the Mormon Women's Forum, and is a trustee of The Mormon Alliance and thereby has co-edited a number of volumes of *Case Reports of the Mormon Alliance* (the latter focusing on the church's regularly inadequate handling of sexual abuse cases as well as its overall authoritarian excesses). There activities yield only a very partial sense of her resumé.

Anderson was excommunicated in 1993, accused of apostasy, but never told exactly to what that charge referred. (In her case, most Mormon-watchers know it was on account of her active speaking and the 1993 *Dialogue* article in which she chronicled what she perceived to be church leaders' repressive treatment of LDS intellectuals.) She is also considered beyond the official pale for publicizing and criticizing the Strengthening Church Members Committee in Salt Lake City's church headquarters (a bureau which keeps files on dissenters, repeat troublemakers, and persons suspect in similar terms.).

Anderson's 1993 excommunication was more severe in consequences than the terms of disfellowship John Heinerman experienced (as described in Chapter 3). She cannot enter any Mormon temple, fill any church position, receive or participate in any sacrament, or stand up in a ward meeting service to offer a prayer or testimony. She has had permanent temple "sealings" to her husband and son suspended until she should properly atone and reapply (like Sonia Johnson) for re-baptism.

Lavina Fielding Anderson, as a symbol of dissent and defiance, is precisely why the LDS Church feels a need to maintain its Strengthening Church Members Committee internal police files. Ostling and Ostling (1999: 354-5), holding sterling reputations for journalistic objectivity, concluded about the committee, "The files are only one aspect of a meticulous system of internal discipline through which contemporary Mormonism operates more like a small cult than a major denomination. . . . Such discipline of rank-and-file members in other churches is virtually unknown."

Which is the point of why Anderson, despite official attempts to marginalize her from LDS Church life, still considers herself a faithful Mormon who sustains both Joseph Smith as a true prophet and the *Book of Mormon* as divinely delivered in the midst of the current hierarchical regime.

Thus, hierarchical church laity in both the Roman Catholic and LDS churches make an action-meaningful distinction between regimes and the faith traditions, between their eternal churches and the current temporal organization staffed with fallible managers (despite the latters' claims otherwise). Maintaining defiance in the face of perceived wrongdoing earns each dissident an empowerment based on the mutual support of like-minded survivors within a "wounded community." In this way consciousness-of-kind and normative justification for opposition to the power-dependent status quo is cultivated.

Such survivors address what they see as violations of the sacred social exchange by insensitive elites. They seek solace in the root values of their faith traditions and can proof-text (i.e., select applicable, context notwithstanding) scriptural passages for their cause. Indeed, elites usually underestimate the fact that scriptural references are a double-edged sword: these are tools for renewal and reform as well as for social control. The American black civil rights movement demonstrated that fact in the segregated South fifty years ago.

In such ways are AAVMs born and healing proceeds.

It may be tempting to conclude that the Roman Catholic hierarchy is more open than its LDS equivalent to considering such reforms as broker accountability. But as we have seen, so far—once past the self-congratulating pronouncements—the latter's effort has been clumsy and half-hearted. One faith is older, larger, with more experience in allowing theological nuance depending on its audiences. The other faith is younger, aggressively expanding, certainly showing no signs in its leadership of diffidence. Perhaps age explains flexibility and the willingness to compromise. Perhaps it does not. The iron law of oligarchy only suggests that each camp in such asymmetrical power arrangements faces a conflict, rather than familial, model for action.

Congregations and Denominations

The counterreformation of which I wrote at the beginning of this chapter and will again is most clearly seen underway in the healing of individual congregations and their respectively larger denominations in the aftermath of scandals' turmoil. It is still useful to consider polity as a contextual factor, but some refinement must be made: from the (evangelical) Protestant *congregational* to the intermediate *moderately hierarchical* (such as various types of Lutherans, Presbyterians as well as United Methodists) to the *ecclesiastical hierarchical* (principally varieties of Catholics and the Latter-day Saints).

In the congregational style of congregational healing (in some cases, there *is* no denomination, or perhaps a loose confederation, fellowship, or convention, such as Southern,

American [Northern], and other Baptists' healing remains narrowly biblical in its prescriptions for change. There are few structural reforms envisioned, at most the removal of a pastor. Scriptural standards of God-liness and servanthood in leadership, equality of spirit, and discipline without hierarchy are emphasized. A good example is Blue's (1993: 150-1) reference to the Apostle Paul's Second Letter to the Corinthians 1:24:

> This humble self-denigration sums up Paul's function as leader. He casts himself as one who works with the Corinthians in a servant role rather than one who stands above them in a ruler role. He emphasizes his function as servant rather than his office as apostle.

Shupe (1995: 120) remarks on the interesting reversal occurring in hierarchical religious groups attempting to contain scandal and victims. Victim vulnerability/disadvantage, on the one hand, and empowerment, on the other, actually relate to one another in a U-curve. That is, "victims initially are in a power disadvantage confronting relatively impermeable organizational structure, but eventually (and ironically) they obtain a structural focus for redress that aids their mobilization of grievances." *Moderately hierarchical* denominations, moreso than their more con-gregational cousins, are likely to create victims' advocacy groups out of pre-existing caucuses and lay interest groups (such as leadership quorums or women's inner-denomination associations) that already have standing and recognition. Such groups, as will be noted shortly, do not exist in nearly as adversarial relations to elites as they do in ecclesiasti-cal hierarchies.

This can be seen in cases such as the Lutheran Laity Movement for Stewardship, which was later carried over into the Evangelical Lutheran Church in America, as William O. Avery analyzed in *Empowered Laity* (1997) and seen in the interest group mobilization in denominations as diverse as the Unitarian-Universalistic Church and the United Methodist Church (Norwood, 1974) (see also Shupe, 1995: 102-4 for additional details).

Healing for congregations and denominations is much more a socio-logical and less a theological matter outside the congregational model. Graham and Fortune (1993) point out in the journal *Pastoral Psychol-ogy* that congregations witnessing the turmoil of a clergy malfeasance crisis require empowerment to mend. Healing often does not naturally or automatically happen with time. The psychic energy spent and anguish generated meanwhile takes a toll.

Therapist Nancy M. Hopkins (1991: 249) advocates immediate intervention with the congregation in the crisis aftermath as well as with primary victims and their families. Otherwise, congregations can by default retreat into denial and/or anger. She warns that "a clergyperson's individual crisis does not happen in isolation, but rather in response to upsets in the balance (homeostasis) of any of the systems to which he or she belongs."

This can be found to be the common case in what Haskin (1995) and Hopkins (1995) term "afterpastors" or "non-offending clergy" (McDonough, 1995), often the clergyperson who newly comes into a pastoral assignment where congregants or parishioners are still reeling from a scandal and must deal with the mess left by a predecessor. There is a predictable honeymoon of relief with the laity, but it can be quickly followed by hurts that were never effectively addressed. Says Haskin (1995: 157):

> When there is public knowledge of the wounds in the congregation but no process to help the congregation heal, the pressure on the afterpastor to "fix" the congregation can be enormous. [If many in the congregation are in denial that healing even needs to take place] the afterpastor is often the target of the anger or rage that the members of the congregation are avoiding to admit exists.

Similarly, Friberg (1995) writes of "wounded congregations" (a favorite metaphor in this literature); Knudsen (1995) considers the social psychological practicalities of congregational dynamics and politics; and Harold Hopkins (1995) examines the wider ripple effects of local scandals on denominations. Probably the most comprehensive look at such group-level healing has been offered by G. Lloyd Rediger, an ordained Presbyterian minister who wrote *Ministry and Sexuality* (1990) after working for nineteen years as a counselor with the Office of Pastors Services in Madison, Wisconsin (under the auspices of the ecumenical Wisconsin Council of Churches). During that time, Rediger came into contact with troubled (and trouble-making) clergy from *thirty* denominations, and he provides a detailed protocol for the group-level intervention so often called for.

Ministry and Sexuality reads like a Protestant equivalent to Sipe's *1990 A Secret World: Sexuality and the Search for Celibacy* treatise on Catholic priests, but minus Sipe's extensive statistics. Rediger has separate chapters on such clergy problems as sexual addiction, adultery, incest, pedophilia, rape, sexual harassment, homosexuality, masturbation, transvestism, and so forth. He devotes a fair amount of emphasis to the "era of sexual transition" (which really has not concluded) and the strain it imposes on the (usually) married pastoral position. At the book's beginning he muses: "Maybe there is a third sex—clergy. If this is true, it is the clergy role, not the clergyperson, that is the third sex" (p. 1). There is because clergy are still captives of what Bratcher (1989) termed "the walk-on-water syndrome," being held to a higher standard, or "the star factor" in Rediger's words.

Thus, "contemporary society still imagines that clergy are somehow different from other persons, that clergy do not have normal human appetites and needs, and that they are spiritually and morally superior to ordinary mortals" (Rediger, 1990:1). Pastors are constantly confronted with opportunity structures for deviance from their image. As a result, Rediger charges both congregations and denominations with complicity when the pastors falls *if* they ignore this reality. Indeed, Rediger is as hard on denominational officials as groups in the AAVM have been critical of Catholic bishops:

> denominational officials are also responsible. They worry about the massive disruption that occurs in a denomination when sexual malfeasance is discovered and dealt with openly. More than this, some bishops and executives are involved in sexual irregularities themselves. Therefore, there is a tendency by some denominational executives to avoid, deny, and even cover sexual malfeasance. (1990: 2)

Rediger, in his group-level protocol, suggests first a ten-point "Outline of a Professional Ethic" for pastors structured after the Ten Commandments (p 109), emphasizing discipline and love toward God/self/others; couched in wisdom sought through prayer and contemplation; avoiding abuse of body/mind/spirit; continued rejuvenation of humor along with self-reflection; and so forth. Then he moves on to an eight-point set of guidelines for congregations and their fiduciaries to manage scandal (pp. 116-18). Some are obvious but are often overlooked in the passion of crisis:

1. Get the facts straight and as soon as possible (but not precipitously) to avoid victim isolation.
2. Obtain independent, authoritative denominational representation ASAP to help manage an investigation.
3. Immediately assess who are the wounded and begin ministering to their needs.
4. After identifying the perpetrator(s), establish limits, treatment, and conditions of reinstatement or termination.

5. Do not let the congregation on its own, without independent input, blindly determine legal procedures and ramifications.
6. Assess "damage control" efforts (not damage—that should have been done earlier in Point 1).
7. Learn potential misconduct's warning signals.
8. Damage control is necessary but not sufficient. It is not of itself healing. Include church fiduciaries for intervention and strategize about "the legal liabilities that often inhibit confessions, testimony, and forgiveness."

Rediger also provides "Prevention Guidelines," each of which is a spin-off of the acronym PREVENT (for example, preparation, evaluation—or accountability and periodic pastoral review, values—or the importance of everyone's needs in the crisis, and so forth), and finally Seven Basic Principles that he refers to as "Beyond Prevention" in the sense they address the pastor-congregation and system generally (pp. 123-26). They also simultaneously prevent clergy misconduct while encouraging Christian organizational excellence. These are as much sociological axioms for providing honesty, trust, and morale as they are guidelines for fostering traditional notions of spirituality. While they are shown here codified, they can be found variously in many of the other writings cited.

The implicit assumptions in the moderately hierarchical writings of Rediger and others are that individual victimization is more than simply a pastoral failing. It is also an organizational failure, and while meeting the immediate needs of hurting individuals is paramount, there must be an accompanying house cleaning in upper levels and creation of guidelines and new procedures of review. The latter must instill permanent, not stopgap, structures of prevention.

One of these structural issues, hinted at in several places by Rediger, addresses financial and legal liabilities that become salient in multi-level healing and reform. Other than pertinent sections of the 1985 Doyle-Mouton-Peterson warning to the Catholic Church, there is only one other explicitly detailed source that addresses these matters. It is the 1986 (distinctly Protestant-oriented) *Clergy Malpractice* by H. Newton Maloney, Thomas C. Needham, and Samuel Southard. Written before either of the two waves of Roman Catholic priest pedophile scandals or even the televangelist scandals of the late 1980s, its detailed suggestions and warnings are as relevant (or more so) today as then:

> Churches and clergy have been sued and will continue to be sued for liabilities arising out of the manner in which they conduct their professional duties. Public pressures, arising from consumer discontent, will in all likelihood gradually erode court resistance to directly trying cases charging clergy malfeasance. (p. 25)

Healing efforts in ecclesiastical entities meet different fates, though all are as yet undecided. Thus far the LDS hierarchy has been fairly successful in marginalizing those who declare themselves victims of authoritarian and sexual abuse, leaving them in a self-reinforcing ghetto of dissent where healing occurs to a degree among those individuals but has yet to obtain any kind of progress toward structural change such as the Catholic Church experienced in 2002. Perhaps the Latter-day Saint organization, despite its geographic diversity, has as yet too monolithic a recent theological culture and so far has provided only a few "options" for believers within a power pyramid. This would be a much different experience from the older Catholic ecclesia with its vast tradition of different orders and ministries.

As far as the Catholics, stirrings of a more profound counterreformation are now being heard. The pedophile scandals someday may be seen as having served as catalyst. Gibson (2004: 2) concurs that

> the scandals may be a blessing, in that it concentrated the collective Catholic mind. . . . the shock of the revelations can also serve a broader purpose in alerting Catholics to the equally dangerous preexisting condition of the church, and pointing the way toward a solution.

The "preexisting condition" for Gibson, as it has become particularly for a number of American Catholics, is the bishops' abuses of authority concomitant with an obsession for secrecy, ecclessiolotry, and even clericalism.

Two illustrative emerging phenomena working within and toward this counterreformation are Voice of the Faithful and The Interfaith Sexual Trauma Institute.

VOTF, the centrist AAVM group described in Chapter 4, maintains three explicit structural goals in keeping with its motto "Keep the Faith, change the Church:"

1. greater accountability of decision makers
2. transparency of the decision making process, and
3. shared responsibility of hierarchy and laity in making decisions

Founded in July 2002 in the backwash of the Boston Archdiocese scandals, the group is made up predominantly *not* of "renegade" Catholics (i.e., the type of "renegades" the Sunstone crowd appears to be to the LDS Church elites) but of concerned laypersons, most of whom are not victims. At that July conclave, after tentative probing earlier that year, approximately 4,200 members from about 40 states and a few other nations met in Boston. Given the access of the internet, fellow AAVM travelers, sympathetic donors, and more serious watchers undoubtedly number in the tens of thousands.

VOTF also illustrates how healing efforts and seeking redress in the Catholic Church have evolved beyond the first groups coalescing during the late 1980s and early 1990s. Earlier the case of Jeanne M. Miller, founder of VOCAL (later The Linkup), and her uphill battle even for minimal recognition from the Chicago Archdiocese, was described. SNAP is another example. Such groups did not garner instant lay appreciation or even a modicum of respect from many fellow believers. Based on interviews, Gibson (2004: 111) recalls:

> for more than a decade Clohessy [head of SNAP] and his fellow victim advocates had been ducking the spitballs of the lay faithful who were furious at them whenever they revealed a priest's misconduct. "A few years ago the best we could hope for from the laity was silence, not to actively oppose us," Clohessy said. ". . . Now they're in the game."

Perhaps because of its outspokenly self-proclaimed faithfulness to the larger Catholic tradition, if not always to the current regime of leaders, VOTF is becoming a force with which to dialogue. For example, David O'Brien, professor of Roman Catholic Studies and director of the Center for Religion, Ethics, and Culture at Holy Cross College in Worcester, Massachusetts was invited to speak to VOTF's National Representative Council. In his talk on December 13, 2003, presented on VOTF's website (www.twincities-Votf.org/obrien.stm/), O'Brien addressed the group's concerns and reinforced their constructive attempts to implement the group's three primary goals. He advised that they regard the priest sex scandals as a social movement opportunity, not a *raison d'etre*; to keep as close an identity with Church teachings and internal policies as possible; to watch their alliances with "marked" liberal dissidents such as Call to Action's members; to recognize the realities of careerism and politics that underlay platitudes issued by coopting elites; and to continue to address victims and priests' concerns. He was specific in tactics: encourage Catholic workers in schools, hospitals, charities, and parish committees who deal with finances, education, and oversight committees (attend their meetings, network with them, write letters and lobby them); do independent assessments of diocesan victim responses and treatment; seek to challenge and engage Catholic leaders across a host of institutions; and make a presence known at such pivotal levels as the United

States Catholic Conference of Bishops' National Advisory Committee meetings. "Find out who's on it and visit them," O'Brien counseled.

That agenda is more ambitious than the earlier AAVM groups would have dared to dream.

Gibson (2004: 342-50) concludes *The Coming Catholic Church* with attention to three levels of reforms: structure, policy, and attitudes. Structure equals governance, one major reform goal of VOTF. That includes lay diocesan review boards and broadly based diocesan councils, personnel move input, and lay financial oversight. Policy, more sensitive, involves issues such as increased liturgical roles for laity (including women), discipline, and current church limitations on sacramental involvement for divorced and remarried Catholics. Attitudes of acceptance, both by laypersons and clergy, remain the most delicate area of change. A major concern for all is how to accomplish it without sacrificing the most valuable and beloved parts of tradition and without "Protestantizing along the way.

These are ambitious considerations, particularly for a worldwide ecclesia that is increasingly Latino, African, Asian, and poor, "encompassing not only the rich panoply of American Catholicism—a fractious and diverse family that grows bigger and more boisterous every year—but also the one billion *other* Catholics in the world who happen to call Rome home and who have other, much different priorities" (Gibson, 2004: 15).

Alternately, The Interfaith Sexual Trauma Institute (ISTI), in its own words "facilitates the building of healthy, safe, and trustworthy communities of faith" (see website www.osb.org/isti/). Founded in 1994, it is located at St. John's Abbey and University at Collegeville, Minnesota and run by the Order of St. Benedict. Like the Center for the Prevention of Sexual and Domestic Violence in Seattle, Washington or the Boston Psychoanalytic Society and Institute, ISTI holds conferences, offers consultations, and makes available instructional materials related to (in ISTIs case, strictly) clergy abuse. It publishes the ISTI *Sun*, the institute's newsletter, as well as selected monographs on victim and congregational healing intervention. (Various ones are cited in this chapter. It holds major annual conferences on its Collegeville campus, and these are important for integrating issues of healing at victim, congregational, and denominational levels, albeit with less publicity than a VOTF or SNAP.

Consider just the 1999 National Conference held before the sensational 2002 Boston revelations. It had as its theme "Sex and the Abuse of Power in Religious Systems," hosting plenary discussion sessions, keynote speakers, and conference workshops. (Presenters are "conference faculty.") Like its other conferences, the 1999 National Conference was self-described as:

> Working from a multi-perspective, multi-disciplinary model, the 1999 National Conference offers a comprehensive approach to dealing with clergy sexual misconduct after and, even more importantly, before it occurs. Designed specifically to address the concerns of those who serve in leadership positions—those who will face victims, offenders, and congregations in crisis—this conference provides up-to-the-date information in dynamic workshops focused on prevention, healing, and long-term change.

Four thematic "tracks" of three workshops each provide a sense of conference content:

Track 1 Theme: Abuse Reduction
(Preventing Abuse, Lessons from Bad History and Good Sense, Respectful Intervention with Victims)

Track 2 Theme: Congregational Healing
(Spiritual Issues for Congregations, Congregational Recovery: What Religious Can Do, Long Term Systems Change)

Track 3 Theme: Victim Concerns
(Abduction of Fidelity: Breaking Traumatic Bonding, Shame Healing for Victims, Sexual Healing: Reclaiming Your Healthy Sexual Self)

Track 4 Theme: Dynamics of Power Abuse
(Pastor Power: Covenant to Care or License to Abuse?
What We Know about Offenders, Voices of Survivors)

It is important to reiterate that such conferences, with their integrated "macro" and "micro" levels of content, were occurring before the 2002 Boston scandal was being publicized. *And* that these conferences were held under the auspices of a Roman Catholic order, indeed, even inaugurated by it. Such small histories may one day make up a larger counterreformation narrative.

Healing for Broker-Perpetrators

The Reverend Jim Bakker, televangelist superstar convicted of twenty-four counts of fraud and conspiracy for taking more than $3 million from his followers through the PTL television ministry, spent five years in a federal prison before early release. He has since low-balled his new electronic outing with a cheap cafe-TV studio holding a 260-seat audience and produces, in many ways by hand-to-mouth and charity, on a daily basis "The New Jim Bakker Show." "This is the lowest-budget show in America," he has said. In his autobiographical recounting of his fall from grace during the late 1980s, entitled *I Was Wrong* (1996), he contritely begins his introduction:

> THE WORDS "I WAS WRONG" DO NOT COME EASILY TO ME. For most of my life I believed that my understanding of God and how He wants us to live was not only correct but worth exporting to the world. One reason I have risked putting my heart into print is to tell you that my previous philosophy of life, out of which my attitudes and actions flowed, was fundamentally flawed. God does not promise that we will all be rich and prosperous, as I once preached. When I really studied the Bible while in prison, it became clear to me that not one man or woman—not even prophets of God—led a life without pain. (1996: 1)

A cynic might observe that the defrocked Assemblies of God minister was a loose cannon barely under his denomination's discipline during his television heyday, so he had little to lose trying to jumpstart a new ministry with his ex-con label. Besides, any revivalist can tell you that the crowd is a sucker for a tearful *mea culpa*, some good old time repentance, and a humble comeback. They bought it from Bakker's fellow Pentecostal Jimmy Swaggart after his dalliances with prostitutes just as the fictitious revival tent masses cheered on the whisky-drinking womanizing protagonist in *Elmer Gantry*. The bigger the sin, the greater the repentance; and, presumably likewise, the forgiveness.

On perpetrators, professional therapists concern themselves with healing the offender's family members the same way they would for an abuse victim's secondary victim unit (Legg and Legg, 1995) or profiling and categorizing "wounding pastors" into types based on pathologies (Irons and Roberts, 1995). The focus of both related approaches, however, is typically the individual's own moral, psychological self. For example, "The goal of treatment is revitalization of the God-given gifts of faith and hope" (Irons and Roberts, 1995: 49). This is what more overtly religious writers (particularly in the congregational polity tradition) refer to as "personal restoration."

A more significant, role-related sociological issue is the possibility of an abusive (most often in sexual matters) minister's restoration to leadership in a local church or denomination. There is mixed evidence and experience in the writings of both congregational and hierarchical traditions. A running theme throughout all is that while the equation of pastoral atonement equals confession of sin plus repentance plus evidence thereof, not all pastoral failures are equally serious. Some say the latter factor should not matter; others are adamant that sexual sin qualitatively differs in its implications for future leadership.

The Roman Catholic change in such perspectives over time, which initially resulted in all the strain and AAVM mobilization described earlier, is instructive. Earlier in the post-World War II era, the church founded (through orders and other moral entrepreneurial agencies) hospitals, retreats, and institutes to deal mainly with a limited range of priests' problems. These included alcoholism, burnout, and depression, dealt with at such places as the Villa Louis Martin, a two thousand-acre retreat at Jemez Spring, New Mexico, founded in 1969 by the Servants of the Paraclete; the House of Affirmation in Massachusetts; or the St. Luke Institute in Silver Spring, Maryland. Essentially, ignorant of the causes, nature, and extent of the pedophilia problem within the clergy, bishops used such places to dump their problem priests with a short-term "out-of-sight/out-of-commission" strategy but a long-run optimism to again place these men into functioning assignments. The protocol was often no more than prayer, meditation, and penance (with the exception of St. Luke).

The realization that pedophiles cannot easily, if ever, be "cured" (any more than those with the disease of alcoholism can) came too late. Meanwhile, particularly in the case of pedophiles, precipitous releases to return to similar pastoral duties in similar populations as before, were made. The result, as in the classic example of Father James Porter, was gross recidivism and, in the instance of the Santa Fe Archdiocese which was home to the Villa Louis Martin (closed in 1993), bankruptcy.

Rehabilitation, the church now appreciates, is more than theologically empowered acceptance and forgiveness of sin. Compulsions do not yield easily to mere will power.

Now, in addition to the much publicized removal of offenders from active priesthood, less penance and more cutting-edge cognitive psychology and experimental aversion therapies are employed, such as at the St. Luke Institute and the bucolic Vianney Renewal Center in Dittmer, Missouri. The latter facility's staff included four licensed therapists (who are also under contract with the Federal Bureau of Prisons). Those patients declared safe for release are monitored and periodically reevaluated with personalized lapse-prevention/fall-back safety plans. One counselor told a reporter of the Center's zero-tolerance failure standard: "the goal here is no more victims." Since the Center's opening in 1988, it claims there have been no recorded incidences, *and no patients returned to active ministry* (Wittenauer, 2006). Most live and die at Vianney.

Restoration to ministry has been the subject of much debate among congregational polity and moderately hierarchical polity spokespersons since the 1980s' sex and money scandals involving television preachers. Well-known authors/spiritual leaders Tim LaHaye (1990) and Kenneth Kantzer (1987), in popular books and prestigious outlets like *Christianity Today*, have answered the question, "Ought/Can once abusive ministers be restored to leadership?" with a resounding "Yes!" The very essence of God's mercy, goes the argument, is that *no* sinner ever goes so far beyond the pale as to become unredeemable.

But redeemable *as what*? The strongest argument against "open restoration" has been made by John H. Armstrong, with evangelical Protestant credentials from Wheaton Graduate School (M.A.) and a doctorate in ministry from Luther Rice Seminary. In his book, *Can Fallen Pastors Be Restored?* (1995), Armstrong examines these frequently encountered positions on the issue, particularly if sexual sin is involved:

1. Immediate (less than one year's time) restoration to pastoral office is feasible.
2. "Pastoral restoration" first requires "personal restoration" of the minister with his family and then a longer time of moral rehabilitation, perhaps one to three years.
3. Personal restoration is, of course, desirable from a Christian standpoint, but *no* pastoral restoration to leadership can occur.

Armstrong's reasons for choosing the third option are grounded in Old and New Testament references, including those of Paul and later Christian leaders who often confronted leadership problems not appreciably different from modern ones. The consensus of most contemporary Christian writers, Armstrong admits, is "most agree that they can be restored, not only to the church visible, but also to the public ministry of Word and sacrament and thus to the office of pastor" (P. 44)

Some argue that a once-fallen pastor can be an even more effective witness because of his (rarely her) first-hand experience with certain sins and intimate knowledge of God's mercy and Jesus' promise of redemption. However, Armstrong contends the opposite position: "Many of God's people. . . . have nagging doubts about offering every repentant pastor full restoration to pastoral ministry" (p. 45). All sins, Armstrong claims, are not equal, and the sexual transgression of adultery—which undermines pastoral authority and "brutally violates" spouse, children, congregation, denomination (if there is one), and the overall "bride of Christ on display before the world"—tops the list of taboos. (Pedophiles, not a pressing Protestant issue compared to Catholic, is not mentioned.) "Adultery is not simply a 'slip-up' but a massive, often planned, rebellion" (p. 49).

Armstrong's unremitting stance, by which the Bakkers, Swaggarts, and others would come up short, is the Pauline one that to be qualified for pastor authority a man must have an "unassailable" moral reputation. He reiterates the sharp distinction between personal life and career, but goes no further into any structural remedy:

> I am convinced that men who fall sexually while in the pastoral ministry generally should remove themselves immediately, if for no other reason than to make sure that they protect themselves from further failure that often recurs if they remain in office." (p. 105)

On the process of restoration, Armstrong concludes: "The goal is to aid the former pastor in restoration to God, to the local church, and to proper relationship with his family; it is not restoration to his former office" (p. 199).

Nobody in this brief review, no matter what their prescriptions at whatever levels of healing or leadership servant-hood restoration, believes they have had the last word. Certainly one cannot during an era of counterreformation when church spokespersons are still thinking through what exactly to do about clergy malfeasance in all its aspects.

Conclusion

Hopefully, some enterprising thesis-hungry graduate students will be investing tremendous amounts of time and attention to in-depth studies of specific scandals and clergy responses in the ways Pullen (1998) did with Santa Barbara's St. Anthony's Seminary Support Group or Nason-Clark (1998, 1991) has done with a Newfoundland scandal in Canada. The area needs more analyses than can be provided by journalistic reports or even journalists writing books.

Meanwhile, the trend in even ecclesiastical hierarchies is not always from conservatism toward liberalism. In America's Episcopalian denomination the incoming 2007 leader, Nevada Bishop Katherine Jefferts Schori, supports gay relationships in a church already torn by issues such as female and gay clergy. In 2006, seven dissenting conservative dioceses (Central Florida; South Carolina; Fort Worth and Dallas, TX; Fresno, CA; Pittsburgh; and Springfield, IL) were debating the likelihood of secession from the national denomination in protest. Dallas alone had seventy-seven congregations; the Plano parish, one of the largest, had already announced plans to depart.

Calls for change can run both ways.

This chapter has attempted to sketch a larger counterreformation underway, one in which clergy elites of whatever level feel account-ability pressures from below. They are being told uncompromisingly in many cases to forget their oligarchic hubris and authentically accept the twenty first century as one of power reform. No faith tradition, despite what ecclesiastical leaders in the Roman Catholic and Latter-day Saint churches are fond of insisting, fails to evolve far beyond its first genera-tions. Garry Wills, in *Why I Am A Catholic* (2002: 2) says, "That is a claim that can be made only with the help of tendentious readings of history, suppression of evidence, or distortion of the evidence." The various lay interest groups crying out for reform, assisted by fast-paced media cover-age and the internet, are engaged in precisely what mid-twentieth-century sociologist C. Wright Mills termed "the sociological imagination," i.e., seeing the general in the particular or reinterpreting specific cases as part of broader patterns (Wright and Etzioni, 1999).

6

Fallout from Clergy
Malfeasance Revelations

A cartoon I read in a newspaper post-Boston 2002 showed a voice coming down from a cloud (presumably God's) saying "Thou Shalt Leave the Kids Alone!" and Moses, still chiseling the Ten Commandments on stone tablets, replying "Do you really think we need to say that?" During that same time period acerbic cartoonist Wiley Miller, in his popular Sunday comic *Non Sequitor,* ran several panels about a Dark Ages waif named Homer who saved a young girl marooned in a cage on a small island for the heresy of having "said no to a bishop." The following Sunday rescuer Homer is tied to a stake by a dark cowled mob. Before they put him to the torch, the following Homer-cowled inquisitor dialogue ensures:

> Homer: But all I did was save a girl. . . . Who says that's blasphemy?
>
> Inquisitor: The Bishop . . . and to question him is the same as questioning the infallible Word of God!!
>
> Homer: Uh...Who told you that?
>
> Inquisitor: Hmmm . . . Now that you mention it, that decree was made by the bishop.
>
> Homer: Didn't that make any of you are little suspicious about his motives?

[The mob pauses in silence.]

> Inquisitor: [To the mob shouting "Burn the Blasphemer!!"] Well now. . . . that would be questioning the bishop, wouldn't it?

Almost immediately two letters to the editor appeared in *The Fort Wayne Journal Gazette* which had published the cartoon. One was a complaint, published New Year's Day, 2003 from a reader in the town of Kendallville (just north of Fort Wayne) chiding the editors:

Making comic strip jokes out of Catholic bishops—by inference is completely out of line! My dad was editor of the Winona Herald published in Winona, Minn., back in the 1930s. He was non-Catholic and my mother was Catholic, but I know he would never had allowed this comic strip to be published and released to the public.

(The reader is absolutely right—see Jenkins, 1998, cited in Chapter 2 and his "culture of clergy deviance" hypothesis that helps answer the question, "Why clergy malfeasance scandals now?")

Another reader took that first reader to task in his/her own letter to the editor of January 7, 2003:

[After summarizing the Kendalville letter's complaint:] Well, that is just rubbish, isn't it? We know that all members of the clergy back then were paragons of moral virture [sic]. Just as they are now.

Psychiatrists and analysts from Sigmund Freud on have told us that humor can be a defense mechanism to help cope with things that really are not funny at all, a sort of "whistling in the dark" tactic to allay anxiety. I tried to make such a point in the final chapter of my first book on clergy malfeasance (Shupe, 1995: 135-6) with three very raunchy Catholic priest pedophilia jokes, all told to me in a Notre Dame-theme bar by admitted Catholic laypersons. I barely convinced the book's publisher to leave them in after one editor threw a fit, scrawling across the offending manuscript page, "These jokes will *not* appear in this book!" (Beware, those jokes are not polite.)

Such items illustrate one form of the "fallout" (defined by a dictionary as "any incidental results or side effects") from arguably the most sensational scandal in not only the largest Christian denomination in America but also in both their histories. Gallows humor, perhaps, but these snippets of popular culture had nowhere near the trenchant implications as other forms of fallout.

A Feeding Frenzy amid Clergy Malfeasance Revelations

Respected University of Virginia political scientist Larry J. Sabato wrote in his book *Feeding Frenzy* about "attack journalism" and its penchant for incessant prying into public figures' lives and laying waste to reputations. He deliberately chose the dramatic shark mob metaphor:

The term *frenzy* suggests some kind of disorderly compulsion, or agitated activity that is muscular and instinctive, not cerebral and thoughtful. In the animal world, no activity is more classically frenzied than the feeding of sharks, piranhas, or bluefish when they encounter a wounded prey. The attack-fish with extraordinary acute senses first search out weak, ill, or injured targets. On locating them each hunter moves in quickly, to gain a share of the kill, feeding not just off the victim but also off its fellow hunters' agitation. . . . the frenzy can spread, with the delirious attackers wildly striking any object that moves in the water, even each other. (1993: 6)

Sabato, of course, was concerned about the investigative press' relation to political scandals, but in the following sentence from his book simply substitute *religious* or *ecclesiastical_* for *political*, and one sees the similarity to the media metaphorically "seizing" American religion's dark side activities in its "jaws" during the past two decades:

> . . . a feeding frenzy is defined as the press coverage attending any political event or circumstance where a critical mass of journalists leap to cover the same embarrassing or scandalous subject and pursue it intensely, often excessively, and sometimes uncontrollably. (1993: 6)

Journalist Howard Kurtz, in his reflective book *Media Circus*, refers to the same phenomenon as "pack journalism" ("pack" presumably implies through metaphor wild predatory beasts) and sums it up: "The herd instinct is one of the strongest forces in journalism" (1994: 20).

Enough of animal comparisons—the media did not create these scandals, much less the serious misconduct and serial depredations underlying them. But continued revelations fed to the public have unquestionably conditioned how they, as well as the pollsters and insurers, have responded.

In all this media fascination with a heretofore-sacrosanct institution being knocked down several pegs is something the media itself rarely addresses; to many reporters and editors, religion is a mysterious if not merely unfamiliar estate. Jeffrey K. Hadden and I two decades ago described this handicap or bias often present in media spokespersons making any sense of religious events, much less criminogenic ones:

> The typical mass-media commentator, print journalists, television's roving reporters and anchor persons, and most editors—are also captive to a secular mindset that is predisposed to exclude religion from news except when it is bizarre or sensational. . . . Nor is the typical communicator well equipped to assess what information about religion may cross his or her desk. There are only about 250 religious newswriters in the United States. To the extent that religion is covered, the majority of journalists find themselves covering it between reporting assignments on natural disasters, crime sprees, traffic accidents, garden shows, and country fairs. . . . Reporters are ill prepared to probe beyond the surface of events. (1998: 42-3)

Citing studies by George Gallup, Jr. and others, Hadden and I noted that religion reporters were found to be not often personally devout or religiously active, certainly much less than the average American (1998: 206-12). We concluded:

> Journalists are not, as a group, very religious. Furthermore, they interact daily with colleagues who also feel indifferent or negative about religion. (1998: 211)

Thus, it is prudent to keep in mind a "feeding frenzy rule of thumb." That is, just as in secular crime where street crime has less overall serious harm than white collar and corporate types (though the former is often more eye-catching and even glamorous), so media coverage devoted to clergy deviance emphasizes sexual malfeasance because it makes "lurid" copy at the expense of covering the larger, more devastating harm caused by economic and even authoritarian abuse. After examining such scandals' fallout, I conclude with what it portends for the future.

Fallout from the Televangelist Scandals

The television preachers, or televangelists as Hadden and Swann (1981) christened them, were their own religious and economic force. Though many had at least titular allegiances with denominations, from the Reformed Church to Presbyterians to Independent Baptists to Southern Baptists to Roman Catholics to Pentecostals, they were essentially free of the latters' control. They financially contributed to, rather than depended on, these denominations. Their radio and television programs and networks were essentially privately run fiefdoms, or *parachurches*, named so after the great nineteenth-century evangelistic organizations created by men like Charles Grandison Finney and Dwight L. Moody, and early twentieth-century giants like Billy Sunday and Aimee Semple McPherson.

Early in the development of broadcasting, evangelists (both Protestant and Catholic) realized the unparalleled potential to fulfill Jesus Christ's Great Commission as declared in the last verses of the Gospel of Mark: "You must go out to the whole world and proclaim the gospel to every creature" (Phillips, 1972: 106). These moral and economic entrepreneurs were quick to begin purchasing airtime once the airwaves were declared by the federal government to be monitored as a public trust. In a 1960 landmark decision rendered by the proprietary Federal Communications Commission, local radio and television stations could sell time slots to churches and parachurch ministries yet still receive credit for the "public interest" (or "sustaining") airtime they were required to turn back to communities in exchange for their FCC-approved licenses. Soon after the "electronic church" began featuring its lucrative ministries mimicking alternately the big orchestra sounds and colorful stage settings of Broadway and the folksy talk-show formats of Johnny Carson and

Mike Douglas. Soon all the major televangelists from Jimmy Swaggart, Jerry Falwell, Jim Bakker, Ernest Angley, W. V. Grant, Jr., and Robert Tilton also struck a goldmine formula that merged material prosperity theology in their sermonizing with ongoing telethon-style fundraising. It all appealed mightily to "heartland" USA listeners and viewers of the modestly educated middle and lower-middle classes. When many of the largest televangelists became mixed up in scandals of corruption, their falls took down enormous numbers of victims with them (see, for example, Hoover, 1988; Frankl, 1987; Shupe and Stacey, 1982).

The televangelist scandals, pieces of which have been referred to in earlier chapters, involved more than a few electronic preachers during the late 1980s and early 1990s. The three most contiguous ones involved, first, Oral Roberts, the Tulsa, Oklahoma-based faith-healing Pentecostal. In March 1987 he claimed that God had in a vision explicitly given him a time-limit of one month to raise $8 million for Roberts' ministry or else God would kill him. Technically Roberts committed no crime, but the audaciousness and poor taste of this appeal generated a landslide of negative scrutiny from both the media and a great many appalled mainstream clergy—but Oral Roberts raised his money by April 1.

Then Jim and Tammy Faye Bakker, he with the boyish grin and she with the garish make-up and challenged singing voice, in 1987 were caught up in a web of clerical stewardship misdeeds:

Jim, it was learned, had performed illicit sex, or adultery with (if not raped) a Praise the Lord (PTL) network secretary, Jessica Hahn, and promised to pay her $175,000 for her silence. After her public disclosure of the deal due to stopped payments, she went on to pose nude in *Playboy* magazine in November, 1987 (article title: "Jessica Hahn: Born Again") and a second time in September, 1988 after plastic surgery to her face and breasts (article title: "The New Jessica Hahn: The Photos You've Been Waiting For");

The Bakkers, along with various of their lieutenants, had been literally helping themselves to cash at the cartons in the mailed donation-counting room, little of which was ever declared as personal income from the ministry (Jim Bakker was charged with income tax evasion.);

Jim Bakker had been soliciting funds from PTL audiences with much fanfare for non-existent overseas missions (Bakker was also charged with mail and wire fraud.);

The Bakkers engaged in building a sort of spiritual theme park/hotel/recreational complex they called Heritage Village USA. They vastly oversold time-sharing units in condominiums and the Heritage Grand Hotel at $1,000 each. They sold 120,000 of these Life Partnerships for only 50 planned rooms in buildings never completed. (See Hadden and Shupe, 1988: 8-12, 126-29 for further financial details of PTL.)

And a third scandal involved Jimmy Swaggart, old-style Pentecostal preacher and musician, with his parachurch headquartered in Baton Rouge, Louisiana. He had previously implicated a rival evangelist, Marvin Gorman, with a prostitute, thus ruining Gorman's ministry—at the same time that Swaggart was highly critical of Jim Bakker for the latter's lustful encounter with Jessica Hahn. In retaliation, Gorman (after winning a $1.85 million lawsuit for defamation against Swaggart) had private investigators photograph Swaggart leaving a cheap New Orleans motel with his own prostitute. Swaggart was ordered by his Assemblies of God denomination to desist from active ministry for one year as punishment. He refused and quite the Assemblies of God (Matthews, 1998; Martz and Carroll, 1988: 13).

There were other smaller, regional scandals, such as the trio of Dallas, Texas-based televangelists Larry Lea, W. V. Grant, Jr., and Robert Tilton, who were exposed as fraudulent fundraisers (ABC, 1991), to name a few more. Thus, within a five-year period, high-profile Protestant evangelists—evangelicals, charismatics, and fundamentalists—and the naive viewers whose money they had based their corrupt ministries upon, had a lot of self-reflecting to do (ultimately, Bakker and Grant only from prison cells).

It was only as Bakker was tried and then sentenced to prison that the economic scale of PTL's massive financial corruption eclipsed his philandering with Hahn. By the twenty first century, an aging Swaggart has made a very modest comeback on television, and his sexual peccadilloes seem a thing of the past to a new, if meager, audience (Matthews, 1998). Tilton, who took his followers' contributions while he tossed their appeals and heart-felt letters away into a dumpster, is still on cable channels, but, like Bakker, a very pale shadow of a once preeminent televangelist.

But during the late 1980s televangelists paraded across television news shows like Ted Koppel's *Nightline* on ABC (the Bakkers were on a record eleven times), and the media reporters, who rarely even watched these mostly conservative evangelical Christian celebrities, were left to ask the public (much of it equally bemused) its reaction to the whole brouhaha.

In a 1987 *New York Times* poll, it was found that 65 percent of Americans held an unfavorable opinion of televangelistics, 73 percent were nonviewers (Clymer, 1987). A *USA Today* poll found 90 percent of Americans disapproved of televangelists' fundraising techniques; 71 percent said they believed the televangelists were really just out to enrich themselves (Kelley, 1987). Worse for television ministers in general, in the 1987 *New York Times* poll, of those who reported having sent money previously to such evangelists 35 percent now expressed unfavorable views about them, and in the *USA Today* poll a little over one-fourth (26 percent) of those having previously contributed said it was unlikely that they would again.

Understandably, Oral Roberts found that towards the end of 1987 his ministry's revenues were off $1.5 million per month, while Jimmy Swaggart saw a *monthly* decline accelerate to $2.5 million (figures which provide some idea of how much pre-scandal tax-free money was being infused into those parachurches).

But the fallout from the scandals began to show up, significantly enough, in some of the larger ministries which had not experienced scandal and/or had absolutely no relation to Roberts, the Bakkers, Swaggart. Jerry Falwell's *Old Time Gospel Hour*, a staple of televangelism with his outspoken political and social conservatism and fundamentalist Baptist theology, reported income losses in 1987 of $2 million per month. Marion G. "Pat" Robertson, at the time a serious candidate for the Republican presidential nomination in 1988, as reported by the *Washington Post* in March, 1987 was having to lay off 470 employees (200 of whom were permanent full-time) from his Christian Broadcasting Network. He forecast on "The 700 Club" program (whether a desperate-sounding plea for continued giving or not) that CBN's revenues were already down $12 million and would probably bottom out at a $28 million loss by year's end. Robertson's push for the presidential nomination suddenly plummeted in public opinion polls (Chandler, 1987). Robertson was quoted as saying: "In the history of American Christianity we have not seen anything like this. The scandal has hit the evangelical world like a bombshell" (*Washington Post*, 1987).

Even the television ministry of Anaheim, California's Dr. Robert Schuller of the Reformed Church, one of the few televangelists with an earned doctorate and who was about as far removed theologically and geographically from the Bakkers, Roberts, Swaggart, and the others as possible, was affected. Arbitron viewer ratings in Spring, 1987 dropped, and Schuller had to lay off 20 percent of the staff of his Sunday program *Hour of Power*. In the process, his ministry lost millions of dollars. In 1987 a *Los Angeles Times* poll concluded that every television preaching personality had lost ground in the arena of public reputation since the scandals. Two years later this was also the assessment of the evangelical

Protestant flagship magazine *Christianity Today* (which had run dozens of news items and some essays on the scandals and their economic-moral implications for Christian stewardship in ministry): "Most religious broadcasters are no longer asking the question of *whether* they've been hurt by scandals within their industry, but of how much" (*Christianity Today*, 1989).

The scandals prompted the National Religious Broadcasters (NRB) professional association to establish its Ethics and Financial Accountability Commission (EFICOM) in January, 1987 and asked the Evangelical Council for Financial Accountability to monitor it. EFICOM's first move after developing a set of financial ethical guidelines was to give NRB members three months to comply or leave the association. Several hundred did.

Ethical guidelines did not prevent later scandals and NRB conflict with the FCC or criticisms of EFICOM's slowness to enforce meaningful audits. Sociologists Jeffrey K. Hadden and Anson Shupe, who at the time were writing *Televangelism: Power and Politics on God's Frontier* about the force of evangelical voters in the coming 1988 presidential election, summed it up:

> This negative image of televangelists did not emerge overnight. . . . But certainly the scandals damaged the credibility of contemporary religious broadcasters, and stereotypes to one side, the negative sentiment was by no means limited to nonviewers" (1988: 16)

And finally, yes, there were plenty of not-so-gentle parodies of the scandals as skits on *Saturday Night Live* and in cartoons, including *"I Am Not A Televangelist!": The Continuing Saga of Reverend Will B. Dunn*, a collection by 1988 Pulitzer Prize winning cartoonist Doug Marlette of the *Atlanta Constitution* (Marlett, 1988; see also Hadden and Shupe, 1988: 6).

Meanwhile, millions of sincere viewers over some years sent these video grifters and hypocrites many more millions of dollars to subsidize their shenanigans. The electronic religious frauds were classic examples of affinity corporate crime, complete with accessories after the fact on ministry "supervisory" boards and behind the scenes acting in the sycophant role during the televangelistic excesses.

Fallout from the First Wave of Roman Catholic Scandals (1986-1998)

For the past thirty years E. Burke Rochford, Jr., professor of sociology and anthropology at Middlebury College, has followed the fortunes of the International Society for Krishna Consciousness (Hare Krishnas) in North America as well as worldwide. He is the leading expert on that Hindu sect's episodic clergy malfeasance since its founder, A. C. Bhaktivedanta Swami Prabhupada, died in 1977. The charismatic leader left an incompletely determined line of guru succession, and particularly during the 1980s there emerged exposures of (and arrests and imprisonments due to) leadership involvement in pedophilia, adultery, homosexuality, drug running and possession, directing rival guru murders, and murders of dissenters (Rochford, 1998). All the ingredients for sensational scandal were there.

But aside from scholars in religious studies (such as Melton, 1986: 241-63) and social scientists engaged in the arcane pursuit of new religious movements as well as relatively few investigative journalists (such as Hubner and Grusan, 1988), the scandals mostly never reached above the radar line of mass media in the U.S. (except locally where Krishna members were clustered, as in West Virginia, and parts of Texas and California). Most editors and reporters ignored the events or dismissively concluded they were unworthy of much attention because they occurred in some Asia-based cult. Ironically, about the same time (and even some years earlier) thousands of young persons were being quietly victimized by more mainline Roman Catholic priests. Soon it was becoming known regionally, nationally, and even internationally—beginning in 1985 with the Father Gilbert Gauthe scandals in Louisiana—as the greatest religious scandal of modern times. This tapered down (but never completely tapered off) by 1998.

Enough has been covered in previous chapters concerning the stellar Catholic clerical deviants in the First Wave (i.e., the Porters, Holleys, and others). The media reaction, too, has been summarized: the majestic tradition of the Roman Catholic institution and its history in the U.S. simply proved overwhelming for many editors and journalists. Hence, they were unprepared to interpret the rash of scandals as anything more than episodic in the "few bad apples" perspective. A larger, systematic cover-up, both in this country and elsewhere, by church oligarchs was unthinkable.

But the polls showed what Catholics in particular were thinking about the shocking revelations. On August 10, 1997, a USA Today/CNN/Gallup national poll of 788 U.S. Catholics reported that, by a margin of 2 to 1, respondents believed that church officials conducted themselves during the scandals as if they cared more for public relations and church image than doing anything meaningful to solve the problem of clergy sexual misconduct. A total of 53 percent said the bishops had done a bad job of handling the abuse scandals, with only 35 percent saying the church had done a good job; 64 percent responded that the church was more concerned with salvaging its reputation; 58 percent said they would not accept an offending priest assigned to their parish even if he had undergone treatment for his problem (*USA Today*/CNN/Gallup Poll, 1993).

Newsweek magazine conducted a poll in summer, 1993 finding that two-thirds of the American Catholics sampled thought their church had treated abusive priests "too leniently" in the past and that such troubled priests posed a serious problem. Defrocking and expulsion from the ministry, not counseling (and retention), was their preferred solution (Press, et al., 1993). Likewise, a NBC poll announced on the *NBC Nightly News* program one year earlier had found *in the general population* that 63 percent of those sampled answered negatively to the question, "Is the Church doing enough?" and 61 percent believed that such abuse happened often. The latter statistic was an indicator that not only Catholics were attending to the spectacle (NBC News, 1992).

In 1992 the priest-psychologist Stephen J. Rossetti directed a study based on 1,810 completed questionnaires of mostly (85 percent) active North American laypeople but including 797 respondents in religious vocations (314 priests and also sisters, brothers, deacons, and others). The sample was drawn from the mailing list of Twenty-Third Publications in Mystic, Connecticut, which prints books and other materials of interest to Catholics. When asked if "my diocese has been affected by a case(s) of a priest sexually abusing children" and if "a priest in my parish has been accused," 35 percent of the 1,013 lay respondents answered "No" to both questions, 55 percent said their diocese had been affected (but their own parish priest had not been accused), and 10 percent said they had experienced their own parish priest being charged with sexual abuse. A total of 58 percent felt the church was not dealing adequately with the abuse problem, and 62 percent said they had not been adequately informed by the church hierarchy of what was happening. Even more, 70 percent, said they wanted the problem dealt with openly and not concealed.

The trust issue was significant in Rossetti's survey. In *parishes* where a priest had been charged with sexual abuse, only 44 percent of the lay respondents felt priests could be trusted. The situation was only relatively better among respondents further removed from actual first-hand knowledge of local scandal: 48 percent in *dioceses* where scandal cases had occurred felt priests could be trusted, and only 59 percent affirmed their trust in dioceses where *no* such scandals had occurred. The "clincher" question dealt with whether or not respondents would allow a son or daughter to go on vacation with a priest. Of those with scandals experienced at diocesan or parish levels, 43 percent gave an "unqualified" yes response. Of those with a priest scandal in their diocese, only 33 percent said "yes," and of those who had witnessed a parish priest charged, only 26 percent responded affirmatively (Rossetti, 1996: 24-44).

By June, 1993 editors of *The Missing Link* newsletter of Chicago-based The Linkup (one of the first national AAVM groups), could take some bittersweet satisfaction in such lay acceptance of leadership complicity and awareness of the priest abuse problem. They wrote:

> The earth may be moving! God knows, we've been churning it enough! (Miller and Kagan, 1993)

One of the reasons internal to the Roman Catholic Church, of course, was the enormous financial burden imposed by victim lawsuits against it during the early 1990s. A perusal of the Associated Press and other sources of these reported lawsuits by 1993, for example, shows the Archdiocese of Chicago having spent $2.8 million on cases (while running a $4.5 million deficit); the Archdiocese of Santa Fe begging parishes for cash as it dealt with dozens of lawsuits that could run costs as high as $50 million and force the archdiocese to file for Chapter 11 bankruptcy relief; the Diocese of Lafayette, Louisiana, where the First Wave of scandals started with Father Gilbert Gauthe had already paid anywhere from $5 million to $10 million; the Diocese of Camden, New Jersey, where nine priests ran up complaints by nineteen men and women to a cost of $3.2 million; or the Archdiocese of Milwaukee, which had set aside $2 million for anticipated settlements over its scandals but was now looking at over half a million dollars more in costs. There were a number of other local scandals and payments of a smaller variety, i.e., $100,000 or less here and there. (See Shupe, 1995: 92-4 for a brief review of such "bargaining" or utilitarian strategies by the church during the early 1990s.)

In some cases, like the Santa Fe Archdiocese, several insurance companies sued the archdiocese in federal court, claiming negligence when the church oversaw the reassignments of known pedophile priests to parishes at the same time they were patients at the Servants of the Paraclete treatment facility. The archdiocese countersued the companies in state court alleging broken contracts and further complicating an embarrassing moral and legal fiduciary mess (Owren, 1994).

Worse, some priests began accusing other priests of past abuses, as occurred in Belleville, Illinois in 1994. There nine priests left their parishes while under investigation for sexually molesting youths. But of the thirty-nine persons claiming to be victims, three were themselves currently priests (Associated Press, 1994). And a spokesperson in the AAVM accused some in the church hierarchy of trying to turn general lay opinion against victims. Frank Martinelli, co-chair of the Wisconsin Action Network for Survivors of Clergy Abuse, wrote in the Stamford, Connecticut *Advocate*:

> Church leaders, in some instances, are tacitly encouraging a backlash against the victims of clergy abuse. In the absence of strong statements of support from the church for the victims, the shock of parishioners who hear allegations of abuse against a trusted priest quickly turns to anger against the victims. (Martinelli, 1993)

Meanwhile, daily life became more complicated for the majority of non-deviant clergy who encountered a new atmosphere—no matter how rarified in parishes with no prior molestation problems—of wariness, both on the part of parishioners toward the once automatically assumed sacrosanct clergy person and by clergy themselves in a sort of preemptive self-defense. It also spread to Protestant leaders who were learning harsh lessons from watching the Catholic Church's experience (See, e.g., Shupe, 1995: 102-3). As one *Chicago Tribune* reporter summed it up:

> As the number of sex abuse charges against the clergy grows, some priests and ministers are becoming reluctant to touch, counsel, hug, or even be alone with members of their congregations. Church leaders have sent directives telling their clergy to be exceptionally careful in being alone with women or children. Priests and ministers are advised to keep their office doors open, even when discussing private matters, or to replace solid wood doors with those with windows so someone can always see into the office. (Griffin, 1993)

To be sure, during this First Wave of sex abuse accusations there were some "bright lights" of acquittal and reconciliation for leaders. Some were local and exiguously reported. A church deacon in Jackson, Michigan at the North Sharon Baptist Church was acquitted of raping three boys in a church washroom and during campouts. The accusation appeared to have been the result of community fear and hysteria in the vein of the adolescent girls' reckless denunciations of mostly elderly citizens during the Salem, Massachusetts witch-scare of the 1680s (*Chicago Tribune*, 1993).

Some cases were more visible and attracted national attention, if only for a while. The most famous of these was that of Chicago's Cardinal Joseph Bernardin, who was once considered a possible candidate for pope.

The cardinal was generally considered an affable man if only grudgingly accepting that his church fiefdom, like many others in the U.S., had a serious problem within its clergy ranks. In early 1992, after much hounding by AAVM groups like The Linkup and SNAP, the prelate appointed a three-person commission (that included a judge and a social worker from outside the ecclesiastical bureaucracy) to examine several decades of lay accusations of priest sexual abuse. They scanned the personnel files of 2,252 priests serving the archdiocese since 1963 and found the cases of thirty-nine priests against whom there were credible complaints. In response, the cardinal created a twenty-four-hour toll-free telephone hotline within the archdiocese with a nine-person review board (including a clinical psychologist, psychiatrist, social worker, lawyer, a computer programmer, and three priests) which could make preliminary decisions on temporarily removing accused priests for further investigation within forty-eight hours of receiving complaints. In addition, Bernardin instructed there to be a reconsideration of recruiting and professional training of seminarians (Steinfels, 1992).

With general goodwill and a proactive record in the abuse matter, it is therefore an understatement to say that an accusation against Bernardin himself of committing sexual abuse in earlier days was a bombshell both staggering and initially horrific to Catholics and non-Catholics alike. On November 12, 1993 a thirty-four year-old gay man, Steven Cook, was dying of AIDS and came forward to allege that while he was a high school student preparing for seminary some fifteen years earlier in Cincinnati, he had been molested by a priest. Moreover, he maintained that during a liaison he had been sodomized by the then-Archbishop of Cincinnati Joseph Bernardin. The Ohio statue of limitation had run out, but Cook only came forward (he claimed) after he had received hypnotic counseling that unlocked repressed memories of the sexual exploitation. Cook claimed he had suffered the effects of the abuse after high school in ways such as homosexual promiscuity and drug use. He retained a lawyer and sued Bernardin, the other priest (who, along with Bernardin, denied it all), and the Cincinnati Archdiocese for $12 million.

The Cable News Network (CNN), in hindsight probably precipitously, aired repeatedly that day a much advertised hour-long interview with Cook in a special reported entitled "Fall from Grace" (into which the network quickly edited bits of Cook's interview). The broadcast was a shocker, and Chicago's media witnessed its own feeding frenzy that lasted, on and off, for over a year before the suit against Bernardin was dropped.

The case is instructive for the curvilinear trajectory of reaction to a local scandal. From the beginning, Bernardin took the high road by maintaining his complete innocence. He stated, "I've led a chaste life" (Hirsley, 1993a). Bernardin even expressed compassion for the ailing Cook, prayed for him, and offered to travel to Cincinnati to meet with him (Hirsley and Carlozo, 1993). Though no one in the Cincinnati hierarchy admitted any wrongdoing, the archdiocese offered to pay Cook's medical bills (Associated Press, 1993).

But quickly the strength of the Cook accusation began to crack. Cook's claim that he only recently recalled this sex abuse in 1993 under therapy contradicted a 1985 statement he made to Philadelphia police about having suffered priest abuse (Crawford and Carlozo, 1993). By spring, 1994 Cook had announced that he was no longer so confident in the reliability of those "repressed memories" as he initially had been. It began to look increasingly like he had been the victim of so-called "repressed memories" being suggested to him in a dubious new form of therapy under criticism at the time. For example, one psychiatrist opined in the *Los Angeles Times* that there were pressures for faster, more cost-effective treatments that were increasingly resulting in pseudo-recovered memories (Metzner, 1993). Garry Wills, a noted Catholic historian, also warned that such repressed memories were legally not testable and a problematic way to help an adult cope with current problems, and they also might commit an injustice against someone unfairly accused (1993).

The CNN story quickly fell under attack by fellow professionals. The national Catholic biweekly *Commonweal* denounced "Fall from Grace" in a 1993 editorial, calling it "cheap-shot journalism" and trading on the lurid prospect of a churchman with a sterling reputation being a closet homosexual:

> CNN failed. Its story is not enterprising; it was mostly a rehash. . . . It was . . . unfair and unprofessional. In no small measure, it depended on the now almost pervasive view that the Catholic church, along with other groups who defend culturally conservative values—especially in matters sexual, reproductive, and familial— is fair game for public pilloring. (*Commonweal*, 1993)

As the CNN report unraveled, in the eyes of many Bernardin was lionized as a local leader above the fray, a man with dignity and "class" (Hirsley, 1993b). A backlash against the allegations emerged, newsworthy of its own accord, and perhaps part of a general discomfort with the entire First Wave of frenzied clergy malfeasance allegations. Some Chicago talk shows became defensive of Bernardin, a local personality maligned by outsiders. Callers on talk shows to which I personally listed in 1993 referred to Steven Cook as a liar motivated only by greed. One *Chicago Tribune* editorial was entitled "Bernardin Bears His Cross." That same day another "coincidentally timed" editorial extolled the importance to the city of Catholic schools (Bryk, 1993). Chicagoans began to pull together behind "their" cardinal. One Chicago freelance journalist, Jim Bowman, wrote in his "Report from Chicago" column for *Commonweal*: "Chicago is 99 percent behind Bernardin, and you know about the 1 percent only spectrally" (Bowman, 1993: 6). *Chicago Tribune* religion writer Michael Hirsley entitled his column "Bernardin Shows All How to React" only one week after Cook's allegation surfaced (Hirsley, 1993b). Even Barbara Blaine, head of the Chicago-based AAVM group SNAP, was quoted as saying: "He has set a perfect example of how to respond to allegations. He had aggressively defended himself without attacking victims" (Bowman, 1993: 6).

Within a relatively short time, the accusations were basically rescinded by Cook who shortly thereafter died of AIDS. Some time later, Bernardin announced he was diagnosed with terminal pancreatic cancer and made a graceful peace with Chicago and the public before he passed away. It was an apparent case of false accusation, a terrible (if brief) journey for the cardinal to endure, and a temporary respite from the otherwise non-stop shocking revelations of real elite malfeasance only tapering off during the mid to late 1990s.

Fallout from the Second Wave of Roman Catholic Scandals (2002-Present)

Some portion of this volume's conceptual substance, if certainly not all its examples, has been in response to the Second Wave of priest pedophilia scandals which reawakened public awareness about such malfeasance after the 2002 Boston uproar. Even though A. W. Richard Sipe had warned Catholics, in his 1990 book entitled *A Secret World,* that a significant number of their leaders were not celibate, the media feeding frenzy of 2002 touched every corner of North America with accounts of similar priest malfeasance and bishopric cover-up. The United States Conference of Catholic Bishops' halting remedial steps only added to the sensation.

Enough cases and examples of this wave have already been cited to provide a background. There were still the anomalous occurrences, such as an Indiana order of Franciscan friars suing the Los Angeles Archdiocese for sending a pedophile priest to them without warning and the Diocese of San Bernardino suing the Archdiocese of Boston for the same reason (Associated Press, 2003). Also, there were polls aplenty, both of the stalwart faithful and of the angry and disillusioned. A 2002 *Los Angeles Times* poll of Catholic clergy nationwide found "deep-seated anger" at both the bishops and in some cases the media. Wrote a *LA Times* journalist:

> In written comments submitted with their poll responses, many priests expressed the view that the bishops delayed dealing with the crisis and thus compounded the problem by adopting a "zero tolerance" policy, the Charter for the Protection of Children and Young People, that denies accused clerics their rights to due process (Stammer, 2002).

More than three out of five priests surveyed said they believed most of the allegations against fellow priests were true; 53 percent thought the church had been too lenient with their errant fellows; and 73 percent also thought the media had been too negative. Meanwhile, two teenage females did their own non-scientific survey of Catholic youths through the Indianapolis Archdiocesan Youth Council (in a city which has had its own share of deviant religious tumult) and concluded: "Despite the recent media coverage of some priests' prurient behaviors, many young Catholics remain dedicated to their faith and unwavering in their support of their clergy" (Bieseckert and Smith, 2003).

But the reams of remaining issues of the Second Wave are not with public opinion but with financial ramifications—insurers' hesitation at paying hefty settlements and lay financial giving to the church.

Insurers' Hesitation

Earlier in this chapter, the scenarios of the Archdiocese of Santa Fe being sued in federal court by its insurance carriers for negligence in allowing known clerical predators to continue in active ministry, and the archdiocese in turn countersuing the carriers, was mentioned. Such cases were quintessential and legion during the Second Wave.

It had come up before. In 1990, during the crest of the First Wave, the Minnesota Archdioceses of St. Paul/Minneapolis and Winona faced a civil judgment of more than $1 million created by a sexual abuse case involving a minor during the 1970s. When these two archdioceses expected their general liability policies to cover the expenses, they were met with refusal. Since the offending priest possessed a fifteen-year history of serial abuse, and that was known to the respective hierarchical superiors, they should have expected more abuse incidents and thus violated their policies by negligence. The archdioceses spent six years in court, finally reaching the 8th U.S. Circuit Court of Appeals only to find ultimately that they—not the insurance companies—should pay the judgment. In the words of the *Washington Post's* Edward Walsh, the case "was in many ways a harbinger of the problems the Catholic Church would face" (Walsh, 2002).

The Archdiocese of Milwaukee likewise sued fourteen insurance companies in 1994, the latter refusing to make payments in nine cases involving pastoral sexual misconduct. The insurers argued that the church hierarchs knew of the abuses but failed to take appropriate actions, saying "the misconduct was intentional and thus not covered by existing policies. In its suit the archdiocese demanded not only compensatory damages to pay the settlement for the nine cases but also punitive damages for breach of contract" (*Citizen-Journal*, 1994). The courts were not impressed.

The Protestant denominations, with their own scandals during the period of the First Wave, encountered that same insurance problem. In 1994, journalist Jenny Owren wrote interdenominationally concerning sexual abuse by pastors and the coming insurance crisis for churches:

> Some religious and mental health officials are concerned that as insurers take an increasingly hard-line approach to settling lawsuits or renewing liability coverage, abusive clergy seeking help and their victims will be forsaken. . . . For local churches of all denominations, the bottom line is often rising insurance costs and limited or no coverage for clergy sexual abuse. (1994)

One president of an Albuquerque, New Mexico insurance company felt that the particularly acute payment crisis in that state made it difficult, if not financially unfeasible, for churches to buy general church insurance (and downright impossible to acquire pastoral coverage). He told Owren, "We don't want to cover churches. The lawsuits are causing a ripple effect throughout insurance companies that insure churches" (Owren, 1994). As a result of such issues, even the evangelical magazine *Christianity Today* featured an article that bluntly considered, "Will Your Church Be Sued?" (Taylor, 1997).

During the Second Wave insurance costs, risk, and denial of coverage were an even more palpable concern for Catholic and Protestant leaders. In 2004, after the Boston Archdiocese's much publicized $85 million settlement with 522 clergy sex abuse victims, the Lumbermens Mutual Casualty Company refused to pay the damages on the grounds that the church's settlement arrangement was a "voluntary payment" to which Lumbermens was not obligated to contribute. The archdiocese alternately maintained that $59.3 million of that settlement was covered by a period of time when Lumbermens was that archdiocese's sole insurer. And there was another $1.7 million from a period when Lumbermens' coverage overlapped with that of another insurer. Soon the Kemper Insurance Cos. group, Lumbermens' lead underwriter, became involved, and a litigious battle repeated many times elsewhere was underway (*Fort Wayne Journal Gazette*, 2004).

One solid, interdenominational look at this insurance crisis was made by journalist Sherry Slater of the *Fort Wayne Journal Gazette* in 2002. This investigation was *apropos* since that mid-western city has long been a national center of life insurance (and similar) companies. Slater provided an important reminder against any consideration of church insurance risks: the September 22, 2001 terrorist attacks in New York City affected the *reinsurance* industry (which sells policies to various insurance companies to cover *their* risks in the event of really large claims) across the nation. An estimate $60 billion was paid in insurance settlements because of 9/11, and those payments, along with sexual molestations by church fiduciaries, were major factors in more recent church insurance rates. Still, as she discovered, deviant religious leaders contributed their fair share by 2002.

For example, North Carolina-based Christian Ministry Resources conducts annual surveys and has found occurrences of child abuse in virtually all religious denominations, averaging seventy allegations per week. (CMR is a tax and legal advice publisher that serves more than 75,000 congregations.) It found that generally local congregations were paying more in 2002 than ever before to protect themselves from the fiscal devastation caused by pastor misbehavior. The Fort Wayne-based Brotherhood Mutual Insurance Company, one of the U.S.' three primary insurers of approximately 330,000 Protestant Churches, was licensed in 2002 in 49 states, which it did to about 30,000 churches and various ministry clients. Accusations of child molestation by pastors in various denominations (not least of all the Catholic Church),

> have halted Brotherhood Mutual's coverage of more than $1 million, so-called excess coverage. After September 11, reinsurance companies quit underwriting excess coverage policies for sexual acts.

As a result, Brotherhood Mutual sells basic coverage as an option for $300,000 on top of its commercial property and liability policy. A local church can qualify to raise its coverage to a limit of $1 million if it pays higher premiums and demonstrates it has a strong screening program for both staff workers and volunteers. Church Mutual, based in Merrill, Wisconsin, offers basic coverage ranging from $300,000 to $500,000 and even up to $1 million if a church can pass an underwriter's review (similar to what Brotherhood Mutual requires). In 2002, Church Mutual insured 75,000 churches but would not offer excess coverage for pastor sexual malfeasance (Slater, 2002). Meanwhile, in 2003 *Christianity Today* presented as a feature article an interview with a tax/law expert on the same liability issue (Hammer, 2003).

Five years later the insurance situation was the same. The three largest national insurance companies for churches—Church Mutual Insurance Co., GuideOne Insurance Co., and (again) Fort Wayne's Brotherhood Mutual Insurance Co.—handle about 224,000 Protestant churches in the United States. By 2007 Church Mutual and Brotherhood Mutual were able to offer statistics on claims. Church Mutual reported receiving an average of 100 sex abuse cases per year involving minors at the hands of clergy over the past decade. GuideOne said it had received an average of 160 reports of sex abuse against minors every year for the past decade. And Brotherhood Mutual relayed the information that it had received an average of 73 new reports of child sex abuse and other misconduct by clergy for each of the past fifteen years. Spokespersons for the three companies agreed the most claims are settled privately and rarely make the media reports (French, 2007).

To be sure, Catholic bishops were not passive in the face of enormous victim lawsuits and insurers' hesitation. They challenged through diocesan lawyers victims' claims and resisted prosecutors' demands for personnel files and clerics' testimonies. Mark Chopko, general counsel for the U.S. Conference of Catholic Bishops, said that about one thousand persons had made new claims against the church just in 2003, and attorneys for the church had an obligation to distinguish legitimate claims from those otherwise (Zoll, 2003g). In this sense, lawyers for the church and insurers' legal representatives became allies, for many insurance contracts require a "vigorous" defense that can include examining on the witness stand victims' sexual and religious histories, hiring private investigators, and other intrusive investigations that may seem harmful to victims (not to say unpastoral) and their sympathizers. It is not surprising that the hoary matter of the constitutional separation of church and state was often dragged into the courtroom (often unsuccessfully) as one defense tactic for contesting claims, at least delaying procedures and even creating legal precedents (Zoll, 2003g).

But what recourse do large religious institutions have when finally confronting huge legal settlements (and insurers are hedging) due to clergy malfeasance? The Roman Catholic Church's answer is three-fold: take out loans, sell off assets, or declare bankruptcy:

- The Diocese of Santa Rosa, California had a $16 million debt from priest sexual misconduct cases and sold property as well as took out bank loans (and solicited donations) of at least $7 million;
- the Diocese of Dallas, Texas, hit hard by the depredations of the Reverend Rudy Kos, mortgaged and sold property to cover the $11 million in a $30 million victim settlement not covered by insurers;
- the Diocese of Tucson, Arizona, where four priests were accused of pedophilia and there was an undisclosed financial settlement, claimed it would have to borrow from a bank or parish accounts to cover the remaining uninsured costs;
- otherwise, from Boston to various dioceses in California, parish schools closed, charitable services cut back, and Catholic lay populations faced increasingly frequent, even desperate appeals for cash. (Zoll, 2003f)

Bankruptcy, which occurred in the dioceses of Portland (OR), Tucson (AZ), San Diego (CA), Davenport (IA), and Spokane (WA), is a third option. The Catholic Church insider authors Doyle, Sipe, and Wall have clearly resented what they regard as the disingenuous manner in which bishops presented this final option to laity, i.e., as if such a drastic step was ultimately the result of money-hungry victims drove further than necessary by equally greedy attorneys:

> Church officials claim their good faith offers of generous settlements have been rejected, leaving them no choice but to file for bankruptcy. They obviously hope to turn public opinion against the clergy abuse victims. Yet by trying to portray the victims and their attorneys as money-grubbers, diocesan officials are denying the reality that the vast majority of victims have shown over and over again, that it's not the money they're after, but justice. (Doyle, Sipe, and Wall, 2006: 257)

These authors name names in pointing out how the Roman Catholic hierarchy's spokespersons have hired expensive public relations firms to spin the victim abuse problems and reframe *themselves* as victims. For example, the Los Angeles Archdiocese used, following its own twenty first century scandals, Michael Sitrick and Associates, the same firm that represented Enron, the troubled Charles Keating of savings and loans fraud fame, and various actors in the tobacco industry (Doyle, Sipe, and Wall, 2006: 258).

Ultimately, however, the authors regard bankruptcy as a form of dodge to spare open diocesan records during processes of "discovery" from being publicized in civil suits:

> Contrary to the impression some bishops are trying to create, filing for bankruptcy is *not* a last-ditch survival effort on the part of the church. It is a sophisticated way of avoiding more painful revelations about internal corruption and a potential for limiting victims' compensation. (Doyle, Sipe, and Wall, 2006: 259)

Whether or not any church or group is actually brought to its financial knees, however, the truth is that the First Wave of scandals caused instances of diocesan/church clashes with insurance carriers; the Second Wave changed their relationships forever.

Financial Giving

A good measure of the grassroots impact of all this scandal, not just on Roman Catholic laity but also on rank-and-file Protestants, is giving to the collection plate. It is a reasonable question to ask if not just seeing a religious group's public reputation besmirched but also considerable sums of money going toward victim settlement payouts would have an effect on financial donations.

In fact, at times the overall picture is counter-intuitive: parishioners and congregants, seeing a beloved institution financially hurting (for whatever reason) may rally to support it. Consider conservative northeast Indiana, for example, where the flagship Roman Catholic institution of higher education, the University of Notre Dame, is located. It was reported in 2003 by Joe Ryan, chief financial officer of the Fort Wayne-South Bend Roman Catholic Diocese, that despite all the national scandals (and a few local) as well as a stagnant economy for the lower and middle classes, church-goers donated $1.3 million *more* to local churches than in 2002. Moreover, the sixteenth annual Bishop's Appeal (which is a fund-raising drive collecting money for priests' retirement and recruitment, charities, and schools and teachers' salaries) brought in $5.2 million. Ryan summed up his perception of the situation: "People like their priests" (Iacone, 2003).

Still, such figures are totals, of course, and some persons may have been contributing disproportionately more to make up for a possible shortfall caused by those disgruntled and not giving at all. Was this a regional fluke? Thinking about the Rossetti study mentioned earlier in this chapter, does having clergy problems *outside* the perimeters of the local parish or at least not in one's own congregation really affect this average donor?

Two larger studies help provide indications, if not conclusive answers.

Shupe, Stacey, and Darnell (2000) conducted a victimization survey in 1996 of randomly selected urban and suburban neighborhoods in the Dallas-Fort Worth metroplex using the U.S. Census (stratified into high, middle, and low average income levels). Both Protestants (80 percent) and Roman Catholics (20 percent) were represented. One major hypothesis related to financial giving was disconfirmed: financial giving did *not* decline with increased awareness of clergy malfeasance at either local or national levels. Interestingly the researchers initially supposed that Roman Catholics would be more aware of clergy abuse than Protestants given the extraordinary amount of media coverage of the Roman Catholic pedophile scandals during the First Wave. But it was the Protestants, not the Catholics, who were more aware of the minister misconduct. Moreover, in that group *as the awareness of clergy scandals at either the local or the national levels increased, contributions also increased* (Shupe, Stacey, and Darnell, 2000: 236-7). On the point of the sampled respondents who reported they had personally been abused physically, sexually, or intimidated, they were asked, "Did the abuse result in stopping your donations or financial gifts to the ministry?" A total of half of the twenty-four persons indicated they had stopped attending and/or stopped giving money to the given ministry (pp. 221-2). But that small figure only represents *direct* experience and perception of victimization, not simply general awareness of the problem.

As another example from that Texas study, among respondents who said they had never heard or read about clergy abuse, about nine percent made financial contributions to radio and television ministers. Among respondents who claimed to hear or read frequently of ministerial abuse through the local media (and there had been a number of sensational regional cases during that decade in Texas, not to mention the televangelist scandals) 21 percent said they had nevertheless made financial contributions to radio or television ministers. Thus, the implication is that awareness or even experience of abuse at the hands of a pastor is not a good predictor of decline in religious donor behavior.

Pursuing the post-2002 Boston scandal implications for Catholic giving at parish/diocesan/national church levels, we can make use of the 2002 FADICA(Foundations and Donors Interested in Catholic Activities, Inc.)-Gallup-Zech Study with a national sample of 1,001 Catholic respondents. The study was sponsored by FADICA along with the George Gallup Organization and Charles E. Zech of Villanova University (hereafter, FADICA, 2002). Its findings suggest that post-2002 Boston scandals financial perceptions and actual giving among Catholic laypersons are not uniform:

- Less than half (45 percent) of the regular church-attending Catholics rated their bishops high on financial stewardship;
- approximately two-thirds agreed that their church should be more financially accountable and that the costs of priestly sexual abuse were a source of concern;
- two-thirds (68 percent) desired an independent, publicly released audit of finances at parish, diocesan, and national levels;
- 79 percent respondents wanted each diocesan bishop to reveal publicly the financial details of settlements after sexual abuse lawsuits;
- more than half (55 percent) were afraid the costs of such settlements would curtail the church's overall charitable, educational, and evangelistic missions.

Most interesting for the old attitudes-versus-behavior divide in social psychology, the majority of respondents said they wanted more diocesan alternatives for Catholic contributions and indicated they would reduce giving if it was learned that their contributions were going to payout settlements to sex abuse victims. *Yet* relatively few parishioners contacted had actually acted on these sentiments. Within the sample, 6 percent of respondents had stopped giving to their parishes, 13 percent stopped donating to diocesan collections, and 18 percent ceased sending money to national collections. *Any financial protest declined the closer the question reached at the local church community level.* Indeed, 87 percent of the regular-attending Catholics had made no changes in contributing at the parish level, 79 percent had not changed their contributions to diocesan causes, and 80 percent had similarly not changed giving habits concerning national causes.

Thus, there is no simple unidirectional effect of clergy scandals on financial giving that can be discovered at this time. Despite some post-2002 Boston scandal concerns about the financial stewardship of leaders (as with the Catholics) or enhanced pre-2002 awareness of the clergy malfeasance problem (as with the Protestants), such factors did not automatically translate into a decline in giving. In fact, giving seems to have remained reasonably constant, sometimes increased if anything. Perhaps members rallied in defense of their local churches and church traditions, perceiving scandals as the result of a cruel, secular media, or they might have adopted the "few bad apples in the barrel" rationalization. Certainly all the evidence in this chapter points to the pattern that scandal in one's local church or parish, i.e., the membership unit with which most persons most readily identify, has the most impact. Overall, giving after the scandals seems to have remained reasonably constant, sometimes increased. The financial contribution process after two un-precedented national religious crises appeared resilient.

From Feeding Frenzy to Counterreformation

Writing about the 1960s and 1970s when the context of social move-ment mobilization differed dramatically from conditions of the twenty first century, sociologist Jo Freeman observed:

> Enormous resources are required to reach, let alone mobilize, aggrieved groups that are atomized and scattered throughout the population. Those that are concentrated can be mobilized fairly easily, which is one reason why students are so readily available to so many movements. (1979: 176)

As we have seen, the availability of the internet changed all that. Potential activists today need not be as clustered geographically as they were during the minority rights/environmental/anti-war protests of that earlier era. The struggling AAVM groups during the First Wave of Catholic priest scandals, which depended on long distance telephone, conventional mail, Xerox machines, faxes and modems took more than a decade to achieve less national mobilization than have the post-2002 Second Wave scandal-driven groups (like Voice of the Faithful) in a single year. Today anyone with computer access is automatically included in the pool of potential activists and sympathizers.

Likewise, aggrieved victims in desperate Protestant denominations can more readily find solace and common cause electronically on websites within individual faith communities. For example, at a West African boarding school in Mamou, Guinea, where Presbyterian missionary parents placed their children while in the field, sexual and physical abuses occurred at the hands of caretakers during 1950-1971. Victims, now-adults in 2002, could find each other for potential activism at www.mksafetynet.ejb.net. Here they could find lists of recent newspaper articles and relevant books, a statement of core values, policies to be implemented in reporting and dealing with child abuse, related internet AAVM links, correspondence, a site map, and so forth. At present, they have had over 11,000 "hits." Similarly, at the website www.reformation. com, Protestant volunteers have been compiling information on their own brand of Christian victims of clerical sexual abuse. Created during the late 1990s, by Fall 2006 the website had received well over 13,000 "hits" and listed over 838 cases including ministers, priests, and miscellaneous fiduciaries of Baptist, Episcopalian, Lutheran, Methodist, Presbyterian, and independent/charismatic churches listed totally by denomination as well as individually.

To be sure, part of the recent upsurge in AAVM mobilization is due to a shift in the media attention to clergy malfeasance. As Berry and Renner (2004: 73) describe journalists reporting on the first Wave of Catholic priest molestations during the mid-1980s to 1990s:

> The coverage of clergy sex abuse by the major Eastern dailies was marked by a reaction to events rather than well-planned investigative work. Talk shows led by Phil Donahue and Geraldo Rivera were in the forefront of covering the issue.

Even Diane Sawyer's pioneering *Prime Time Live* reporting at the time of Father James Porter (ABC, 1992) dealt with the abuse as a regional (New England) scandal, not a national crisis. It was as if there was a widespread skepticism or even disbelief that a religious institution with such a reputation for charity, education, and other good works could possess anything more than a very limited rogue element and secrecy obsession among a minority of clergy who did such heinous things to an entire class of victims. Accordingly, while there were some full-time religious news writers and criminal investigative reporters, such as at the *Boston Globe*, who had the backgrounds and sustained focus to follow stories over time, many reporters were pulled off their usual general beats and thrown into covering an unfamiliar subculture for what was considered to be a short-run, if sensational, phenomenon.

Thus, social movements of the twenty first century, unlike their counterparts in the latter half of the twentieth century, have possessed a greater savvy in their movement strategies concerning organizational communications, which in turn affects coalescing of movement ideology. Consider the following quote, again from sociologist Freeman, writing about the issue of resource mobilization with another generation's student movements in mind (and substitute *religious* for political): "Finding leverage points within the political system generally requires some intimate knowledge of its workings and so is an alternative available only to those not totally alienated from it" (1979: 185). The current counterreformation already has those "insider" activist-critics, from Lavina F. Anderson and Michael Quinn in the LDS Church, to the more outspoken Catholics such as the AAVM groups described above, from activist spokespersons like Barbara Blaine and David McCholessey, to knowledgeable authors like Jason Berry, Garry Wills, A. W. Richard Sipe, Andrew M. Greeley, and Thomas P. Doyle.

The effects of clergy scandals in the U.S.' largest and most visible Christian denomination (but also for Protestant ones on a smaller scale, I would argue) can be visualized over time as two curvilinear relation-

Figure 3
Late Twentieth Century

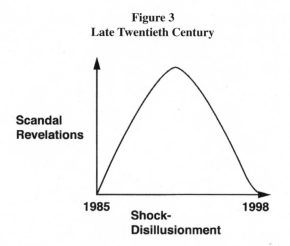

ships. Figure 3 illustrates the relationship between scandal revelations and laity/public disillusionment during the First Wave period from 1985 until the mid- to late-1990s. It resembles what statisticians call a "normal" or bell curve. Figure 4 illustrates the same variables' relationship following 2002 to the present. In Figure 4, the curve is not only skewed heavily along the left axis, but the curve displays more of a gradual slope toward the present time. Here the abrupt media feeding frenzy may have subsided, the initial shock dissipated and some desensitization crept in, but now the media (as well as many congregants) are more vigilant and mindful of possible recurrences.

Figure 4
Early Twenty-First Century

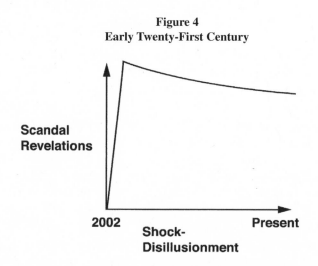

And there is an enervating function performed by such media attention for many activists in seeing sacred institutions struggling to implement counterreformation even as they try to save face. As sociologist Harvey Molotch has observed, in members' eyes, media coverage, consistent or frenzied, can

> enliven the movement and increase morale. . . . there is a special euphoria that comes from seeing in mass media the results of their own actions. It provides for a sense of dignity and effectiveness—regardless of the type of coverage received. (1979: 32-3)

But perhaps a less visible, more corrosive effect is not enervating and does not result in a coordinated social movement, which should give observes pause to believe that the worst effects of the Second Wave (or any other wave) of scandals are over. In a rare introspective look at his personal reaction to reporting on the 2007 Los Angeles Archdiocese scandals and $660 million claims settlement, *L.A. Times* religion journalist William Lobdell wrote of his adult conversion to, and then disillusionment with, Roman Catholicism and its leaders' handling of the clergy malfeasance issue:

> When editors at the Los Angeles Times assigned me to the religion beat, I believed God had answered my prayers.
> As a serious Christian, I had cringed at some of the coverage in the mainstream media. Faith frequently was treated like a circus, even a freak show. I wanted to report objectively and respectfully about how belief shapes people's lives. Along the way, I believed, my own faith would grow deeper.
> But during the eight years I covered religion, something very different happened.

Lobdell dug into his new assignment enthusiastically, covering human interest stories (Orthodox Jews to Mormons to mundanely heroic acts, such as "the elderly church organist who becomes spiritual mentor to the man who tried to rape, rob, and kill her"). With encouragement from his wife, he converted to Catholicism and threw himself into participating in that denomination as believer and journalist as well. Then in 2002, he began following a Roman Catholic sex scandal. At first he thought the victims could and should get over their past hurts.

> But then I began going over the documents. And interviewing the victims, scores of them. I discovered that the term "sexual abuse" is a euphemism. Most of these children were raped and sodomized by someone they and their family believed was Christ's representative on Earth. That's not something an 8-year-old's mind can process: it forever warps a person's sexuality and spirituality.

Lobdell became more disillusioned with the Church's denials and/or rationalizations alongside its leaders' pious claims for loyalty and obedience.

> Clearly, I saw now that belief in God, no matter how grounded, requires at some
> point a leap of faith. Either you have the gift of faith or you don't. It's not a choice.
> It can't be willed into existence. And there's no faking it if you're honest about the
> state of your soul. (Lobdell, 2007a)

Lobdell went on to follow scandalous details of, among others, a Catholic priest, the Monsignor Michael Harris. It was a classic case. There were repeated church denials by the church even as it appeared that Harris, a parochial high school principal, was a serial molester. As more students stepped forward with accusations and lawsuits, other parents and students rallied behind the priest. In a school rally for Harris they sang "For He's a Jolly Good Fellow" as an airplane overhead towed a banner reading: "We Love Father Harris." Harris' lead defense attorney (predictably) denounced all accusers in the media as "sick individuals." Lobdell, however, found that "church leaders remained silent as the alleged victims were savaged. Some of the diocese's top priests—including the cleric in charge of investigating the accusation—threw a going away party for Harris." (Harris never really admitted his guilt but announced he was taking a leave of absence, reportedly because of stress.)

Lobdell sadly concluded:

> At the time I never imagined Catholic leaders would engage in a widespread practice
> that protected alleged child molesters and belittled the victims. I latched onto the
> explanation that was least damaging to my belief in the Catholic Church—that this
> was an isolated case of a morally corrupt administration. And I was comforted by
> the advice of a Catholic friend: "Keep your eyes on the person nailed to the cross,
> not the priests behind the altar." (Lobdell, 2007b)

Conclusion

I have argued in previous chapters that a counterreformation is underway within some churches, particularly in the more hierarchical ones and not always gracefully or whole-heartedly on the part of leaders. This counterreformation also embraces the various levels of healing needed for individuals, congregations thrown into confusion and/or division, and entire denominations that may be rethinking clerical accountability and lay authority.

Churches are societies written small, susceptible to oligarchic concentration of power that can only be forestalled by vigilance or challenged by the reclamation of democratic rights. This was the message (albeit pessimistic) of Robert Michels. In all this mix, the mass media and victim mobilization play symbiotic roles.

Readers may now see why I did not adopt a more constructionist approach in framing my analysis. It is because the very concept of reactance, as provided by the classical labelists a generation ago, at critical points neglected the factor of power in the process of label attachment. This gives us the best clue as to why clerical secondary deviance could fester as a problem for so long, unapprehended by so many laypersons and outside observers.

For example, in Howard S. Becker's edited volume of essays *The Other Side,* early labeling theorist John I. Kituse (1964: 97) offers two sentences integral to that sub-disciplinary approach. The first statement few sociologists, especially post-modernists, would contest:

> Forms of behavior *per se* do not differentiate deviants from non-deviants; it is the responses of the conventional and conforming members of the society who identify and interpret behavior as deviant which sociologically transform persons into deviants.

However, consider its follow-up sentence (Italics are mine.):

> Thus, in the formulation of deviance proposed here, if the subject observes an individual's behavior *and defines it as deviant but does not accord him differential treatment as a consequence of the definition, the individual is not sociologically deviant.*

In light of the ways in which religious elites generate and sustain privileges of authority *vis-à-vis* laity, the latter statement seems in hindsight either incredibly naive or inapplicable. Clergy are believed to be "called" to their vocations by supra-human agencies; they are venerated for the domestic and financial sacrifices they often undergo in addition to their possession of special wisdom about sacred matters. As has been shown, they have a concomitant power to obfuscate deviance, if not their own than that of others, by denial, the inherent "credibility of office" that adheres to them, or intimidation.

Clergy malfeasance is not about victimless crimes, a category with which constructionists are most comfortable. What if real victims never accept their victimization as "appropriate" or successfully repress their misgivings but are afraid to whistle-blow or are incapable of telling? Are the perpetrators less deviant sociologically because a public reaction wider than the audience of one victim never materialized close to the time of the act? It makes little sense to claim so. That is why an understanding of the current controversies over rogue clerics is served better by political sociology than by the social constructionism now in vogue. As Saint Paul declared to his fellow religionists in 1 Corinthians 4: 20-21, "The kingdom of God is not a matter of talk, but of power."

Thus, the ultimate sociological power of perpetrators is to stifle labels, which is to say they can manage to escape social control. The constructionist approach ignores the eventual possible empowerment of victims to appear with accusations to jumpstart the labeling process even decades after an offense. It is a process that an investigative media and an invigorated victim pool can invent, or reinvent, as needed.

Epilogue:
Waiting for the Next Big Scandal

During the writing of this book in 2006, several colleagues expressed some surprise that I was "helping keep the subject alive." Their line of thought went that the 2002 scandal in the Archdiocese of Boston was mostly over except for some victims' financial settlements, that the United States Conference of Catholic Bishops had "solved their problem," and that the phenomenon I term clergy malfeasance had largely subsided. To be kind, these are social scientists, adept within their own sub-specialties, who know very little of larger organized religion's presence in American society. Had I assumed in 1995 that the "First Wave" of scandals (as I have referred to it) was so episodic I would never have written my first book on the subject.

Once attuned to the general problem of clergy deviance, the evidence of continuing controversy is everywhere, not merely the local youth pastor found *in flagrante delicto* with an adolescent, but also at regional and national levels. For example, in mid-October of 2006 it was announced that the Organization of Concerned Priests in the Diocese of Manchester, New Hampshire, a local clerics' group, had itself registered as a non-profit in order to raise aid for diocesan pastors forced from ministry by accusations of child molestation. Its immediate goal was to ask fellow Catholic clergy to each donate a minimum of $1000 to its "Mercy Fund" (*Fort Wayne Journal Gazette*, 2006).

At the national level in an October, 2006 meeting in London, Roman Catholic bishops from England and Wales rejected a British Broadcast Corporation (BBC) documentary claiming that the current Pope Benedict XVI, as Cardinal Joseph Ratzinger in charge of the Congregation for the Doctrine of the Faithful (formerly the Office of the Inquisition) from 1981-2006, had orchestrated a system of cover-up of child molestation. The bishops declared the BBC documentary "Sex Crimes and the Vatican" as "false and entirely misleading," reflecting, as it also did, badly on Pope John Paul II despite reliable independent evidence to support that contention (Berry and Renner, 2004: 1-105).

Seeing venerated leaders as having something appallingly worse than clay feet is indeed troublesome for communities of faith as well as religionists writ large. My own form of spirituality, Zen Buddhism, was not spared during the "First Wave." *Roshi* Philip Kapleau (*Roshi* is a honorific Japanese term for "master," similar to a "sensei" which is more familiar to Americans) wrote in 1977 about recent scandals within three large Zen Buddhist centers in the U.S. These scandals had involved most nonascetic, lavish lifestyles of some teachers, sexual harassment of female members, alcoholism, and adulterous affairs compromising some teachers. Part of the fallout was the defections of some shocked and disgusted senior students and the forced resignation of one *roshi*. Lamented Kapleau:

> Most disillusioning for many is the fact that the sexual transgressions were not by monks who had taken vows of celibacy and were feeling the strain of those vows, but by married roshis living with their spouses and children—priests who had pledged to uphold the Buddhist precepts and to make them the moral basis of their lives. . . . It is particularly distressing to see some of Zen's contemporary exemplars brought low by such difficulties. Yet each of us needs to take personal responsibility for his or her actions (1997: 150-51).

No community of faith is exempt. Leadership reinforces its office and accompanying privileges. That is the systemic source of recurring malfeasance. Robert Michels in *Political Parties* emphasized, "With the institution of leadership there simultaneously begins, owing to the long tenure of offices, the transformation of the leaders into a closed caste" (1969: 196). And his final sentence in that volume (p. 408) offered a prognosis of dismay at the cyclical prospects of elites solidifying power, the periodically rising masses insisting on remedying checks, and then elites reconsolidating their non-accountability: "It is probable that this cruel game will continue without end."

References

American Broadcasting Company. 1996. "Judgement Day," "Prime Time Live." Narrated by Diane Sawyer.
——. 1992. "Secret No More," "Prime Time Live." Narrated by Diane Sawyer.
——. 1991. "The Apples of God's Eye," "Prime Time Live." (November 21) Narrated by Diane Sawyer.
ABC News, 1992. "America Close Up," *ABC Nightly News* (August 11).
Albuquerque Journal, 1993. "Archbishop Denies Rape Allegation." *Albuquerque Journal* (March 24).
Adler, Patricia A. and Peter Adler. 1997. *Constructions of Deviance: Social Power, Control, and Interactions*. Second edition. New York: International Thomson Publishers.
Allport, Gordon W. 1950. *The Individual and His Religion*. New York: Macmillan.
Anderson, Lavina F. 1993. "The LDS Intellectual Community and Church Leadership: A Contemporary Chronology." *Dialogue* Vol. 26 (1): 7-64.
Anderson, Lavina Fielding and Janice Merrill Allred. 1997. "Information About the Mormon Alliance." In Lavina Fielding Anderson and Janice Merrill Allred, eds., *Case Reports of the Mormon Alliance, Vol. 2, 1996,* pp. xvi-xix. Salt Lake City, UT: The Mormon Alliance.
Armstrong, John H. 1995. *Can Fallen Pastors Be Restored: The Church's Response to Sexual Misconduct*. Chicago: Moody Press.
Assembly of First Nations. 1994. *Breaking the Silence*. Ottawa: First Nations Health Commission.
Associated Press. 2007a. "Pastor to Plead Guilty in Indianapolis Welfare Case." July 14.
——. 2007b. "Church Says Ex-Trustee, 71 Stole $28,000 during Masses." July 28.
——. 2003. "Bishops to Vote on Abuse Policy." (November 13).
——. 2002. "Boston Archdiocese Considers Bankruptcy in Face of Lawsuits." (August 9).
——. 2001. "Judge: Church Must Release Records of Sex Abuse Complaints." (February 9).
——. 2000. "Priest Admits Abusing Boys but Says the Boys 'Threw Themselves at Him.'" (October 9).
——. 1998. "'Lyons Says He's No Monster,' Has No Comment on Charges." (November 1).
——. 1994a. "Archdiocese Offers the Pay Accuser's Bills." *State Journal-Register* (January 16).
——. 1994b. "Priests among Those Alleging Abuse by Priests." *State-Journal Register* (May 7).
——. 1993. "Indiana Franciscan Order Sues L.A. Archdiocese" (April 6).
Ayella, Marybeth F. 1998. *Insane Therapy: Portrait of a Psychotherapy Cult*. Philadelphia: Temple University Press.

Avery, William O. 1997. *Empowered Laity: the Story of The Lutheran Laity Movement.* Minneapolis: Augsburg Fortress Press.

Baglo, Ferdy. 2001. "Canadian Churches Seek to Resolve Abuse Cases." *Christianity Today* (July 21).

Balch, Robert W. 1995. "Charisma and Corruption in the Love Family: Toward a Theory of Corruption in Charismatic Cults." In Mary Jo Neitz and Marion S. Goldman, eds., *Sex Lies, and Sanctity: Religion and Deviance in Contemporary North America,* pp. 155-79. Greenwich, Ct: JAI Press.

——. 1988. "Money and Power in Utopia: An Economic History of the Love Family." In James T. Richardson, ed., *Money and Power in the New Religions,* pp. 185-221. Lewiston, NY: Edwin Mellen Press.

Barnhart, Joe E. 1988. *Jim and Tammey: Charismatic Intrigue Inside PTL.* Buffalo, NY: Prometheus Books.

Barron, Bruce. 1987. *The Health and Wealth Gospel.* Downers Grove, IL: InterVarsity Press.

Barrouquere, Brett. 2002. "Canada Tough on Abusive Clergy." *Washington Post* (April 30).

Beal, John P. 1992. "Doing What One Can: Canon Law and Clerical Sexual Misconduct." *The Jurist* Vol. 52: 642-83.

Becker, Howard S. 1963. *Outsiders.* Glencoe, IL: The Free Press.

Belluck, Pam. 2002. "Cardinal Told How His Policy Shielded Priests." *New York Times* (August 14).

Berry, Jason. 1992. *Lead Us Not Into Temptation: Catholic Priests and the Sexual Abuse of Children.* New York: Double Day.

Berry, Jason and Gerald Renner. 2004. *Vows of Silence: The Abuse of Power in the Papacy of John Paul II.* New York: Free Press.

Biesecker, Emily and Stephanie Smith. 2003. "Indiscretions of Clergy Don't Sway Faithful." *Indianapolis Star* (March 16).

Blankenship, Michael B., ed. 1993. *Understanding Corporate Criminality.* New York: Garland Publishing.

Blanshard, Paul. 1949. *American Freedom and Catholic Power.* Boston: Beacon Press.

Blue, Ken. 1993. *Healing Spiritual Abuse.* Downers Grove, IL: InterVarsity.

Blumhofer, Edith. 1993. *Aimee Semple McPherson: Everybody's Sister.* Grand Rapids, MI: William B. Eerdmans.

Bonavaglia, Angela. 1992. "The Sacred Secret." *MS* (March/April): 4-5.

Boorstein, Michelle. 2006. "Priest, Victim of Abuse Draws Ire for Revelation." *Washington Post* (April 29).

Boston Globe. 2002. *Betrayal: The Crisis in the Catholic Church.* Boston: Little, Brown and   Company.

Boswell, John. 1981. *Christianity, Social Tolerance, and Homosexuality.* Chicago: University of Chicago Press.

Bowman, Jim. 1992. "Cardinal Joseph Bernardin: A Shepherd Enfolded by His Flock." *Commonweal* (December 3): 5-6.

Boyd, Malcolm, 1986. *Gay Priest: An Inner Journey.* New York: St. Martin's Press.

Bradlee, Ben, Jr., and Dale Van Atta. 1981. *Prophet of Blood.* New York: Putnam's.

Brady, Noel S. 2001. "Mormons Pay $2 Million in sex-Abuse Settlement: Kirkland Family Says Church Knew Molester's History." *East Side General* (September 17).

Bratcher, Edward B. 1984. *The Walk-on-Water Syndrome.* Waco, TX: Word Books.

Broadway, Bill. 2001. "Faith-based Investment Scams on Rise." *Washington Post* (August 20).

Brodie, Fawn M., 1995. *No Man Knows My History: The Life of Joseph Smith the Mormon Prophet.* Second edition. New York: Alfred A. Knopf.

Bromley, David G., ed. 1988. *Falling from the Faith: Causes and Consequences of Religious Apostasy.* Newburg Park, CA: Sage.

Bromley, David G., and Anson D. Shupe, Jr. 1981. *Strange Gods: The Great American Cult Scare.* Boston: Beacon Press.

Bromley, David G. and Bruce C. Busching, 1988. "Understanding the Structure of Contractual and Covenantal Social Relations: Implications for the Sociology of Religion." *Sociological Analysis* Vol. 49 (Summer): 15-32.

Brown, DeNeen L. 2002. "In Canada, A Tougher Stand on Clergy Sex Abuse." *Washington Post* (October 15).

Brown, Mollie. 1994. *Victim No More: Ministry to Survivors of Sexual Abuse.* Mystic, CT: Twenty-Third Publications.

Bryant, Howard. 2005. *Juicing the Game.* New York: Viking.

Bryk, Anthony. 1993. "Catholic Schools Valuable Example." *Chicago Tribune* (November 16).

Bullough, Vern, ed. 1982. *Sexual Practices in the Medieval Church.* Buffalo: Prometheus Books.

Burks, Ron and Vicki Burks. 1992. *Damaged Disciples.* Grand Rapids, MI: Zondervan.

Burkett, Elinor and Frank Bruni. 1993. *A Gospel of Shame: Children, Sexual Abuse, and the Catholic Church.* New York: Viking Press.

Burnham, Kenneth C. 1979. *God Comes to America: Father Divine and the Peace Mission Movement.* Boston: Lambeth Press.

Cafardi, Nicholas P. 1993. "Stones Instead of Bread: Sexually Abusive Priests in Ministry." *Studia Canonica* Vol. 27: 145-72.

Caleca, Linda Graham and Richard D. Walton. 1997. "The Bishops' Justice." *The Indianapolis Star* (February 17).

Callahan, Daniel. 1965. *Honesty in the Church.* New York: Charles Scribner's Sons.

Campbell, Linda. 1997a. "Woman Says Bailey Used Her for Sex Acts Over 3-Year Period." *Fort Worth Star-Telegram* (January 8).

———. 1997b. "3.7 Million Verdict Faults Bailey." *Fort Worth Star-Telegram* (January 18).

———. 1996a. "8 Women Seek $14 Million from Ex-Pastor." *Fort Worth Star-Telegram* (December 3).

———. 1996b. "Bailey Denies Seducing Women." *Fort Worth Star-Telegram* (December 5).

Canseco, Jose, 2005. *Juiced: Wild Times, Rampant 'Roids, Smash Hits, and How Baseball Got Big.* New York: ReganBooks.

Careless, Sue. 2002. "Legal Bills Sink Canadian Diocese." *Christianity Today* (January 7): 20.

Carleton, W.A. 1970. *The Growth of the Early Church.* Nashville, TN: Convention Press.

Carnes, Patrick. 1991. *Don't Call It Love: Recovering from Sexual Addiction.* New York: Bantam.

Cava, Marco R Della. 2002. "Gays Tell Bishops: Don't Blame Us." *USA Today* (June 12).

Chadwick, Owen. 1972. *The Reformation.* New York: Penguin Books.

Chandler, Russell. 1987. "Bakker Scandal Damages Standing of TV Preachers." *Los Angeles Times* (March 31).

Chicago Tribune. 1993. "Church Deacon Acquitted in Sex Abuse Case" (December 4).
Christianity Today. 2001. "Health Plan Accused." (April 2): 23.
——. 1996a. "Ex-Treasurer Accused of Embezzling" (November 11): 103.
——. 1996b. "Ex-Treasurer Admits Embezzling." (March 4): 69.
Clayton, Mark. 2002. "Sex Abuse Spans Spectrum of Churches." *USA Today* (May 5).
Citizen-Journal. 1994. "Archdioces Sues for Insurance Payments." *Arlington Citzen-Journal* (December 26).
Catholic League for Religious and Civil Rrights. 2004. *Sexual Abuse in Social Context: Catholic Clergy and Other Professions.* Special Report by the Catholic League for Religious and Civil Rights (February).
Cloward, Richard A. and Lloyd E. Ohlin. 1960. *Delinquency and Opportunity: A Theory of Juvenile Gangs.* New York: The Free Press.
Clymer, Adam. 1987. "Survey Finds Many Skeptics Among Evangelists' Viewers." *New York Times* (March 31).
Cohen, Gary. 2001. "Dark Clouds Over a Guru to the Stars." *U.S. News & World Report* (May 28): 35.
Coleman, James William. 2002. *The Criminal Elite: Understanding White-Collar Crime.* Fifth edition. New York: Worth Publishers.
Commonweal. 1993. "CNN's Fall from Grace." *Commonweal* (December 3): 3-4.
Conway, Jim and Sally Conway. 1993. *Sexual Harassment No More.* Downers Grove, IL: InterVarsity Press.
Cooperman, Alan. 2006. "Sex Abuse Scandal Hits Orthodox Jews." *Washington Post* (May 29).
——. 2002. "Bishops Warned on Change." *Washington Post* (November 12).
Cozzens, Donald. 2000. *The Changing Face of the Priesthood.* Collegeville, MN: Liturgical Press.
Crawford, Jon and Lou Carlozo. 1993. "New Credibility Hurdle for Cook." *Chicago Tribune* (November 20).
Daichman, Graciela. 1990. "Misconduct in the Medieval Nunnery: Fact, Not fiction." In Lynda L. Coon, Katherine J. Haldine, and Elisabeth W. Sommer, eds., *That Gentle Strength: Historical Perspectives on Women in Christianity,* pp. 97-117. Charlottesville, VA: University of Virginia Press.
Daniels, Bruce. 1993. "Archdiocese May Face Bankruptcy." *Albuquerque Journal* (January 17).
Darrand, Craig Tom and Anson Shupe. 1983. *Metaphors of Social Control in a Pentecostal Sect.* Lewiston, NY: The Edwin Mellin Press.
Dart, John. 1986. "Divisions Threaten Krishna Cult." *Dallas Times Herald* (July 27).
Davies, Horton. 1972. *Christian Deviations: The Challenge of the New Spiritual Movements.* Third edition. Philadelphia: Westminster Press.
DePalma, Anthony and David J. Wakin. 2002. "Parishes Lack Lay Oversight on Finances." *New York Times* (July 8).
Dettro, Chris, 2004. "Priest Will Not Face Charges in Case of Money Stolen from Edwardsville Church." *State Journal-Register* (November 11).
Djilas, Milovan. 1998. *Fall of the New Class: A History of Communism's Self-Destruction.* New York: Alfred A. Knopf.
——. 1957. *The New Class: An Analysis of the Communist System.* New York: Praeger.
Dow, James. 1986. *The Shaman's Touch.* Salt Lake City, UT: University of Utah Press.
Doyle, Thomas P. 2001. "Roman Catholic Clericalism, Religious Duress, and Clerical Sexual Abuses." Oklahoma City, OK: Unpublished Paper Manuscript.

——. A. W. R. Sipe, and Patrick J. Wall. 2006. *Sex, Priests, and Secret Codes.* Los Angeles: Volt Press.

Duncan, Wendy, Jr. 2006. *I Can't Hear God Anymore: Life in a Dallas Cult.* Rowlen, TX: VM Life Resources, LLC.

Dziech, Billie Wright and Linda Weiner. 1990. *The Lecherous Professor: Sexual Harassment on Campus.* Urbana: University of Illinois Press.

Eaton-Robb, Pat. 2005. "Archdiocese Settles Abuses for $22 Million." Associated Press (December 1).

Echols, Mike. 1996. *Brother Tony's Boys.* Buffalo, NY: Prometheus Books.

Eichenwald, Kurt. 2005. *Conspiracy of Fools.* New York: Broadway Books.

——. 2000. *The Informant.* New York: Broadway Books.

Eisenberg, Carol. 2003. "Catholic Prelates Meet in St. Louis." *Newsday* (June 19).

Ekech, Peter. 1974. *Social Exchange Theory: Two Traditions.* Cambridge, MA: Harvard University Press.

Emerson, Richard M. 1970. "Power-dependent Relations." In Marvin E. Olson, ed., *Power in Societies* pp. 44-53. New York: Macmillan.

Enroth, Ronald M. 1992. *Churches That Abuse.* Grand Rapids, MI: Zondervan.

Etzioni, Amitai, 1961. *A Comparative Analysis of Complex Organizations.* New York: Free Press.

Foundations and Donors Interested in Catholic Activities. 2003. *Nationwide Survey of Catholic Parishioners on Financial Accountability and Support.* Washington, DC: Foundations and Donors Interested in Catholic Activities, Inc. (conducted in association with The Gallup Organization and Dr. Charles E. Zech, Villanova University).

Fager, Chuck. 2001. "Greater Ministries Leaders Get Lengthy Prison Time." *Christianity Today* (October 1): 20-1.

——. 2000. "'Gifting Clubs' Shut down." *Christianity Today* (November 13): 23-4.

——. 1999a. "$100 Million Missing in Greater Ministries Scandal." *Christianity Today* (October 4): 19-20.

——. 1999b. "Baptist Foundation Faces Investment Fraud Charges." *Christianity Today* (October 25): 18-9.

——. 1999c. "$12 Million Fraud Scheme Parallels Greater Ministries." *Christianity Today* (February 8): 14-5.

——. 1999d. "Judge Orders Gift Refunds." *Christianity Today* (March 1): 21.

Feldmeth, Joanne Ross and Midge Wallace Finley, 1990. *We Weep for Ourselves and Our Children: A Christian Guide for Survivors of Childhood Sexual Abuse.* San Francisco: SanFranciscoHarper.

Feuerstein, Georg. 1991. *Holy Madness.* New York: Paragon House.

Fialka, John. 1995. "Unholy Acts: Church Officials's theft Dismay Catholics." *Wall Street Journal* (July 27).

Fiegugh, Debra. 2003. "Denomination thwarts Bankruptcy." *Christianity Today* (May): 25.

First Nations. 1994. *Breaking the Silence.* Ottawa: Assembly of Nations.

Firestone, David. 2001. "Child Abuse at a Church Creates a Stir in Atlanta." *New York Times* (March 3).

Flaccus, William, 2007a. "L.A. Archdiocese to Pay $600 Million in Abuse Claims." Associated Press (July 15).

——. 2007b. "L.A. Archdiocese Apologizes for Clergy Sex Abuse." Associated Press (July 16).

Fort Wayne Journal Gazette, 2007a. "Pastor in Gay-Sex Scandal is Heterosexual, He Avows." (February 7).

——. 2007b. "Ohio Youth Pastor Gets 2 Years for Sex with Teen." (February 8).

——. 2006. "Priests Raise Money for Accused Clergy." (October 14).

——. 2004. "Boston Diocese Sues Insurer on Abuse Claims." (March 7).

——. 1998a. "'Frugal Gourmet' Settles Suits." (July 3).

——. 1998b. "Faith Investors Short changed." (October 27).

Fortune, Marie. 1989. *Is Nothing Sacred?* San Francisco: Harper Collins.

Frame, Randy. 1995. "The Post-New Era Era." *Christianity Today* (July 17): 60-1.

——. 1989. "Surviving the Slump." *Christianity Today* (February 3): 23-4.

Frankforter, A. David. 1978. *A History of the Christian Movement: The Development of Christian Institutions.* Chicago: Nelson-Hall.

Frankl, Razelle. 1987. *Televangelism: The Marketing of Popular Religion.* Carbondale, IL: Southern Illinois University Press.

Franklin, Stephen. 1987. "Murder, Abuse Charges Batter Serenity at Big Krishna Camp." *Chicago Tribune* (September 27).

Freeman, Jo. 1979. "Resource Mobilization and Strategy: A Model for Analyzing Social Movement Organization Actions." In Mayer N. Zald and John D. McCarthy, eds., *The Dynamics of Social Movements: Resource Mobilization, Social Control, and Tactics* pp. 167-189. Cambridge, MA: Winthrop Publishers.

French, Rose. 2007. "Protestant Sex Abuse Cases Noted." Associated Press, June 15.

Frend, W.H.C. 1987. *The Early Church.* Philadelphia: Fortress Press.

French, Ron. 1993. "Shattered Trust." *Fort Wayne Journal Gazette* (December 12).

Friberg, Nils C. 1995. "Wounded Congregations." In Nancy Myer Hopkins and Mark Laaser, eds., *Restoring the Soul of A Church* pp. 55-74. Collegeville, MN: The Liturgical Press.

Friberg, Nils C. and Mark R. Laaser. 1998. *Before the Fall: Preventing Pastoral Sexual Abuse.* Collegeville, MN: The Liturgical Press.

Garrow, David J. 1981. *The FBI and Martin Luther King, Jr.* New York: Penguin.

Geiselman, Art. 1993. "Parishes Weren't Told of Priests' Problem" *Albuquerque Journal* (March 16).

Gellner, Ernest. 1988. *Plough Sword and Book: The Structure of Human History.* Chicago: University of Chicago Press.

Giles, Thomas S. 1995. "'Double -Your-Money' Scam Burns Christian Groups." *Christianity Today* (June): 40-1.

——. 1993. "Coping with Sexual Misconduct in the Church." *Christianity Today* (January 12): 48-49.

Goodstein, Laurie and Stephanie Strom. 2007. "Embezzlement is Found in Many Catholic Dioceses." *New York Times* (January 5).

Gordon, Donna. 1993. "When the Sacred Becomes Profane." *World* (January-February): 20-24.

Gordon, James S. 1987. *The Golden Guru.* Lexington, MA: Stephen Greene Press.

Gottliev, Bob and Peter Wiley. 1984. *America's Saints: The Rise of Mormon Power.* New York: Putnam.

Gottlieb, Bob and Peter Wiley. 1982. "Mormon Infighting Intensifies as "Theologians Vie for Power." *Daily Californian* (April 6): 20.

Greeley, Andrew M. 2004. *Priests in the Pressure Cooker: the Sociology of a Profession Under Attack.* Chicago: University of Chicago Press.

——. 1992. "Clerical Culture and Pedophilia." Taped address to the first Annual Conference of VOCAL (Victims of Clergy Abuse Linkup), Chicago, October 16.

Griffin, Jean Latz. 1993. "Clergy Abuse Cases Taking their Toll on the Ministry." *Chicago Tribune* (December 16).

Hadden, Jeffrey K. and Anson Shupe. 1988. *Televangelism: Power and Politics on God's Frontier.* New York: Henry Holt.

Hadden, Jeffrey K. and Charles E. Swann. 1981. *Prime Time Preachers: the Rising Power of Televangelism.* Reading, MA: Addison-Wesley.

Hall, John R. 1989. *Gone From the Promised Land: Jonestown in American Cultural History.* New Brunswick, NJ: Transaction Publishers.

Halsey, Peggy. 1987. "What Can the Church Do?" In Mary D. Pellauer, Barbara Chester, and Jane Boyajian, eds., *Sexual Assault and Abuse: a Handbook for Clergy and Religious Professionals* pp. 219-24. San Francisco: Harper SanFrancisco.

Hammer, Richard. 2003. "Law and Disorder." *Christianity Today* (May): 48-51.

Hardett, Carolyn. 1998. "Dozens of Parishioners Turn Out to Support Lyons." *Sarasota Herald-Tribune*, (July 7).

Harding, Richard. 1993. Letter from Richard Harding, Attorney-at-law, Pasadena, CA to Anson Shupe. December 3 and prior telephone conversation, November 19.

Haskins, Darlene K., "Afterpastors in Troubled Congregations." In Nancy Myer Hopkins and Mark Laaser, eds., *Restoring the Soul of a Church* pp. 155-64. Collegeville, MN: the Liturgical Press.

Heineman, Uta Ranke. 1990. *Eunuchs for the Kingdom of Heaven.* Translated by Peter Heinegy. New York: Doubleday.

Hemrick, E. and Dean Hoge. 1991. *A Survey of Priests Ordained Five to Nine Years.* Washington, DC: Seminary Department of the National Catholic Education Association.

Herbert, Ross. 1998. "Real Estate Investment Failure Targets Churchgoers." *Christianity Today* (November 16): 31-2.

Hirschi, Travis. 1993. "A Control Theory of Delinquency." In Delos H. Kelley, ed., *Deviant Behavior* pp. 164-72. New York: St. Martin's Press.

Hirsley, Michael. 1993a. "I've Led A Chaste Life, Bernardin Says." *Chicago Tribune* (November 13).

——. 1993b. "Bernardin Shows All How to Act." *Chicago Tribune* (November 19):164-72.

Hirsley, Michael and Lou Carlozao. 1993c. "Bernardin Case Probers Want to Meet His Accuser." *Chicago Tribune* (November 16).

Hoffman, Lisa. 1983. "Beatings, Sex Inflicted on Faithful, 6 Charge." *Miami Herald* (February 27).

Homans, George C. 1967. "Fundamental Social Processes." In N. J. Smelser, ed., *Sociology* pp. 27-78. New York: Wiley.

——. 1961. *Social Behavior: Its Elementary Forms.* New York: Harcourt, Brace and World.

——. 1958. "Social Behavior as Exchange." *American Journal of Sociology* Vol. 63 (August): 597-606.

Hoover, Stewart M. 1988. *Mass Media Religion: The Social Sources of The Electronic Church.* Beverly Hills, CA: Sage.

Hoover, Thomas. 1988. *Zen Culture.* London: Routledge.

Hopkins, Harold. 1995. "The Effects of Clergy Sexual Misconduct on the Wider Church." In Nancy Myer Hopkins and Mark Laaser, eds., *Restoring the Soul of A Church* pp. 116-39. Collegeville, MN: The Liturgical Press.

Hopkins, Nancy Myer. 1998. *The Congregational Response to Clergy Betrayals of Trust.* Collegeville, MN: The Liturgical Press.

——. 1995. "Further Issues for Afterpastors." In Nancy Myer Hopkins and Mark Lasser, eds., *Restoring the Soul of A Church* pp. 165-72. Collegeville, MN: The Liturgical Press.

Hopkins, Nancy Myer and Mark R. Laaser, eds. 1995. *Restoring the Soul of A Church.* Collegeville, MN: The Liturgical Press.

Horst, Elisabeth A., 1998. *Recovering the Lost Self: Shame-Healing for Victims of Clergy Sexual Abuse.* Collegeville, MN: The Liturgical Press.

Huber, John and Lindsey Gruson. 1988. *Monkey on A Stick: Murder, Madness, and the Hare Krishnas.* New York: Harcourt Brace Jovanovich.

Iacone, Amanda. 2003. "Area Catholics Donate $3.8 million to Diocese." *Fort Wayne Journal Gazette* (May 31).

Iadicola, Peter and Anson Shupe. 2003. *Violence, Inequality, and Human Freedom.* Second edition. New York: Rowman and Littlefield.

Irons, Richard and Katherina Roberts. 1995. "The Unhealed Wounders." In *Restoring the Soul of A Church* pp. 33-51. Collegeville, MN: the Liturgical Press.

Isely, Paul J. 1997. "Child Sexual Abuse and the Catholic Church: An Historical and Contemporary Review." *Pastoral Psychology* Vol. 4 (No.4).

Ives, Christopher. 1992. *Zen Awakening and Society.* Honolulu: University of Hawaii Press.

Jacobs, Janet Liebman. 1989. *Divine Disenchantment: Deconverting from New Religions.* Bloomington, IN: Indiana University Press.

Jenkins, Philip. 2002. *Mystics and Messiahs: Cults and New Religions in American History.* New York: Cambridge University Press.

——. 1998. "Creating a Culture of clergy Deviance." In Anson Shupe, ed., *Wolves Within the Fold: Religious Leadership and Abuses of Power* pp. 118-32. New Brunswick, NJ: Rutgers University Press.

——. 1996. *Pedophiles and Priests: Anatomy of A Contemporary Crisis.* New York: Oxford University Press.

Johnson, David and Jeff VanVonderen. 1991. *The Subtle Power of Spiritual Abuse.* Minneapolis, MN: Bethany House.

Johnson, Pual. 1976. *A History of Christianity.* New York: Atheneum.

Johnson, Paul E. And Sean Wilentz. 1994. *The Kingdom of Mattias: A Story of Salvation in the 19th Century.* New York: Oxford University Press.

Johnson, Sonia, 1981. *From Housewife to Heretic.* Garden City, NY: Doubleday.

Journal Gazette, 1991. "Life After Faith Assembly." *Fort Wayne Journal Gazette* (March 31).

Judd, Alan, 2001. "Church Faces Abuse Probe over Whipping of Children." *Atlanta Journal* (March 22).

Kaplan, David E. and Andrew Marshall. 1996. *The Cult at the End of the World.* New York: Crown Publishers.

Kapleau, Philip. 1997. *Awakening to Zen: the Teachings of Roshi Philip Kapleau.* New York: Simon & Schuser.

Karmen, Andrew. 1990. *Crime Victims: An Introduction to Victimology.* Second edition. Pacific Grove, CA: Brooks Cole.

Kee, Howard Clark. 1980. *Christian Origins in Sociological Perspective.* Philadelphia: The Westminster Press.

Kelly, Niki. 2007. "Pastor Misused $12,000 in Grants, State Audit Finds." *Fort Wayne Journal Gazette* (May 4).

Kelley, Jack. 1987. "Roberts, Bakker in Disfavor." *USA Today* (April 1).

Kennedy, Eugene. 2001. *The Unhealed Wound.* New York: St. Martin's Griffin.

Kennedy, John W. 2002. "Mormon Scholar Under fire." *Christianity Today* (March): 22, 24.

——. 1995. "Probe of Mission Schools Demanded." *Christianity Today* (May 14): 60.

Kisala, Robert. 1998. "The AUM Spiritual Truth Church in Japan." In Anson Shupe, ed., *Wolves within the Fold: Religious Leadership and Abuses of Power* pp. 33-48. New Brunswick, NJ: Rutgers University Press.

Kituse, John I. 1964. "Social Reaction to Deviant behavior: Problems of Theory and Method." In Howard S. Becker ed., *The Other Side* pp. 87-102. New York: The Free Press.

Knowlton, David Clark. 1996. "Authority and Authenticity in the Mormon Church." In Lewis F. Carter, ed., *The Issue of Authenticity in the Study of Religions* Vol. 6 pp. 113-34. Greenwich, CT: JAI Pres.

Knudsen, Chilton. 1995. "Understanding Congregational Dynamics." In Nancy Myer Hopkins and Mark Laaser, eds., *Restoring the Soul of A Church* pp. 75-101. Collegeville, MN: The Liturgical Press.

Krakauer, Jon. 2003. *Under the Banner of Heaven.* New York: Doubleday.

Kramer, Andrew. 2001. "Attorney: More Suits Against LDS Church Likely." Associated Press (September 6).

Kramer, Joel and Diana Alstad. 1993. *The Guru Papers: Masks of Authoritarian Power.* Berkeley, CA: Frog, Ltd.

Krebs, Theresa. 1998. "Church Structures that Facilitate Pedophilia among Roman Catholic Clergy." In Anson Shupe, ed., *Wolves within the Fold: Religious Leadership and Abuses of Power* pp. 15-32. New Brunswick, NJ: Rutgers University Press.

Kroeger, Catherine Clark and James E. Beck, eds. 1996. *Women, Abuse, and the Bible.* Grand Rapids, MI: Baker Books.

Kurtz, Howard. 1994. *Media Circus.* New York: Time Books.

Kusmer, Ken. 2005a. "Victims Push Archbishop on Abuse Case." Associated Press (September 23).

———. 2005b. "Forum Hosts Contentious Cardinal." Associated Press (September 21).

Laaser, Mark R. 1995. "Long-Term Healing." In Nancy Myer Hopkins and Mark Laaser, eds., *Restoring the Soul of A Church* pp. 232-50. Collegeville, MN: The Liturgical Press.

———. 1992. *The Secret Sin: Healing the Wounds of Sexual Addiction.* Grand Rapids, MI: Zondervan.

Ladurie, Emmanuel Leroy. 1978. *Montaillou: The Promised Land of Error.* Translated by Barbara Bray. New York: Braziller.

Lango, Gabriel. 1966. *Spoiled Priest.* New Hyde Park, NY: University Books.

Lavallee, Mary Lou. 1995. "Communicating with the Wider Community." In Nancy Myer Hopkins and Mark Laaser, eds., *Restoring the Soul of A Church* pp.173-83. Collegeville, MN: The Liturgical Press.

Lavole, Denise. 2006a. "Jury in Priest's Slaying Saw Video." Associated Press (January 13).

———. 2006b. "Archbishop Facing New Crisis." Associated Press (January 14).

———. 2003a. "Boston Paper Trail Shows Long Pattern of cover-Up." Associated Press (March 22).

———. 2003b. "Church Property Now Collateral in Sex Scandal." Associated Press (December 21).

Lebacqz, Karen and Ronald C. Barton. 1991. *Sex in the Parish.* Louisville, KY: Westminster/John Knox Press.

LeBaron, Verland M. 1981. *The LeBaron Story.* Lubbock, TX: Verland M. LeBaron.

LeBlanc, Douglas. 2002. "Crumbling Family Values." *Christianity Today* (January 10): 20-6.

Legg, Ann and Derek Legg. 1995. "The Offfender's Family." In Nancy Myer Hopkins and Mark Laaser, eds., *Restoring the Soul of A Church* pp. 140-54. Collegeville, MN: The Liturgical Press.

Lemert, Edwin M. 1958. "The Behavior of the Systematic Check Forger." *Social Problems* Vol. 6 (Fall): 148-49.

Lemire, Christy. 2006. "Haggard Decries Gays in New Film." Associated Press (November 7).

Lewis, Sinclair. 1927. *Elmer Gantry.* New York: Grosset and Dunlap.

Linder, Eileen. 1998. *Yearbook of American and Canadian Churches.* Nashville, TN: Abingdon Press.

Lindsay, Jay. 2004. "Ex-Boston Archbishop's Appointment to Rome Basilica Stirs Up Controversy." *State Journal-Register* (April 16).

Lindsey, Robert. 1988. *A Gathering of Saints.* New York: Simon & Schuster.

Liska, Allen E. 1981. *Perspectives on Deviance.* Englewood Cliffs, NJ: Prentice-Hall.

Lissen, Robert 1958. *Living Zen.* Translated by Diana Abrahams-Curiel. New York: Grove Weidenfeld.

Lobdell, William. 2007a. "Scandals Drain Faith of Believer." *Los Angeles Times* (August 4).

———. 2007b. "Church Denials About Sdex Abuse Difficult to Grasp." *Los Angeles Times* (August 4).

Loviglio, Joann. 2005. "Philadelphia Clergy Probe Finds Blame, No Charges." Associated Press (September 22).

Lutheran, The. 1996a. "N.C. Bishop Resigning. Admits Misconduct." (July): 42.

———. 1996b. "New York Pastor Suspended." (July): 42.

Lutz, Brenda J. 2004. "A Report of Sexual Harassment Policies in Fort Wayne, Indiana Churches." Unpublished manuscript, Department of Sociology, Indiana-Purdue University Fort Wayne, (May).

Maloney, H. Newton, Thomas C. Needham, and Samuel Southard. 1986. *Clergy Malpractice.* Philadelphia: Westminster Press.

Maris, Margo. 1995. ". . . that which is hidden will be revealed" (Luke 12:2)." In Nancy Myer Hopkins and Mark Laaser, eds., *Restoring the Soul of A Church* pp. 3-22. Collegeville, MN: The Liturgical Press.

Marlette, Doug. 1988. *"I Am Not A Televangelist!": The Continuing Sage of Reverend Will B. Dunn.* Atlanta, GA: Longstreet Press.

Martinelli, Frank. 1993. "Problem of Sexual Abuse Long-Standing in Church." *Fort Wayne Journal Gazette* (November 17).

Martz, Larry and Ginny Carroll. 1988. *Ministry of Greed.* New York: Weidenfeld & Nelwon.

Martz, Ron. 2001. "OFCS to Take 10 More Kids from Members of Atlanta church in Wake of Abuse Probe." *Atlanta Journal* (March 20).

Mattingly, Terry. 1993. "Pope's Moral Views Collide with U.S. Culture, Catholicism." Scripps Howard News Service (August 21).

Matthews, Joe. 1998. "Jimmy Swaggart Is Still Preaching, But Few Are Listening." *Baltimore Sun* (December 12).

Mauss, Armand L. 1994. *The Angel and the Beehive: the Mormon Struggle with Assimilation.* Chicago: University of Illinois Press.

———. 1975. *Social Problems as Social Movements.* Philadelphia: J. B. Lippincott.

Mauss, Marcel. 1967. *The Gift: Forms and Functions of Exchange in Archaic Societies.* Translated by Ian Cunnison (Original Publication in 1925). New York: W. W. Norton.

Maxwell, Joe. 1995. "Ministers Pursue Disputed Funds." *Christianity Today* (August 14): 56.

McCaghy, Charles H., Timothy A. Capron, J. D. Jamieson, and Sandra Harley Carey. 2006. *Deviant Behavior: Crime, Conflict, and Interest Groups.* Seventh edition. Boston: Pearson/Allyn and Bacon.

McConkie, Bruce R. 1978. *Devotional Speeches of the Year: BYU Devotional and Addresses.* Provo, UT: Brigham Young University Press, p. 9.

McDonough, Kevin. 1995. "The Effects of the Misconduct Crisis on Non-Offending Clergy." In Nancy Myer Hopkins and Mark Saaser, eds., *Restoring the Soul of a Church* pp. 102-15. Collegeville, MN: the Liturgical Press.

McLoughlin, Emmett. 1962. *Crime and Immorality in the Catholic Church.* New York: Lyle Stuart.

McManus, Michael J. 1994. "Abuse After Bernardin." *Christianity Today* (April 25): 14-15.

Melton J. Gordon. 1986. *Encyclopedic Handbook of Cults in America.* New York: Garland Publishing.

Merton, Robert K. 1938. "Social Structure and Anomie." *American Sociological Review* Vol. 3: 672-82.

Metzner, Richard J. 1993. "A Legitimate Therapy Suffers Ripoffs." *Los Angeles Times* (December 3).

Michels, Robert. 1959. *Political Parties.* First published in 1915. New York: Dover Books.

Miller, Jeanne M. 1998. "The Moral Bankruptcy of Institutionalized Religion." In Anson Shupe, ed., *Wolves within the Fold: Religious Leadership and Abuses of Power* pp. 152-72. New Brunswick, NJ: Rutgers University Press.

Miller, Jeanne M. and Andrew B. Kagan. 1993. "Message from The President." *The Missing Link* (July 1): 1.

Missing Link, The. 1966. "Downward Accountability." Chicago, IL: The Linkup: Survivors of Clergy Abuse, 15.

Moll, Rob. 2007. "Abusive Clergy." *Christianity Today,* (March: 52-6).

——. 2005. "The Fraud Buster." *Christianity Today* (January): 28-33.

Molotch, Harvey, 1979. "Media and Movements." In Mayer N. Zald and John D. McCarthy, eds., *The Dynamics of Social Movements: Resource Mobilization, Social Control, and Tactics* pp. 71-93. Cambridge, MA: Winthrop Publishers.

Moore, Carrie A. 2001. "Lawyer Blasts LDS Church." *Desert News* (September 5).

Mosca, Gaetano. 1939. *The Ruling Class.* Translated by Hannah D. Kohn and edited and revised by Arthur Livingston. New York: McGraw-Hill.

Murphy, Caryle. 2006. "50 Years Later, An Abuse Victim Confronts Priest." *Washington Post* (April 22).

Naifeh, Steven and Gregory White Smith. 1988. *The Mormon Murders.* New York: Weidenfeld and Nicolson.

Nash, Jay Robert. 1976. *Hustlers and Con Men.* New York: M. Evans and Company.

Nason-Clark, Nancy. 1998. "The Impact of Abuses of Clergy Trust on Female Congregants; Faith and Practice." In Anson Shupe, ed., *Wolves within the Fold: Religious Leadership and Abuses of Power* pp. 85-100. New Brunswick, NJ: Rutgers University Press.

——. 1991. "Broken Trust: The Case of Roman Catholic Priests in New Foundland Charged with the Sexual Abuse of Children." Unpublished paper presented at the annual meeting of the Society for the Scientific Study of Religion, Pittsburgh, PA., November.

Neff, David. 1995. "How Shall We Then Give?" *Christianity Today* (July 17): 20-1.

News-Sentinel. 1983. "52 Deaths Attributed to Faith Healing." *Fort Wayne News-Sentinel* (May 3).

Nieburh, Gustave. 1994. "Clergy Sex Abuse Insurance Firms Cast Final Judgements." *Fort Worth Star-Telegram* (March 20).

O'Brien, Dennis. 2002. "Another Church Facing Charges of Sexual Abuse." *Baltimore Sun* (May 21).

Olson, Marvin E., ed. 1970. *Power in Societies.* New York: Macmillan.

Ostling, Richard N. 2005. "Bishops Defends U.S. Priests." Associated Press (October 15).

Ostling, Richard N. and Jan K. Ostling. 2002. *Mormon America: The Power and the Promise.* San Francisco: HarperSanFrancisco.

———. 2003. "Catholic Bishops at Crossroad." Associated Press (June 23).

———. 2002. "U.S. Protestants face Sex Abuse Scandals, too, But with Less Publicity." *Fort Wayne Journal Gazette* (April 6).

Ostrum, Carol M.. 1988. "Embattled Pastor Didn't Admit '75 guilty Pleas, Records Show." *Seattle Times* (April 11).

Overland, Nathalie, 1988a. "Chapel Is 'Hands-Off,' Say Church Leaders." *Valley Daily News* (May 10).

———. 1988b. "Battered Christians Search for Life after Barnett." *Valley Daily News* (May 9).

Owren, Jenny. 1994. "Clergy Sex Abuse: Insurance Firms Cast final Judgements." *Fort Worth Star-Telegram* (March 20).

Palmer, Susan J. and Arvind Sharma. 1993. *The Rajneesh Papers.* Delhi: Motilal Banarsidass Publishers.

Palmer, Susan J. and Frederick Bird. 1992. "Therapy, Charisma and Social Control in the Rajneesh Movement." *Sociological Analysis* Vol. 53: 71-85.

Parry, Geraint. 1976. *Political Elites.* London: George Allen & Unwin.

Paulson, Michael. 2004. "Abuse Study Says 4% of Priests in Us Accused." *Boston Globe* (February 17).

Pellauer, Mary D., Barbara Chester, and Jane Beyajian. 1987. *Sexual Assault and Abuse: A Handbook for Clergy and Religious Professionals.* San Francisco: HarperSanFrancisco.

Peterson, Mark E. 1981. "When Shall It Be?" *Church News* (December 12): 16.

———. 2001. "Clergy Push for Reports of Abuse." *Boston Globe* (September 10).

Peterson, Michael, Thomas P. Doyle, and F. Ray Mouton, Jr. 1985. *The Problem of Sexual Molestation by Roman Catholic Clergy: Meeting the Problem in a Comprehensive and Responsible Manner.* Unpublished paper delivered to American Catholic Bishops. (See also www.survivornetwork.org and www.thelinkup.com)

Phillips, J.B. 1972. *The New Testament in Modern English.* Revised edition. Translated by J. B. Phillips. New York: The Macmillan Company.

Pogatchnik, Shawn. 2006. "102 Dublin Priests Suspected of Abuse." Associated Press (March 11).

Poling, James Newton. 1991. *The Abuse of Power: A Theological Problem.* Nashville, TN: Abingdon Press.

Porterfield, Kay Marie. 1993. *Blind Faith.* Minneapolis: Fortress Press.

Press, Aric, et al. 1993. "Priests and Abuse." *Newsweek* (August 16): 12-4.

Pullen, Elizabeth. 1998. "An Advocacy Group for Victims of Clerical Sexual Abuse." In Anson Shupe, ed., *Wolves Within the Fold: Religious Leadership and Abuses of Power* pp. 67-84. New Brunswick, NJ: Rutgers University Press.

Quinn, D. Michael. 1987. *Early Mormonism and the Magic World View.* Salt Lake City, UT: Signature Books.

———. 1992a. "On Being a Mormon Historian (and Its Aftermath)." In George D. Smith, ed., *Faithful History: Essays on Writing Mormon History* pp.69-91. Salt Lake City: Signature Books.

———. 1992b. "One Hundred Fifty Years of Truth and Consequences about Mormon History." *Sunstone* Vol. 16 (1): 12-14.

Rabey, Steve. 1993. "In Search of Catholic Youth." *Christianity Today* (September 13): 68.

Rahner, Mark. 1997a. "Higi: Success, Not a Mess." *Journal and Courier* (February 20).

———. 1997b. "Grieving, Denial Mark Priests' Session." *Journal and Courier* (February 22).

Reavis, Dick J., 1995. *The Ashes of Waco.* New York: Simon & Schuster.

Reuter. 2006. "Bishops Reject Vatican Abuse Cover-up Report." MSNBC Home webpage MSNBC.msn.com (October 3).

Rediger, G. Lloyd. 1990. *Ministry & Sexuality.* Minneapolis: Fortress Press.

Rice, David. 1992. *Shattered Vows: Priests Who Leave.* New York: Triumph Books.

Richardson, James T. 1982. "A Comparison between Jonestown and Other Cults." In Ken Lvi, ed., *Violence and Religious Commitment: Implications of Jim Jones' People's Temple Movement* pp. 21-34. University Park, PA: The Pennsylvania State University Press.

———. 1975. "New Forms of Deviancy in a Fundamentalist Church: A Case Study." *Review of Religious Research* Vol. 16 (Winter): 134-41.

Rochford, E. Burke, Jr. 1998. "Reactions of Hare Krishna Devotees to Scandals of Leaders' Misconduct." In Anson Shupe, ed., *Wolves Within the Fold: Religious Leadership and Abuses of Power* pp. 101-17. New Brunswick, NJ: Rutgers University Press.

Romney, Marion G. 1972. "The Covenant of the Priesthood." *Ensign* Vol. 2 (July): 98.

Rose, Michael S. 2002. *Goodbye, Good Men.* Washington, DC: Regnery Publishing.

Rossetti, Stephen J., 1996. *A Tragic Grace: the Catholic Church and Child Sexual Abuse.* Collegeville, MN: the Liturgical Press.

———. 1990. *Slayer of the Soul: Child Sexual Abuse and the Catholic Church.* Mystic, CN: Twenty-Third Publications.

Rowland, Christopher. 1985. *Christian Origins.* Minneapolis: Augsburg Publishing House.

Rutter, Peter. 1989. *Sex in the Forbidden Zone.* Los Angeles: Jeremy P. Tarcher.

Salt Lake Tribune. 2002a. "LDS Church Is Targeted in Lawsuit" (May 31).

———. 1985. "Elder decries Criticism of LDS Leaders." (August 18).

———. 2002b. "Child Sex Abuse Charge Filed Against LDS-Ex-Bishop." (September 6).

Sasse, Cynthia Stalter, and Peggy Murphy Widder. 1991. *The Kirtland Massacre.* New York: Donald I. Fine.

Schreiner, Bruce. 2002. "Jehovah's Witnesses May Out 4 who Oppose Policy on Abuse." *Fort Worth Journal Gazette* (May 11).

Schroeder, Michael. 2001. "Arizona Officials Allege Anderson Auditors Played Role in Fraud by A Baptist Group." *Wall Street Journal* (April 26).

Schur, Edwin M. 1971. *Labeling Deviant Behavior.* New York: Harper & Row.

Seal, Jeff T., James T. Trent, and Jwe K. Kim. 1993. "The Prevalence and Contributing Factors of Sexual Misconduct Among Southern Baptist Pastors in Six Southern States." *Journal of Pastoral Care* Vol. 47 (No.4): 363-70.

Sennott, Charles M. 1997. *Broken Covenant.* New York: Simon & Schuster.

Shepherd, Gordon and Gary Shepherd. 1984. *A Kingdom Transformed: Themes in the Development of Mormonism.* Salt Lake City: University of Utah Press.

Shower, Neal and John Paul Wright, eds. 2001. *Crimes of Privilege.* New York: Oxford University Press.

Shupe, Anson. 2007. *Spoils of the Kingdom: Clergy Misconduct and Social Exchange in American Religion.* Champaign, IL: University of Illinois Press.

———. 2005. "Philly Priest Pedophilia Inquiry Finds Officials Guilty." *Fort Wayne Journal Gazette* (October 10).

———. ed. 1998. *Wolves within the Fold: Religious Leadership and Abuses of Power.* New Brunswick, NJ: Rutgers University Press.

———. 1995. *In the Name of All That's Holy: A Theory of Clergy Malfeasance.* Westport, CT: Praeger.

——. 1991. *The Darker Side of Virtue: Corruption, Scandal and the Mormon Empire.* Buffalo, New York: Prometheus.

Shupe, Anson and William A. Stacey. 1982. "Correlates of Support for The Electronic Church." *Journal for the Scientific Study of Religion* 21 (December): 291-303.

Shupe, Anson, William A. Stacey, and Susan E. Darnell, eds. 2000. *Bad Pastors: Clergy Misconduct in Modern America.* New York: New York University Press.

Shupe, Anson, Dana Simel, and Rhonda Hamilton. 2000. "A Descriptive Report on the National Clergy Abuse Policy Project." Unpublished paper presented at the annual meeting of the North Central Sociological Association, Pittsburgh, PA, March.

Shupe, Anson and Susan E. Darnell. 2006. *Agents of Discord: Deprogramming, Pseudoscience, and The American Anticult Movement.* New Brunswick, NJ: Transaction Publishers.

Silk, Mark. 2002. "The Media vs. the Church." *Religion in the News* spring: 1-2.

Sillitoe, Linda and Allen Roberts. 1988. *Salamander.* Salt Lake City, UT: Signature Books.

Simon, David. 2006. *Elite Deviance.* Eighth edition. Boston: Parson Education.

Simon, Stephanie. 2006. "Haggard Confesses to Church." *Los Angeles Times* (November 6).

Sipe, A. W. Richard, 2003. *Celibacy in Crisis: a Secret World Revisited.* New York: Brunner-Routledge.

——. 1998. "Clergy Abuse in Ireland." In Anson Shupe, ed., *Wolves Within the Fold: Religious Leadership and Abuses of Power* pp. 133-51. New Brunswick, NJ: Rutgers University Press.

——. 1995. *Sex, Priests, and Power: Anatomy of A Crisis.* New York: Brunner/Mazael.

——. 1990. *A Secret World: Sexuality and the Search for Celibacy.* New York: Brunner/Mazel.

Slater, Sherry. 2002. "Churches Put Faith in Liability Coverage." *Fort Wayne Journal Gazette* (May 19).

Stacey, William A., Susan E. Darnell, and Anson Shupe. 2000. "How Much Clergy Malfeasance is Really Out There? A Victimization Survey of Prevalence and Perceptions." In Anson Shupe, William A. Stacey, and Susan E. Darnell, eds., *Bad Pastors: Clergy Misconduct in Modern America* pp. 187-213. New York: New York University Press.

——. Anson Shupe, and Susan E. Darnell. 2000. "Clergy Malfeasance, Victimization, and National/Local Awareness: Their Effects on Church Attendance and Financial Giving." In Anson Shupe, William A. Stacey, and Susan E. Darnell, eds., *Bad Pastors: Clergy Misconduct in Modern America* pp. 214-38. New York: New York University Press.

Stafford, Tim. 2005. "Good Morning, Evangelicals! Meet Ted Haggard the NAE's Optimistic Champion of Ecumenical Evangelism and Free-Market Faith." *Christianity Today* (November: 40-5).

Stammer, Larry B. 2003a. "Keating Assails Bishops in Fiery Exit." *Los Angeles Times* (June 17).

——. 2003b. "Clergy Abuse Panel Forcing Out Its Leader." *Los Angeles Times* (June 16).

Stapleton, Anne and Nancy Nason-Clark. 1992. "The Power and the Pedestal: Roman Catholic Women in Newfoundland Reassess Their Beliefs and Attitudes in the Aftermath of Scandal." Paper presented at the annual meeting of the society for the Scientific Study of Religion. Washington, DC.

Stark, Rodney. 1981. "Must All Religions Be Supernatural?" In Bryan Wilson, ed., *The Social Impact of New Religious Movements* pp. 159-77. New York: The Rose of Sharon Press.

Stark, Rodney and William Sims Bainbridge. 1985. *The Future of Religion.* Berkeley: University of California Press.

———. 1980. "Towards a Theory of Religion: Religious Commitment." *Journal for the Scientific Study of Religion* Vol. 19 (June): 1145-28.

Stark, Werner. 1967. *The Sociology of Religion,* Vol. Two. New York: Fordham University Press.

Steinfels, Peter. 2003. "Abuse by Priests Under Study by Chicago Diocese." *New York Times* (February 24).

Stiles, Hilary. 1987. *Assault on Innocence.* Albuquerque, NM: B & K Publishers.

Stockton, Ronald R. 2000. *Decent and Order: Conflict, Christianity and Polity in a Presbyterian   Congregation.* Westport, CT: Praeger.

———. 1998. "The Politics of a Sexual Harassment Case." In Anson Shupe, William A. Stacey, and Susan E. Darnell, ed. *Bad Pastors: Clergy Misconduct in Modern America.* pp. 131-54. New York, NY: New York University Press.

Sunstone Magazine. 1994. "Lee Pleads Guilty in child sex-Abuse case." (December): 28.

Sutherland, Edwin H. 1947. *Principles of Criminology.* Philadelphia, PA: J. B. Lippincott.

Suzuki, Daisetz Teitaro. 1980. *The Awakening of Zen.* Boulder, CO: Prajna Press.

———. 1961. *Essays in Zen Buddhism* (First Series). New York: Grove Press.

Sykes, Gresham M. and David Matza. 1957. "Techniques of Neutralization: A Theory of Delinquency." *American Sociological Review* Vol. 22 (6): 664-70.

Taylor, Thomas F. 1997. "Will Your Church Be Sued?" *Christianity Today* (January 6): 42-5.

Theissen, Gerd. 1978. *Sociology of Early Palestinian Christianity.* Translated by John Bowden. Philadelphia: Fortress Press.

Thio, Alex and Thomas C. Calhoun, eds. 2006. *Readings in Deviant Behavior.* Fourth edition. Boston: Pearson/Allyn and Bacon.

Thomson, James G., Joseph A. Marolla, and David G. Bromley. 1998. "Disclaimers and Accounts in Cases of Catholic Priests Accused of Pedophilia." In Anson Shupe, ed., *Wolves Within the Fold: Religious Leadership and Abuses of Power* pp. 175-90. New Brunswick, NJ: Rutgers University Press.

Trott, Jon. 2000. "Is Abuse About Truth or Story...Or Both?" In Anson Shupe, William A. Stacey, and Susan E. Darnell, eds., *Bad Pastors: Clergy Misconduct in Modern America* pp. 155-84. New York: New York University Press.

Turk, Austin T. 1969. *Criminality and Legal Order.* Chicago: Rand McNally.

Turley, Jr., Richard E. 1992. *Victims: The LDS Church and the Mark Hofmann Case.* Champaign, IL: University of Illinois Press.

Turner, Jonathan H. 1998. *The Structure of Sociological Theory.* Belmont, CA: Wadsworth.

Tyre, Peg and Julie Scelto. 2002. "A Fed for the Church." *Newsweek* (November 18): 66.

United Methodist Church. 1990. *Sexual Harassment in the United Methodist Church.* Dayton, OH: Office of Research, General Council of Ministries, United Methodist Church.

Unsworth, Tim. 1993. *The Last Priests in America.* New York: Crossroad.

USA/CNN/Gallup Poll. 1993. "Poll shows Majority of U.S. Catholics Think Bishops Blundered."

USA Today (August 10).

Vaillancourt, Jean-guy. 1980. *Papal Power: A Study of Vatican Control over Lay Catholic Elites.* Berkely: University of California Press.

Wach, Joachim. 1967. *Sociology of Religion.* Chicago: University of Chicago Press.

Wagner, Richard. 1980. *Lay Catholic Preists.* San Francisco: Institute for Advanced Study of Human Sexuality.

Wallace, Harvey. 1998. *Victimology: Legal, Psychological, and Social Perspectives.* Needham Heights, MA: Allyn & Bacon.

Walsh, Andrew. 2006. "No Peace for the Church." *Religion in the News* Vol. 8 (No. 3): 17-9, 24.

Walsh, Edward. 2002. "Insurance A Worry for Catholic Church." *Washington Post* (July 10).

Ward, Kevin J. 2001. "The Path to Healing." British Columbia: Indian and Northern Affairs, Canada: 1-6. Internet: http://www.prsp.Wc.ca/history/history/htm

Washington Post. 1987. "470 Laid Off at Robertson's TV Ministry." (June 6).

Watkin, Daniel J. 2002. "Victims Group Says Nine Dioceses Broke Promise." *New York Times* (July 30).

Watts, Alan W. 1958. *The Spirit of Zen.* New York: Grove Press.

Webb, Al. 2006. "Life after Haggard." *Christianity Today* (December: 13).

Weber, Max. 1964a. *The Sociology of Religion.* Translated by Ephraim Fischoff. Boston: Beacon.

——. 1964b. *The Theory of Social and Economic Organization.* Trans. By A.M. Henderson and Talcott Parson. Glenco, IL: The Free Press.

Weisbrot, Robert. 1983. *Father Divine.* Boston: Beacon Press.

White, Jr., O. Kendall. 1987. *Mormon Neo-Orthodoxy: A Crisis Theology.* Salt Lake City, UT: Signature Books.

White, Daryl and O. Kendall White, Jr. 1996. "Charisma, Structure, and Contested Authority: The Social Construction of Authenticity in Mormonism." in Lewis F. Carter, ed., *The Issue of Authenticity in the Study of Religions* pp. 93-112. Vol. 6 of *Religion and the Social Order* series, David G. Bromley, ed. Greenwich, CT: JAI Press.

White, John and Ken Blue. 1985. *Healing the Wound.* Downers Grove, IL: InterVarsity.

Wiley, John K. 2006. "Top U.S. Catholic Bishop Faces Claim of Sexual Abuse." Associated Press (September 22).

Willerscheidt, Phyllis A. 1995. "Healing for Victims." In Nancy Myer Hopkins and Mark Laaser, eds. *Restoring the Soul of A Church* pp. 23-32. Collegeville, MN: The Liturgical Press.

Wills, Gaary. 2002. *Why I Am A Catholic.* New York: Houghton Mifflin.

——. 2000. *Papal Sin: Structures of Deceit.* New York: Doubleday.

——. 1993. "Bad shrinks Can't End Abuse." *Fort Wayne New Sentinel* (December 3).

Wilson, John. 1998. *Religion in American Society: The Effective Presence.* Englewood Cliffs, NJ: Prentice-Hall.

Wilson, Mike. 1997. "Lyons Survives Challenge." *Christianity Today* (October 27): 191-3.

Witham, Larry. 2002. "Protestant Ministers Face Own Sex Scandals." *Washington Times* (May 3).

Wolff, Kurt H., ed. and trans. *The Sociology of Georg Simmel.* New York: The Free Press.

Woodall, Martha. 1995. "New Era Cases Candy Money." *Philadelphia Inquirer* (June 4).

Wooldridge, Clifton R. c. 1910. *The Grafters of America.* Chicago.

Woodward, Kenneth L., et al. "The Sins of the 'Father.'" *Newsweek*: 60-1.

——. Kenneth L. 1997. "Sex Morality and the Protestant Minister." *Newsweek* (July 28): 62.

Wright, Stuart A., ed. 1995. *Armageddon in Waco*. Chicago, IL: University of Chicago Press.

Wronski, Richard. 2005. "Church Accountant Held." *Chicago Tribune* (December 15).

World Teacher's Message. 1945. "Sustaining the General Authorities." Salt Lake City, UT: Church of Jesus Christ of Latter-day Saints.

Wyatt, Kristen. 2001. "Kids in Foster Abuse After Abuse." Associated Press (March 28).

Yankin, Jonathan. 1992. "Church Settles with 68 People Who Said Priest Molested Them." *Indianapolis Star* (December 2).

Yeakley, Jr., Flavil, R., ed. 1988. *The Discipling Dilemma: a Study of the Discipling Movement among Churches of Christ*. Nashville, TN: Gospel Advocate Company.

Zoll, Rachel. 2006. "Pope Benedict Reprimands Favorite Priest of John Paul." Associated Press (May 20).

———. 2002a. "At Least 300 Church Abuse Suits filed." Associated Press (June 8).

———. 2002b. "Prosecutors Find Bishops' Complicity in Molestings." *Fort Wayne Journal Gazette* (August 24).

———. 2002c. "At Least 300 church Abuse Suits Filed." Associated Press (June 9).

———. 2002d. "Bishops Open Priest Sex Abuse Talks." Associated Press (June 13).

——— 2002e. "Bishops Plan to Oust Preists Coming Apart." Associated Press (September 15).

———. 2002f. "Price of Abuse Costs Dioceses in Land, Loans." Associated Press (March 4).

Index